Motherload

Motherload

MAKING IT ALL BETTER
IN INSECURE TIMES

Ana Villalobos

UNIVERSITY OF CALIFORNIA PRESS

University of California Press, one of the most distinguished university presses in the United States, enriches lives around the world by advancing scholarship in the humanities, social sciences, and natural sciences. Its activities are supported by the UC Press Foundation and by philanthropic contributions from individuals and institutions. For more information, visit www.ucpress.edu.

University of California Press
Oakland, California

Library of Congress Cataloging-in-Publication Data

Villalobos, Ana, 1965– author.
    Motherload : making it all better in insecure times / Ana Villalobos.
        pages cm
    Includes bibliographical references.
    ISBN 978-0-520-27809-7 (cloth) — ISBN 0-520-27809-7 (cloth) —
ISBN 978-0-520-27810-3 (paperback)   ISBN 0 520 27810 0
(paperback)
    1. Motherhood.   2. Mother and child.   3. Security (Psychology)
in children.   4. Security (Psychology)   I. Title.
    HQ759.V536 2014   306.874′3—dc23

                                                    2014012057

23   22   21   20   19   18   17   16   15   14
10   9   8   7   6   5   4   3   2   1

To my mothers, Carole and Michele, who have always listened with rapt attention to my stories.

And to Ofer and our children, Avilev, Talia, and Eliyah, who fill those stories with love.

Contents

Acknowledgments

Of this book's many sources, I am foremost indebted to the mothers whose stories fill its pages. In a society where a woman's acceptance is partly based on her ability to hold up a façade of good motherhood, these women allowed me to enter their worlds of raw truth. This included their exquisitely rapturous heights of love and joy, but also their dark demons of rage, their shame about lacking bonded feelings, their longings to escape, and their longings to hold on forever. Sharing their lived experiences with me was a great gift of trust both to me and to the readers of this book. Some readers may find themselves wishing to emulate one or more of the mothers who populate these pages. Some readers may wince or think, "Those crazy mothers!" and distance themselves from some of their stories. All of this, I believe, is instructive. It is eye-opening to see beyond the circumscribed socially appropriate smile at the park and to hear what is actually going on for that mother and child behind their front door. I thank these women for opening those doors and letting us all in.

As I wrote this book, my own intellectual mother was Arlie Hochschild, whose never-ending wellspring of insights deeply inspired and fortified this research. Arlie's passion to make the world a better place through seeing it sociologically and engaging in intellectual activism with an open, caring, and thoroughly engaged heart has inspired many a researcher, including me. Her imprint on my life and work is among my most treasured blessings. Barrie Thorne and Evelyn Nakano Glenn, who likewise possess an uncanny ability to see through the social matrix into its underlying truth, also gave indispensable support to this research, and just as importantly, taught me it is possible to be a serious research scholar while fully maintaining one's humanity. I wish I could bottle their courage of self and their abilities to profoundly engage the social world, understand its hidden structures, and write it down on a page.

Additionally, Lynn O'Brien Hallstein, Kathleen Gerson, Ilene Philipson, Naomi Schneider, James Cook, Karen Hansen, Laura Miller, Ken Sun, Jillian Harvey, and a number of anonymous reviewers gave their attentive and very helpful feedback to this work, and John Elder used his keen editorial eye to immensely improve the writing flow.

My own mothers, Carole and Michele, assisted greatly in this project as well, as did my father, Tom. They sent me relevant articles, watched the kids so I could go to interviews, and read and commented on drafts. Along with my sister, Beth, and my brother, Sean, they listened to me endlessly discuss my research and writing, and showered me with love and encouragement every step of the way.

Above all, I am grateful for my greatest colleague and comrade of all time, the one whose clarity focuses my creative abandon, whose sociological eye is so penetrating and imaginative and *brilliant* he can discern underlying patterns when I so much as mention my material: my intellectual alter ego and the love of my life, Ofer Sharone. There is no joy sweeter than working alongside my husband on meaningful life projects, be they political, academic, creative, or reproductive. Having three children with Ofer while I conducted this research was certainly our greatest joint venture of all, yet parenting is only one of the many deep, magnificent life projects we share. This research and book could simply not have come into being without his practical, intellectual, and emotional support. When I got stuck in the piles of data, Ofer was there to pull me out and help me think my way out of my stuckness with new insights. When I wanted to quit and felt overwhelmed by the hefty sum of teaching, researching, writing, and coparenting three babies simultaneously in diapers, he was the one who told me without a shred of doubt on his face that

I could do it. He is the greatest ally I have ever had, and I am both humbled and grateful to be sharing my life with such a phenomenal sociologist, activist, and human being.

Finally, and paradoxically, I could not have written this book without my children: Avilev, Talia, and Eliyah. If I had to spend all my time in front of a computer without warm little fingers tugging at my sleeves, without milk spills and unyielding emotional needs and miraculous blossoming life flooding my senses each morning, if I were merely productive without this surrounding landscape of human love and raw beauty personified in my children's relentless wills to grow each day, I would feel like the shell of a researcher, mechanically tapping keys, dehydrated. My life felt vividly alive and three-dimensional before Ofer and I had children, but since their emergence, the thought of a life without them feels unbearably flat. Arlie said more than once that I was too close to what I was studying, with three children under age two while I interviewed mothers of very young children. She was right. She was also right that life is messy, and scholarship is produced by human beings with lives, feelings, and unique perspectives, and sometimes truth emerges from the darnedest places, including one's own lived experiences.

To all of the incredible people who have supported me on this epic venture, thank you for contributing your spirits to this book, to the pursuit of dreams, and to a rich and fulfilling life. You will always have my deepest gratitude and my most abiding love.

1 Introduction

Like so many Americans, Myra Rossi is feeling insecure.[1] Unable to find a suitable job for a year, she has been living off her savings, which are now nearly gone. She worries a lot—about drive-by shootings, nuclear terrorism, and road rage. She thinks it is only a matter of time before the planet will become uninhabitable due to global warming. She doubts she and her boyfriend will make it as a couple. Myra has just had a baby.

With five-pound Giovanna now wriggling in her arms, where does all that insecurity go? Myra has heard again and again—from experts, from friends, and from her own stay-at-home mother—that a baby's security ultimately depends on its early relationship with its mother. She is now that mother, wondering how to fulfill her maternal job description given *this* is the world her child has been born into. If she struggles to "make it all better"[2] and turn the tide of turbulent social forces for this one particular child, a quiet question may go unheard under the gale: What if trying too hard, with such high expectations that the mother-child relationship can indeed make it all better, brings its own set of consequences? Or spoken louder: What if placing a whole society's worth of security needs onto the shoulders of individual mothers backfires and ultimately *undermines* security?

Meanwhile, this moment, she is this baby's mother and needs to figure out how to proceed. Rather than fight the world on multiple security fronts, Myra engages in a simple yet creative act. She pulls out a Lysol wipe to sanitize the counters. It makes her feel a little bit better. She carefully places a clean paper towel under Giovanna's pacifier. She is protecting her daughter. Though Giovanna has never had any health problems, Myra finds her thoughts drawn to all that could go wrong medically, fixating on one particular illness after another, which she calls the problem du jour. Myra's growing obsession with simply keeping Giovanna alive becomes so all-consuming that it appears to absorb her previous economic, social, and environmental insecurities. Perhaps she fixates on this one issue because it seems fairly manageable, given Giovanna's good health so far. In any case, as she engages in all-out warfare against her enemy, *the germ*, she finds herself worrying less about the other things that once seemed so threatening.

Unfortunately, some of those problems are made worse by being ignored. Myra stops worrying about paid work and all but ceases her job search, thus launching herself into a multiyear period of unemployment. She stops worrying about her boyfriend, and three years later, at the time of my final check-in with her, the relationship's long-term prospects remain dubious. She has solved the insecurity puzzle through a laser focus on her baby's health—providing a psychic solution to unmanageable demands—but it exacerbates the real insecurities in her life.

Heather Dover sobs the moment I show up at her door. She is underemployed and living with her two young children and life partner in a subsidized apartment complex that is about to be closed down. Yet that's not what Heather is crying about. She's crying because motherhood has worn her down. Her Herculean efforts to create a sense of safety for her children, to give herself to them day and night as a living security blanket, have left her drained. Heather held her children nearly continuously during their infancies, has slept with them every night since birth, breast-fed each of them for three years, and always tries to "follow their lead," as she puts it, playing whatever they are interested in even when it becomes mind-numbingly tedious.

Like Myra, Heather is using a *security strategy*—a set of mothering practices intended to create security, or at least a sense of security, for one's children or oneself. While Myra focuses on physical security—germs, health, and safety—Heather focuses on emotional security and hopes that lavishing love and comfort on her children will give them a secure inner core no matter what ultimately befalls them. But Heather's security strategy, like Myra's, comes at a cost. For her, motherhood feels like a supreme sacrifice. As she denies her own needs, she finds herself battling feelings of resentment and even rage. "It's just *so hard* sometimes," she tells me, once her crying has calmed enough for her to speak. "I feel like I'm carrying this whole thing and I'm just *fried*." As this book will show, it is not Heather's mothering practices, per se, but her single-minded intensity regarding the security she believes those practices will bring about that can undo the good she is trying so hard to do.

Stepping back from these individual mothers and taking a long-distance view, we see women's use of security strategies in their mothering is an entirely reasonable response to the current social situation. Within the context of an unpredictable economy, uncertainty about marriage, and fraying government safety nets, the last refuge of security upon which society at large projects almost mythical powers to make it all better is the mother-child relationship. Not that the mothering relationship typically *is* a source of ultimate security, but due to a lack of alternatives, we hold out hopes that it will be. Because of this, many mothers today try to shoulder almost impossible burdens. They want so badly to do what is necessary to keep their families safe, but they do not know how to change the economy or to make marriage into a reliably soul-nurturing institution, so they do what they think they *can* do for their families. They can focus their protective energies on insecurity in the emotional realm, like Heather, or on germs, like Myra, and make those the battleground issues upon which the struggle for security is fought. If they can at least right those wrongs, they can feel they are fulfilling their maternal responsibilities and standing between their families and the surrounding perils.

The unfortunate finding of this research, however, and what *Motherload* will repeatedly show, is that heaping mothers with unrealistic security expectations causes them to engage in struggles that actually cause security *repercussions* within the family. The fierceness of a woman's efforts, the vastness of her skills, or her willingness to shoulder such burdens aside, a one-relationship solution to society-sized insecurities simply doesn't work. Furthermore, the contortions required for this type of individualistic solution put great strains upon families that set in motion a cascade of ill-effects. This research documents those ill-effects, born of our hopes for redemptive security projected onto the mother-child relationship, and also documents the much greater ease in families that manage against the odds to take alternative approaches, such as more evenly distributing the responsibility for security among a greater number of players than just the mother.

WHY SECURITY?

Motherload is based on 168 interviews with fifty-one mothers in the United States, thirty-four of whom partook in a longitudinal study during the first three years of their children's lives, beginning in late pregnancy. To capture some of the diversity in American mothers, I interviewed women of various races and ethnicities, wealthy and poor, married and unmarried, lesbian and heterosexual, native-born and immigrant, and who ranged in age from teens to women in their forties. For a full listing of the study participants and a discussion of the research methodology, see appendices A and B.

When I began this research, I intended to examine the effects of various social forces on how women juggle independence and connection in their roles as mothers. I wasn't focusing on security, but the women I interviewed certainly were. In discussing why they chose to mother in the particular ways they did, security came up with such resounding frequency that I simply could not ignore it. For example, mothers such as Heather Dover—who keep their children close, hold them frequently, and attend to their every whimper—typically do so for the sake of security. Likewise, mothers who seem to have just the opposite in mind—who purposefully let their children cry it out in separate rooms, do not gate the stairs, or handle children roughly to toughen them up—also explain these choices as necessary measures for survival in today's challenging world—in other words, as security.

Framing their mothering as a security project makes sense when we recognize these twenty-first-century women almost universally discuss rampant *insecurity* in the world or in their own lives. They have financial worries or see the United States as economically insecure and are concerned for their children's place in it. They see how undependable relationships can be, both their own and those they anticipate for their children. They are concerned about crime, sickness, and accidents. And as mothers, they often feel a level of personal responsibility to remedy all of this for their children. Even before their children are born, many mothers have a how-to in mind—how they hope their particular manner of mothering will, indeed, create some measure of security.

Common as the expressed concern with security is in contemporary mothering, however, there is great variety in what women actually mean by the word. Merriam-Webster's dictionary defines "security" both as "freedom from danger: safety"—which is an objective experience—and as "freedom from fear or anxiety"—a subjective experience. Mothers, too, speak of both objective and subjective experiences of security. They talk about security as protection from accidents, child abduction, or germs. They talk about it as solid paychecks serving as an insurance against men who might abandon them. They talk about it as a feeling of emotional safety with dearly loved ones. They talk about the *sense* of security when something can be counted on to remain in their lives forever and not just as a matter of whim.

Through these discussions, I came to understand that security does not have a fixed, commonly agreed-upon meaning, but rather it is an umbrella concept, similar to "God" or "love." Such concepts are so foundational that almost all people use them to explain their actions and motives, despite having vastly different meanings to different people. All of those widely varying meanings converge and become concentrated in a single potent container symbol—the word—the usage of which is culturally mandated and the substance of which powerfully influences people's choices and how they interpret their lives. As rhetorical theorist Michael McGee argues, human beings are conditioned "not directly to belief and behavior, but to a vocabulary of concepts that function as guides, warrants, reasons, or excuses for behavior and belief."[3] Security has certainly become such a concept in American society today.

It is worth notice and study that security has become a must-invoke concept in the vocabularies of mothers of young children—during the so-called critical years of children's development. But equally worth notice and study is the fact that most of these women see the mother-child relationship not merely as one means through which security (however defined) can be brought to their families but as the primary means. This assumption brings its own set of consequences for families.

While psychologists have been focusing for decades on attachment and emotional security in the mother-child relationship, sociologists have largely failed to delve into their own dimensions of security as they relate to this first and arguably most important social relationship that humans experience. This is a great oversight in the twenty-first-century United States. National security issues, terrorism, economic volatility, job insecurity, psychotherapeutic framings pinning insecurity to early childhood experiences, divorce anxiety, and worries about health and safety all loom large in the national consciousness, yet we know little about the effect of these widely shared forms of insecurity on how parents bring up their children, particularly on how parents attempt to make themselves and their children feel more secure. This book addresses that issue. It shows how mothers manage the threats they see all around them—threats once collectively managed but now frequently viewed as within the purview of individual families—by using a variety of highly patterned security strategies in their mothering. As our collective burdens fall upon mothers and compel them to utilize such strategies, it is an extreme disservice to then dismiss their behavior as "mommy madness" or to fail to recognize the load they are shouldering and the reasonableness of the quest for security underlying their actions.

This research shows how incredibly common it is for mothers within the current social climate to try to carry enormous weight. It also shows how displacing economic, physical, social, and existential fears onto the project of child rearing generally does not make it all better. In fact, despite women's best efforts, it often does just the opposite.

TOWARD A NONPATHOLOGICAL UNDERSTANDING OF
INTENSIVE MOTHERING

There is broad consensus that mothering has intensified during the last four or five decades. Although women's paid work hours have also increased during precisely the same decades, mothers paradoxically spend more time with their children now than they did in 1965.[4] Working mothers today (whose numbers have dramatically increased since the 1960s and who now make up the vast majority of American mothers) spend a higher proportion of that time actively engaged with their children than their stay-at-home counterparts in the past or present.[5] The subjective difficulty of mothering has increased since a generation ago.[6] And both the financial outlay on behalf of children and the emotional absorption in those children are at levels that may be unprecedented in human history.[7] The strength of these trends has stimulated a flood of research and commentary, bringing to light what has been alternately called the "ideology of intensive mothering," "parenting out of control," "hyper-parenting," the ethic of "total motherhood," and "mommy madness."[8]

To date, the most convincing arguments regarding the causes of this sort of extreme mothering are found in the research on class differences. Social class—an amalgam of financial, social, and cultural resources including one's educational background, income, and wealth—has clear ties to security. Those with greater resources can better protect themselves from various social and economic dangers. Yet despite that, the "haves" of our society are anything but relaxed about their social position,[9] and the effects of social class on parenting reveal an unexpected pattern. In fact, the most well-established contributor to mothering intensity is economic anxiety—among the privileged. Well-off parents fear that their children may lose their class status without the boost of intense parental involvement, and sociologist Annette Lareau shows how these parents therefore frequently take a managerial approach to motherhood: hiring tutors, scheduling enrichment activities, and pouring ever greater resources into their progeny to increase the likelihood they will succeed.[10] Likewise, sociologist Margaret Nelson documents how a fear of downward mobility can drive professional parents into "out of control" child surveillance and micromanagement.[11] Both Lareau and Nelson thus offer explanations of why parents on the upper end of the social-class spectrum, with everything to lose, engage in such high-intensity practices.

Sociologists Kathryn Edin and Maria Kefalas show how, at the other end of the class spectrum, poor single women with nothing to lose have everything to gain from motherhood and thus frequently seek their own emotional security, life grounding, and even *salvation* in their relationships with their children.[12] These women, like their middle-class sisters, dream of good jobs and stably employed partners, but for them, that dream is unreachable. Well-paying and meaningful career options are not available in their neighborhoods, particularly to people with their educational backgrounds, and their social networks do not offer them solid prospective partners. With dependable work and partnership foreclosed as avenues to security, they take the route that remains: having a baby and centering their lives on motherhood.

The findings of these two types of class-based study seem to contradict one another, with Edin and Kefalas showing how it is the underprivileged who forefront motherhood and Nelson and Lareau showing how it is the privileged who do so. Taking security as the clarifying concept, however, both of these findings make sense. Resource-rich mothers sometimes bear an eerie resemblance to the poor women Edin and Kefalas describe because the privileged *feel* anxious and insecure as well; it is simply a different form of insecurity. Theirs is a "what if" insecurity about a hypothetical and disastrous future rather than the "what is" insecurity of the poor navigating their current realities. The poor therefore "put motherhood before marriage" for one set of security reasons while the privileged "parent out of control" for a different set of security reasons. The results? A whole lot of focus on mothering at all points on the social map!

As various forms of insecurity have become more pervasive, class no longer suffices as the single dimension with which to understand either security or, relatedly, differences in mothering. It is necessary to broaden our investigation at this point to include how mothering relates to job insecurity (which can occur anywhere along the class spectrum), divorce anxiety, fear of terrorism or child abduction, and the long list of the other security concerns that women repeatedly raised in their interviews with me.

It is particularly urgent to look at this relationship between security and motherhood now, given the historical context in which it is embedded. Indeed, we may have greater compassion for the mothering "madness" of recent decades if we recognize the connection and perfect synchronization between two seemingly disparate phenomena: the advent of a "culture of fear" or "risk society," on the one hand, and the intensification of mothering, on the other.

A radical break took place around the early 1970s when concern with various forms of insecurity began to escalate and we saw the emergence of a "risk society."[13] Just as people's perceptions of risk shot up, we saw a dramatic upsurge in a "child-centered, expert-guided, emotionally absorbing, labor-intensive, and financially expensive" form of child rearing, which sociologist Sharon Hays later termed "intensive mothering."[14] I argue that these historical trends are related and that, as families have felt increasingly under threat (and less and less protected by social safety nets and other forms of support), they have pinned their hopes on intensive mothering as the security solution for their own individual families.

When a child is born, many of today's mothers' first orders of business, whether conscious or unconscious, is to devise what I call a *security strategy*. A security strategy is an ideologically driven set of mothering practices intended to maximize the security derived from the mother-child relationship. How women do this—their actual practices of intensive mothering—varies tremendously. One can hover over one's toddling child lest she stumble (accident prevention), train her to be tough and fit for independent survival (resilience building), or hold and breast-feed her around the clock (physical and emotional comfort giving), to name a few.

I find that these strategic differences directly relate to which particular forms of insecurity are most urgent in the woman's own life, which themselves vary widely. Many women are concerned about economic insecurity—both their own abilities to provide for their families and their children's prospects for eventually getting well-paid jobs. Additionally, doctors, parenting books, and well-meaning friends barrage women with information about potential physical threats to children. Almost all of the mothers I spoke with mentioned concerns about SIDS (sudden infant death syndrome), in which a seemingly healthy baby dies suddenly and inexplicably. Mothers are concerned with toxins, allergens, and germs, and many brought up the common belief that feeding a baby bottled formula rather than breast-feeding deprives the baby of immunological protection against such risks.[15] Many mothers also worry about violence against children or abandoning men—dangers they believe they can mitigate with the proper parenting choices.

A mother may further feel her child's emotional security is at stake. She may believe the child's self-esteem will be compromised if he sees himself as losing or failing, which could in turn make him feel unloved or unwanted. In short, the child is seen as a fragile being who could be scarred for life by improper handling, so his main handler (meaning his mother) had better get it right.[16]

Within this flurry of concerns, the mother flips on the nightly news and sees Al Qaeda's latest terrorist threat, pedophiles tracking smartphone photos of children, the outbreak of a new rapidly spreading strain of disease, and a heartbreaking Day 37 update on the search for a kidnapped girl. This is followed by a report on today's overscheduled, overmedicated, or overweight children, with the commentator saying what a shame it is that kids no longer run around outdoors or create their own play.

A woman who tries to weave a security blanket for her child of such threads may well feel daunted, yet this is only half of the mothering-for-security story, from the perspective of the child's interests. However, children are not the only ones whose security is at stake. A mother is, after all, not merely preparing her child to live in an insecure world; she is living in that world and feeling all that insecurity herself. Her own job security may be eroding as waves of social, economic, and technological change splash over her. Her partnership may be imperiled, or she may not have a partner in parenthood. She may be anxious about highly publicized large-scale threats such as global terrorism. Where, we might ask, are mothers seeking their own safe havens?

Perhaps not surprisingly, my research shows that they are frequently seeking it in the same mother-child relationship that is supposed to provide a safe haven for the child. Fifty-one percent of mothers of minor children rank their children as the single greatest contributor to their personal happiness and fulfillment (whereas only about half as many rank their partners as the most important element, and even fewer point to their careers).[17] Given this priority women place on the mother-child relationship for their own well-being, it would be a great oversight to look at motherhood merely as a form of child socialization in which other-oriented women give to security-hungry children what those children need to survive in an unreliable world. Women need security as well, and for many women, motherhood is a primary source from which they draw their own coping resources.[18] This additional element of the security equation has received far too little attention in the sociological research on intensive mothering, which usually frames women's extreme efforts as being made for the benefit of their children.[19]

Psychological research likewise overwhelmingly focuses on the child's perspective and frames mothers as security *objects*, not as security *subjects*, with their own stakes in an intensive mother-child relationship. However, ignoring a mother's subjectivity and her own security needs and yearnings conceals a crucial aspect of the intensive mothering phenomenon: some women vehemently attach themselves to the mother-child relationship because it makes *them* feel secure.

It is time to update our understanding of intensive mothering. When Hays collected her data in the 1990s, she found intensive mothering to be "child-centered,"[20] but at this point I find that intensive mothers typically go into less detail about their actual children than they do about the mother-child relationship. The twenty-first-century variant of intensive mothering is not as much child-centered as it is "mother-child-centered." Whether geared to the mother's needs or the child's, it is the *relationship* that is endowed with the precious power to produce security, and the correct execution of that relationship on which many mothers focus their energies.

The effects of societal insecurity on the mother-child relationship, then, are arguably twofold. On the one hand, many women do take on the onus of providing security for their children. The combination of perceived threats (high insecurity), the assumption of a "breakable child" (high stakes), and a widely shared belief that mothering determines how a child turns out (high responsibility) can conspire to create anxiety and a somewhat desperate attempt to practice "correct mothering."[21] The assumption is often that the mother-child relationship *should* be able to keep a child emotionally, physically, and economically safe, so the goal is to figure out how to do that and then hold tenaciously to that mothering model.

On the other hand, instability in work, marriage, and other possible sources of security for women themselves prompts many mothers to seek their own security havens within the mother-child relationship, often the one relationship they feel they can count on to be there for the long haul. Here, the focus is on the mother's needs rather than the child's, but again the goal is to maximize security through the right type of mother-child relationship.

Given the security that the mother-child relationship is expected to provide to both the mother and the child, motherhood is becoming a taller and taller order. It is increasingly regarded as *the* relationship to make it all better.

I use the term *motherload* to describe the subjective importance of the mother-child relationship and the power ascribed to it to provide security to the mother, the child, or both. Metaphorically, the motherload is the weight that many women carry into motherhood as they view the mother-child relationship as a singularly powerful form of protection, amelioration, or even salvation in an undependable or seemingly threatening world. And, as I have suggested, this awesomely potent medicine may not be intended to save merely the child; for some women, it is the way to save themselves.

MATERNAL DETERMINISM

In the last several decades, the motherload has become heavier. Plausibly, this could have happened either because threat perception went up and there was an increase in the felt need for security, or because mothers were relegated greater responsibility for providing that security. In fact, both have occurred.

Many parents now view themselves as being "alone in the tasks of raising children and as having sole responsibility for their children's safety and psychological well-being."[22] This sole responsibility is partly due to a "great risk shift" in the last several decades wherein the hazardous consequences of our social and economic organization have been passed from the broader society to private families, who increasingly bear the brunt of society's problems.[23] Anthropologist David Harvey claims this shift began in the 1970s and 1980s when a doctrine of neoliberalism took hold in much of the world.[24] State protections weakened, inequality grew, and families were increasingly forced to find individual solutions to higher and higher levels of risk. But when we say "the family," who precisely is it that we are talking about? In her study of American families today, Sociologist Marianne Cooper finds that it is "the women in these families [who are] expected to be the family's security guards . . . charged with keeping insecurity at bay, while their husbands [are] comparatively less burdened . . ."[25] That is, in the current gendering of family life, security and motherhood have become inextricably linked. However, managing increasing amounts of security work at precisely the historical moment when the state and public sectors have backed off from their own responsibilities puts a great burden on mothers.

While the rise of the risk society and the shift of the burden of that risk from public to private domains have both occurred during the period from the 1970s through the present, maternal determinism dates back much further. Since the late nineteenth century, when Sigmund Freud first pointed the finger of blame for people's troubles at their early, even if unconscious, childhood experiences with their mothers, people seeking to understand their lives have tended to exonerate the society in which they find themselves. Instead, when things go well, they credit themselves and their own individual merits. And when things go badly, one low-hanging fruit they can easily pluck is a "bad mother."[26] In other words, when trying to understand why their own or others' lives fall apart—why some people can't stay partnered, why no one will hire them, why they murder—people typically explain it in terms of personalities rather than social forces, and often view undesirable personalities as the outcome of "improper parenting."[27] This rise of psychotherapeutic framings has led our society to psychologize social problems and to place both the culpability and the burden of remedy in private hands—especially mothers'. During the period between World War II and the late 1950s, women's quality of mothering came to be held responsible for every possible outcome in their offspring, from schizophrenia and male homosexuality to bed-wetting and even color-blindness.[28] Philip Wylie's *Generation of Vipers*, a vitriolic attack on the damage "overbearing mothers" were wreaking on society during this period, argued that our nation was in a deep "nightmare now and mom sits on its decaying throne."[29] Mothers, having been sent home from their wartime jobs and banished to the suburbs, allegedly lacked anything to do and therefore smoked, chewed gum, ate bonbons (*Vipers* was the origin of the bonbon-eating myth about stay-at-home mothers), and created a whole generation of emasculated sons who could no longer contribute to society. In other words, Wylie argued, the downfall of civilization was due to smothering mothers. On the other hand, society at large viewed mothers who *with-held* affection from their children as equally viperous, and the commonly accepted cause of child autism was "refrigerator moms," whose coldness purportedly brought on this dreaded disease in their children. A mother was therefore damned if she did, damned if she didn't during this historical time period, which was arguably the apex of mother-blame: the dark side of maternal determinism in which all that is wrong with either individuals or the social order is due to bad mothers.

In the 1960s through the early 1980s, new ideas flooded the cultural landscape and maternal determinism became wedded to the idea of security—a seemingly more positive spin on the supreme power of mothering, in which the sensitive (i.e., good) mother was viewed as her child's nearly sole security source.[30] Psychologists John Bowlby and Mary Ainsworth brought these ideas to the fore and elaborated the determinative effects of early mothering through their development of attachment theory. This theory states that an infant's attachment security hinges on its relationship with one sensitive and responsive adult (often described as the mother or mother-substitute). For example, Ainsworth discovered that babies' attachments were more "secure" if their mothers quickly and affectionately responded to their cries, held them with tenderness and affection, and breast-fed on demand rather than on a set schedule.[31] Since mothering in this time period was viewed less as viperous and more as a critically needed human good, and as middle-class women's labor force participation was steadily growing, it was now a mother's absence rather than her presence that was primarily pathologized—as what Bowlby called "maternal deprivation."[32] Public awareness of Harry Harlow's famous rhesus monkey experiments added an element of horror to the already-brewing concerns over the security consequences of a mother's absence or insensitivity. In Harlow's experiments, young monkeys without a mother present became crazed and clung to the little rags in their cages as if for dear life. Furthermore, given the choice between a terry-cloth substitute mother and a wire mesh substitute mother with a bottle of formula jutting from its chest, the little monkeys chose to be with the softer, nonfeeding mother any time they were not actively drinking, preferring that sense of comfort over food.[33] The take-home point for many mothers was: It's not about what you can provide; it's about *you*.

Your continuous loving presence is the magic pill your child needs in order to thrive and grow securely.

The deal was sealed in the 1970s when bonding research (now in disrepute due to faulty methodologies and for inferring too much about human babies from baby goats and other animals) showed the long-term consequences to children and to mother-child bonding when there was even a several-minute mother-child separation after the birth.[34]

This near-total responsibility for young children's emotional security that early attachment theorists placed on mothers' shoulders (and in their arms and at their breasts) resonated so well with popular audiences that Bowlby's and Ainsworth's conclusions, along with those of the bonding researchers, jumped the academic fence and were absorbed into the public consciousness.[35] At the same time, a swelling supply of advice books trumpeted the thesis of maternal determinism.[36] One likely reason advice books converged on this thesis relates to sales. Sociologist Ofer Sharone finds that the self-help industry fosters a belief in personal agency, which makes prospective book buyers feel that everything will be okay if they can simply do what the book says.[37] Just as with the selling of deodorant, teeth whiteners, and expensive cars, selling expert parenting books relies on convincing people both that there is a problem to be anxious about and that the product (or, in this case, the form of correct mothering espoused in the book) can solve that problem. The expert parenting literature thus peddles individual control, a distinctly nonsociological view of how the world works, but one that sells books. As such books began to fly off the store shelves and homeward, both the mother's crucial role in providing security to her child and her ability to right a thousand wrongs, if she is willing to mother properly, came to be taken for granted.

The scientific concept of attachment was thus beginning to shape the very behavior it was created to explain.[38] Rather than receiving attachment theory as a descriptive—the observation that a child's attachment security relates to its mother's sensitivity and responsiveness—mothers were instead increasingly receiving it as an imperative: thou shalt make thy child secure. Taking up that yoke of now-pop psychology with vigor (and perhaps fortified by middle-class female guilt about entering the workforce in droves in the 1970s), women exceeded the theory's original intent by assuming responsibility not just for their children's emotional security but for other forms of security as well. For example, mothers often see it as their responsibility—and theirs alone—to steer their children clear of social and academic failures, to mitigate their children's exposure to environmental toxins, to deflect potential crimes against their children, and so on.

The rise of this maternally deterministic view of security in the 1970s and 1980s fit devastatingly well with the forces of neoliberalism shifting risk from society at large to individual families (and specifically to mothers). While the first of these social changes struck on the cultural level—the absorption of psychotherapeutic framings into everyday understandings—the other hit on the socioeconomic level—the privatization of risk. Either of these shifts alone would be grounds to argue for an increased motherload, and their emergence in tandem in different realms of social life only amplified the effect, completely naturalizing women's responsibility for maintaining security, and giving us the perfect set of shoulders on which to place the burden of our social problems.

Furthermore, at the very same moment as we designated Mother as the ultimate security source, the need for security skyrocketed, adding additional weight to the load.

OBJECTIVE INSECURITY

Whether one describes the last several decades using the terms "Risk Society," "The Great Risk Shift," or "The New Insecurity," people today are feeling insecure and there are some fairly compelling reasons why they feel that way.[39]

One common site of insecurity is work. Labor unions, created to protect workers, began rapidly disappearing in the 1970s, and in the 1980s we saw the burgeoning of a new corporate ethic of restructuring and downsizing.[40] In part due to these economic changes, the fear of job loss increased almost fourfold during the last quarter of the twentieth century, such that almost half of American workers were "frequently concerned about being laid off."[41] The recession of 2008 only heightened these fears.[42]

Work insecurity itself is not a new historical development, however. The preeminent sociologist Emile Durkheim, writing in the late nineteenth century, discussed how people in the West once had fairly well-defined life paths, with trades mostly passed down from parents to children.[43] The explosion of nonfamily industrial productivity undid that certainty and created a world abuzz with life options. Without a clear social blueprint for how to live or what to do for one's livelihood, this increase in personal freedom carried with it a new source of doubt for individuals who now had "no choice but to choose how to be and how to act."[44]

The number of vocations has simply exploded in recent years and with it the anxiety of the uncharted path. Parents today have no idea what the world of work will look like when their children are grown. The options are more plentiful, but a lot less is known about them. Furthermore, until recently, once one managed to land in an occupation, the sense of wayfaring uncertainty was generally over. But for the last three to four decades, particularly for the younger cohort of workers, there has been no such thing as landing.[45] That is, today's work insecurity is not merely due to the lack of guidelines, unknowns, and the vastness of the job market as one enters but is also due to one's constantly shifting location within that vast market. This is new. Among mid- to large-sized firms, there is "more hiring, more firing, and more companies doing both at once" than in previous times.[46] While periods of joblessness between positions may be short, even short periods without work or frequently shifting job descriptions create a new tenuousness in people's work lives.

The trend toward job-hopping among younger workers (who are the workers most likely to be parents of young children) has economic repercussions as well. Frequently changing jobs generates greater income instability, which is "almost five times as great as it was in the early 1970s."[47] That means that incomes go up and down more frequently now than in the past. Regarding the down, in a given two-year period, about half of all families will experience a drop in real income, and the amount of that drop has increased dramatically since the 1970s.[48]

Along with the financial roller coaster of increasing income fluctuation comes a fear of material loss and poverty that affects even those who do not actually experience a loss but who see the trends around them and wonder if they will be next. In the quarter century prior to the 2008 recession, home foreclosure rates had already increased fivefold, bankruptcy almost sevenfold,[49] and the recession only caused these figures to further rise.[50] While the national child poverty rate hovers around 20 percent, the threat of poverty affects many more people than that. In fact, given higher income volatility and the increased likelihood that a child will live with a single parent at some point during her upbringing, the *majority* of US children now spend at least one year in poverty by the time they are eighteen years old.[51]

Thus, while the anxiety of the early industrial period might be characterized as "too much to *choose*," today's angst might be characterized as "too much to *lose*." With change a perennial requisite of continued success, the direction of that change could always take one either up or down the social ladder.

If a woman feels threatened in this insecure milieu, where can she turn for refuge? One might expect her to turn to her life partner, both for emotional and financial grounding. Yet even if she is married (and the likelihood of this is decreasing over time), her soul may not rest in that fact, as the half of marriages that will end in divorce make the other half feel less certain of enduring.[52] Indeed, this research shows that marriage not only fails to redress the anxiety over potential losses elsewhere in one's life but it also adds another arena of anxiety over potential loss. With US divorces occurring after a median marriage duration of only 7.2 years, marriage is losing its haven status.[53]

Marriage is not the only relationship on the security chopping block. Community ties, too, are providing less and less shelter from the storm. Political scientist Robert Putnam compiled extensive evidence that civic participation and both formal and informal social associations have declined in recent times and that people have fewer stable social networks on which to depend for support. For example, since 1965 there has been a 40 percent decline in schmoozing among friends, including parties, casual conversations, and simply hanging out together.[54] People are less likely to socialize and spend time with their neighbors and they spend less time in houses of worship.[55] Associations that still exist are often short-term, life-stage specific, and relationships of convenience.[56]

Between job insecurity, economic volatility, marriage unpredictability, and the decline of community support, we see ample evidence of objectively declining bases of security in American society in the last several decades. Pairing this with the cultural view of mothers as security providers that arose during precisely those same decades, the motherload has become heavier since the 1970s.

SUBJECTIVE INSECURITY

Beyond this objective destabilization, a subjective element also contributes to modern fears. There was certainly plenty of economic insecurity during the Great Depression, and American families experienced tremendous mortal fear during the world wars. Furthermore, many more children died of illness and injury in the past than do now. Yet despite recent increases in actual health and safety, the fear of toxins, germs, and accidents has rapidly increased.[57] Likewise, "as crime rates plunged throughout the 1990s . . . two-thirds of Americans believe[d] they were soaring."[58] This is less about objective measures and more about fears. Sociologist Shulamit Reinharz writes: "[I]t is difficult to imagine a public space that does not tell me that I have to fear theft, suffocating others, becoming ill, or being blown to pieces. . . . [T]here is so much information of this sort, people are beginning to think that catastrophes are almost inevitable."[59]

Indeed, sociologists describe the current ethos as a "culture of fear"[60] in which people are "obsessively preoccupied with the conviction that we are living under the threat of hazardous uncertainty."[61] Sociologist Barry Glassner offers a theory of displacement that explains our rising fears as symbolic scapegoats that deflect our attention from the real perils of society: "From a psychological point of view extreme fear and outrage are often projections. Consider, for example, the panic over violence against children. By failing to provide adequate education, nutrition, housing, parenting, medical services, and child care over the past couple of decades we have done the nation's children immense harm. Yet we project our guilt onto a cavalcade of bogeypeople—pedophile preschool teachers, preteen mass murderers, and homicidal au pairs, to name only a few."[62]

This displacement of fear from the failings of a poorly organized society to the crimes of a few deviant individuals within that society depoliticizes our shared insecurities and deemphasizes our collective responsibility both for creating these problems and for solving them. Extreme fear can thereby serve to maintain the status quo. In fact, if one takes a step back from the real perils that Glassner contends are being ignored and the scapegoats onto whom our fear is projected, several differences become apparent. Specifically, attention shifts from problems that are ongoing, that harm millions of people, and that are part of the social organization, and instead we focus on problems that are unexpected events affecting only a handful of people seemingly at random. While a rational calculus of fear would predict that the former problems, affecting many more people over a much longer time, would cause more alarm, it is the latter that arouse a greater emotional response. That is because involuntary one-time-event risks (such as terrorism and nuclear disaster) inspire more fear than ongoing voluntary risks (such as driving, smoking, or poorly funded social programs), even though the voluntary risks generally involve a much greater probability of harm.[63]

In the 1980s, risk scholars developed the *social amplification of risk framework* to explain why some risks are amplified while others are minimized. This framework shows that risks such as terrorism and homicidal au pairs, by virtue of being dreaded events (that is, identifiable incidents that are uncontrollable, viscerally horrible, and fatal), are the types of risk whose dangers people tend to most highly amplify over the actual probability of harm.[64]

Frightening occurrences may also appear more probable than they truly are due to disproportionate media focus on crime, terrorism, deadly bacterial strains, and other disasters. The media amplify everyday forms of insecurity as well, such as divorce. An archival search of the number of articles about divorce published in a set of mainstream magazines such as *Time* and *Newsweek* reveals an average of 51.3 such articles per year in the 1980s, 68.1 in the 1990s, and 75.0 during the first seven years of the 2000s.[65] So although the divorce rate has stabilized, the divorce *discourse* rate continues to rise. Saturated in this discourse and in the glossy chronicling of celebrity divorces in grocery lines, the threat of partner loss appears both omnipresent and *personalized.*

Social media likewise abound with personalized instances of misfortune. In all eras, hearing about a friend's bad luck has caused psychological ricochets, prompting people to wonder if they, too, would contract that illness or lose their corn crops or have their own houses burn down.

However, with the rising accessibility of new communication technologies, the number of personal cautionary tales that people are exposed to is mounting far more quickly than the number of tales themselves. That is, due to the proliferation of Facebook, e-mail, blogs, YouTube, and other technologies for the easy mass dissemination of formerly private information, many of today's incidents of woe have an unprecedented number of witnesses. Witnessing personal loss has powerful effects, causing a sort of "insecurity osmosis" as people absorb other people's tribulations into their own stockpiles of fears.[66] Returning to divorce, sociologist Karla Hackstaff finds that "divorce anxiety—a tangible uncertainty regarding [one's] own and other marriages . . . seems to be fostered by witnessing family or friends going through a divorce."[67] She also finds that, as time goes on, "the felt prevalence of divorce is unmistakably greater" due to this "ripple effect" of repeated exposure.[68] Similarly, regarding work, one layoff among one hundred coworkers results in the other ninety-nine people experiencing job insecurity because, as social theorist Pierre Bourdieu observes, "insecurity acts directly on those it touches . . . and indirectly on all the others, through the fear it arouses."[69]

Thus, the increasing accessibility of highly personal stories of misfortune and today's veritable explosion of witnessing amplify the effects such misfortunes have on subjective insecurity and on the sense that the world is a place where bad things happen.

THE MOTHERING TUG-OF-WAR

While risk scholars engage in lively debates regarding the degree to which today's insecurities are objective phenomena or socially constructed perceptions, *Motherload* examines the unmistakably real effects these insecurities have on how women mother. When an individual feels she cannot count on her job, house, partner, or community to be there for the long term, or when she has an aroused fear of economic loss, crime, or disaster, how does this shape her parenting choices?

If, like most women in this research, she believes the mother-child relationship has special security-producing powers, the question remains how best to structure that relationship to take home the prize. Should she shield her child and turn her family into a safe alternative universe in which the rules are entirely different from the increasingly competitive, threatening, and elusive rules of the world at large? Or should she instead try to promote knowledge and savvy regarding "life out there," including practice at struggle, uncertainty, and standing back up after a punch? Will an intensely independent child succeed where others fail, or will she be stressed, miserable, and alone? Conversely, will a child showered with love, kisses, and a sense of her own goodness have a secure inner core capable of coping with life's certain challenges, or will she be a lamb to the slaughter?

These questions relate to the clearest difference I find in how women expect the mother-child relationship to produce security: namely, through independence or connection. If a mother highlights independence, she may speak of the importance of a child's toughness or flexibility in today's world and may strive to foster his own self-protective abilities, let him take risks (and learn from failures or from getting hurt) and leave him alone in his crib as a baby to learn how to self-soothe. These are not acts of neglect or last-resort measures when she hits her limits but rather deliberate measures intended to expose the child to *just the right* level of difficulty to make him stronger without overwhelming him. In addition to this, a mother's own needs may come into play in her independence orientation if she sees her own security as stemming from sources, such as her paycheck, that involve separation from the child. In either case, she frames her family's security as best served by a degree of carefully meted mother-child independence.

According to multiple social theorists such as anthropologist Margaret Mead and sociologists Robert Bellah and Jerald Wallulis, this tendency to prioritize independence, individualism, and selfhood over connectivity—either in one's children or oneself—is widespread in insecure societies or during times of rapid social change.[70] The logic is simple: if one views connections as ever shifting, insecure, or undependable, then overly depending upon them puts one at risk. Therefore, insecurity promotes independence.

A great amount of evidence supports these theories both regarding what parents believe their children need to survive and what women want for themselves in insecure social contexts. For example, in the 1970s, as the economy weakened and divorce rates shot up, so, too, did women's desires for independence. While we tend to frame the second-wave feminist discourse—extolling paid work as a path to women's independent selfhood—as a *cause* of white middle-class women's changing work patterns in the 1970s, social historian Stephanie Coontz has amassed data showing this discourse may have instead been a *response* to conditions of economic and marital destabilization—which necessitated women to join the workforce.[71] Regardless of the causal link, economic downturn and record-high divorce rates occurred alongside a burgeoning discourse on the value of women's independence, which became an increasingly central component of US womanhood, even beyond the white middle-class feminists who originally gave it voice.[72] By the end of the twentieth century, the vast majority of US women considered independence important in defining themselves as persons, and financial independence was women's top-rated financial goal.[73]

Women also increasingly view independence as crucial for their children. In the half century leading up to the 1970s, the frequency with which parents listed "independence" among the three most desired traits in their children went from only a quarter of parents to more than triple that.[74] This desire has since continued, and while not all ethnic communities view independence as favorably as do whites, US parents as a whole value their children's independence more highly than their kindness, self-confidence, or good study habits.[75]

Given this widespread value of independence and its adaptive logic in periods of undependable ties and rapid social change, it may be surprising that not all women describe their mothering security projects in this way. In contrast with such approaches, or perhaps in *response* to independence-oriented approaches in their *other* relationships, some mothers look to the mother-child relationship as the one and sometimes only realm in which deep dependency can freely reign. Drawing on a wholly different model of security, a mother with a connection-oriented security strategy may speak of the importance of her near-continuous presence in the child's life, of physically holding him to create a sense of security, of responding quickly whenever he cries, or of wanting to sequester the child away from threats in the world, with her there to keep him safe. She may also describe how being physically together with the child or devoting her life to motherhood helps *her* to feel more secure.

These women seem to defy the theories of increasing independence, at least regarding this one particular relationship. Likewise, all of the measures of the intensification of mothering in the last several decades—such as women spending more time with children and being more emotionally absorbed in them—suggest the possibility that the mother-child relationship may not perfectly mirror independence trends in marriage, work, and other relationships.

While these women with a connection-oriented approach to mother-child security cast doubt on generalized theories of increasing independence in times of uncertainty, their approach is perfectly in keeping with attachment theory. Attachment theory, among the most well-established theories in psychology—discussed earlier regarding maternal determinism—has as its most basic claim that a sense of threat propels most people to seek comfort and remedy through *connection* with those to whom they are most attached.[76]

Thus, the premise of both sets of theories is that people, under threat, will seek to become secure. The difference is that mothers can accomplish this either by prioritizing their own or their children's independence (for survival in a world of uncertainty and flux) or by creating a more intense mother-child connection (for solace in that ever-shifting world, as well as to cultivate advantage).[77]

This research thus finds no single US model of parenting for security but rather distinct models that emerge relative to the particular circumstances a woman is facing when she becomes a mother. In the upcoming chapters, I explore these circumstances, as well as the distinctive strategies, expectations, and weighty burdens of mothering they bring forth, and the resulting family dynamics when independence-oriented and connection-oriented mothers try to carry that weight. I also critically examine the assumption underlying all of these strategies that a properly enacted mother-child relationship does, in fact, have the power to make it all better.

PREVIEW OF FINDINGS

While much commentary on the new style of over-the-top mothering seems to imply a monolithic ideology or set of practices to which at least middle-class American women attempt to conform upon birthing a child, I find extreme mothering is far from uniform. Its diversity has, until now, been poorly understood. Yet its many variations include Heather's profusion of love and physical connecting, Myra's Internet-intensive preoccupation with health, and also much-overlooked strategies that seem quite different from either of these, such as intentionally exposing young children to germs, hardship, or various other forms of risk in order to toughen them up to life's travails. None of these women are outliers or anomalies. Their strategies of producing security through their particular mothering practices fall into patterns with those of other women who, unbeknownst to one another, use similar strategies within their own homes.

These strategies vary fundamentally along two dimensions, as depicted in Table 1. First, as just discussed, some strategies use mother-child connection as the primary security-producing tool, whereas others use independence. Second, some strategies are intended to provide security to the child, while others are aimed primarily at the mother's security. So, for example, one mother may use independence to create security for her child, and another may use connection to create security for herself.

Table 1   Mothering security strategies

Security strategy intended to enhance:	Independence Oriented	Connection Oriented
CHILD'S security	Strategy A	Strategy B
MOTHER'S security	Strategy C	Strategy D

Motherload explores this variety of security strategies and argues against a one-size-fits-all understanding of intensive mothering. For each of these different strategies, I include a chapter to explore the various factors that predispose women toward mothering in that particular way, the family dynamics that security strategy tends to foster, and the early outcomes associated with that strategy, including how the mother-child relationship itself tends to fare when a woman uses that strategy versus another.

As I explore this diversity of intensive mothering practices, I also grapple with the important convergence in why mothers engage in such practices: to produce security. Again and again, I heard women share their sense that the world is an undependable, scary, or insecure place in which to live and raise children, immediately followed by their beliefs that a properly managed mother-child relationship should be able to resolve some of that insecurity. That is, they carried motherloads. Yet as widely shared as this assumption is that women who practice (whichever form of) correct mothering *can* make it all better for their children or themselves, my findings call it into serious question. In fact, I never found a single case in which the mother's efforts to remedy a world of insecurity through a single just-right relationship in fact led to the holy grail of security. Instead such efforts frequently led to the opposite.

These findings sound terribly bleak: one more sociological study showing what a mess things are, with no clear way out. But, fortunately, there is more to the data, and more to the story of contemporary US mothering, than that. Yes, this research finds most mothers do struggle under enormously heavy motherloads—but it also finds a sizable minority of women who do not. These mothers remain somehow immune to pressures on mothers to single-handedly make it all better. While they are every bit as caring as women with heavy motherloads, these mothers do not aim to save either their children or themselves from emotional, economic, physical, or other perils by being just the right kind of mother. Without realizing the radical nature of their stance, they break from their fellow mothers by carrying light motherloads. For them, the mother-child relationship is simply one (often very special and lovely) relationship among many.

Like women with heavy motherloads, these mothers, too, often orient their mothering toward independence or connection. I devote one chapter to connection-oriented mothers with light motherloads—a category of women whose very existence reveals that highly connected, even consuming mothering practices can be partaken in without the belief that this is how one *should* mother in order to produce security—and another chapter to light-motherload independence. In these chapters, I analyze both what gives these women their unusual capacity for moderation and also how moderation in expectations about the mother-child relationship, in turn, affects women's adult partnerships, their work, and the mother-child relationship itself. The lives of these women provide a basis of comparison and shed much-needed light on the fact that motherloads vary in weight. Some women do imbue mothering with nearly magical powers to make it all better, but some—bringing up their children in the same place and time—do not. The surprise finding of this research is that the families of women who do not view motherhood as a panacea of security are paradoxically more secure over time. I chronicle their successes and draw on the data to show that the degree to which mothering is a struggle and an ordeal is less a matter of the intensity of the particular mothering practices a woman uses than it is a matter of how much security she expects those practices to create. That is, across class and racial divides, dramatic differences in family well-being trace back to *expectations* of motherhood.[78]

Motherload's core arguments, then, are that security seeking is the driving force of intensive mothering and that a high expectation of security in the mother-child relationship (i.e., the motherload) is what makes mothering so difficult today. It further argues that the motherload, carried with every good intention to produce security through this one uniquely powerful relationship, can unintentionally undermine families' security.

PART I Connection

2 Shielding and Antidote Strategies

MOTHERING THAT SAVES THE CHILD

I feel apprehensive [about crime] . . . and that has certainly affected my feelings towards the boys. I worry that they will not be able to enjoy childhood in the way I did, free from anxiety. I think I probably overcompensate by trying to make sure home is a safe haven for them as much as possible. . . . In such an uncertain world, I sometimes find myself saying, "Don't worry, Mummy's here. I'm always here," which seems a sad thing to have to say.

—Amy Rothschild, twenty-eight-year-old mother

I think the world is going to toughen the girls up enough without me. I think it already has. From the day they were born, they had to face the reality of living in the world . . . I want to create a safe haven, to the degree possible, where they *don't* have to be so tough.

—Pat Rodgers, thirty-year-old mother

Pat Rogers, a married white mother of four-year-old twin girls, has been saving up money for a procedure, and last year she asked the grandparents to chip in for it as their Christmas gifts to the girls. She wants to have electronic locator tags inserted under her daughters' skin so they can be found in case they are ever lost or abducted. Pat also voices great concern over the risk of terrorist attack and believes her job as a mother is to "provide safety, keep them *alive*. . . . [G]etting them to [age] twenty-one safely is my primary goal." She says having children brought out this

31

protectiveness in her. "After we had the kids . . . I had this anxiety or feeling of strong motivation to try to secure the area and make everything safe: get a new, safer car with airbags, put alarms on the windows of the house . . ."

By contrast, Morowa Franklin, a twenty-two-year-old single African American woman pregnant with her first child, has no plans to get an alarm system when her son is born, and certainly not electronic locator tags. Instead she says, "The most important thing a baby needs is to know it is loved." Nine months pregnant and about to give birth, she finds herself without a job, and the child's father lives in Jamaica. She lived with her mother during the middle part of the pregnancy, but they had a falling-out and she is currently living on the couch of a stranger who took Morowa in as an act of kindness and with whom Morowa and her son will live for several months after the birth. Morowa's economic circumstances are dire, with no money, home, or job, and one might expect this to be the focus of her concern relative to her son. Yet that is not the insecurity she speaks about. Unlike Pat, who is afraid of perils from the outside world, the perils Morowa presents as motivating her mothering are those that occur *within* families. She speaks of her own mother's interpersonal failures. "[W]hen I was little, my mother didn't tell me she loved me, and I've always felt that as something missing . . . I want to say those words so my . . . [child will have] a sense of security." She plans to hold her son day and night so as to feel she is providing him security.

Each of these women wants to use the mother-child connection to create security for her children, but the women have two very different models of what security means, why it is needed, and how to accomplish it as a mother. The first meaning is *physical* safety—with a great concern about death, accidents, illness, and danger from strangers—which is most salient for Pat in her efforts to keep her children alive. The second meaning is an *emotional* sense of security, which is ironically most pronounced for Morowa, even though she lives closer to the edge of physical survival than most other informants in this study.

First I will discuss mothers whose concern is primarily with their children's physical safety.

SHIELDING

When we think of a protective mother, certain images may come to mind: a woman gating the stairs, preventing Junior from sucking his germ-laden thumb at the park (or perhaps squeezing a drop of hand sanitizer on it first), or placing scissors out of his reach. She may think, "Watch your step," or "Is that stool stable?" or "Don't get too close to the edge." These images convey one type of danger from which many mothers want to protect their children, namely physical danger. In the twenty-first century, however, bodily protection has an updated version, as new forms of physical danger eclipse maternal worry about the hot stove or choking hazards. Although these classic concerns remain quite evident in practice, the physical dangers women discuss most tend to be of a different type more reflective of risk society. They include fears of such things as child abduction, terrorism, environmental catastrophes, pedophiles, and random crime. For example, Lottie Finch, a thirty-four-year-old white mother, is fairly characteristic in her sentiments: "I imagine people with girls are [more] afraid of kidnappers [than people with boys]. I know I would be! A friend of mine said she'd prefer her nine-year-old daughter walk home alone because when [her daughter] was with my boys, she got so distracted [by them that] the mom was afraid [the daughter] would be careless with traffic and wouldn't look both ways on the street. And I thought, 'You're going to let your nine-year-old girl walk home *alone*?' To me, that's a target for kidnappers. I couldn't believe it!"

Lottie is incredulous that her friend would be more concerned with her daughter's inattention making her an unsafe pedestrian than she was with a potential kidnapping. This incredulity is despite the fact that a child is fifty times more likely to be killed in a car accident than to be kidnapped by a non-family member—and the majority of these kidnapping victims are not killed.[1]

Gwen Savage, a white thirty-year-old mother, discusses the effect of this fear of kidnappers when she says, "People don't let their kids play outside because some weirdo might hurt them. Even if you decide it's safe enough to let *your* kid out, other parents aren't doing this, so there isn't anyone to play with."

Risk, as the term is used in economics, is defined as "the probability of an adverse event (e.g., injury, disease, or death) times the consequences of that event (e.g., number of injuries or deaths, types and severity of diseases)."[2] So why are mothers so afraid of the stray bullet or the kidnapper when the most lethal threat to their children is actually the blue-green minivan in which they drive to swim class?

Recall the *social amplification of risk framework* that suggests some risks are subjectively amplified more than others. Specifically, dreaded (involuntary, catastrophic, and capable of eliciting a strong emotional response) and unknown (new, poorly understood, and seemingly unpredictable) risks are assessed as the most dangerous.[3] Thus, the act of driving one's child to and fro may pose a greater actual danger to the child than the theoretical possibility of, say, abduction by a stranger, but the driving is voluntary, repeated, and seemingly predictable, whereas abduction is both dreaded and unknown, so the latter risk is amplified.[4]

Furthermore, "threat-induced anxiety tends to elevate risk perceptions," and the last several decades have no lack of threat-induced anxiety to heighten people's risk perception.[5] For example, the 9/11 attacks, which caused physical harm to a miniscule percentage of the population, caused an emotional response and *fear* of harm in a far larger percentage. Seeing the images over and over again of the World Trade Center's Twin Towers collapsing, and recognizing in horror what that meant for the thousands of people within them, left a lasting imprint of sorrow, vulnerability, and fear on the American psyche. After the attacks, more than two-thirds of Americans surveyed reported being very or somewhat concerned about their own families, friends, or selves being the victims of a future terrorist attack.[6]

Sociologist Ulrich Beck implicates the media, among other forces, in the amplification of risk: "The power of terrorist actions rises with a series of conditions . . . [including] the global, mass media–informed presence of terrorist risk . . ."[7] For example, in a 2008 presidential primary debate, the presider, ABC News anchorman Charles Gibson, prefaced a question by saying in a somber voice, "The next president of the United States may have to deal with a nuclear attack on an American city. . . . The best nuclear experts in the world say there's a 30 percent chance in the next ten years. Some estimates . . . [are] over 50 percent." Thus, millions of viewers simultaneously considered the high likelihood of an up-coming nuclear attack on an American city.

Jessica Tasker, a white mother of one, explains how this fear affected her family's geographical location. She says that she "wanted [them] to move to Ithaca, New York [over two hundred miles from New York City] . . . but [her] husband felt it was too close to New York City—in his mind a definite target for a nuclear blast." So the family settled elsewhere.

Concern with global environmental risk is also rising, and increasing ocean temperatures, storm intensity, and droughts cause some to wonder if the effects of human activity may eventually disrupt the very habitabil-ity of our planet. Anthony Giddens writes, "For hundreds of years, people worried about what nature could do to us—earthquakes, floods, plagues, bad harvests, and so on. At a certain point . . . we stopped worrying so much about what nature could do to us, and we started worrying more about what we have done to nature. The transition marks one major point of entry in risk society."[8]

Beck defines *risk society* as a state of affairs in which "hazards and in-securities [are] induced and introduced by modernization itself."[9] Encom-passing more than simply a subjectively inflated culture of fear, he distin-guishes today's risk society from prior times partly by virtue of today's world being the first in which complete self-annihilation is possible.

Myra Rossi, the germ-obsessed mother mentioned in the introduction, discusses her perceptions of the "world out there" that her now preschool-age daughter is entering. She says: "I'm concerned there's not going to *be* a world. Global warming is number one . . . the environment is going to cease to ex-ist. Add war, terrorism, random violence—people are just shot—road rage, diseases we can't eradicate. That's what [my daughter] is walking into."

Though some mothers in this study do *not* express insecurity or voice these sorts of apprehensions about life today, the majority do, and it is this majority I discuss now. For many women, the twenty-first century is a frightening time in which to mother and to keep their children physically safe.

Shirley Matheson, a white twenty-seven-year-old stay-at-home mother of a toddler boy, says, "[W]hen I stroller down the sidewalk or, worse, let my three-year-old walk down the sidewalk, I am always afraid a passing car will jump the curb and hit him. I have bad thoughts about drive-by shootings. . . . I panic if I am in a store and he strays down an aisle and I can't see him—this is a fear of someone stealing my child."

Within this fearful emotional context, mothers often carry very heavy motherloads and go to extreme lengths to protect their children. Philosopher Sara Ruddick writes, "[A]s she engages in preservation, a mother is liable to the temptations of fearfulness and excessive control. If she is alone with and responsible for . . . young children, then control of . . . her physical environment is her only option, however rigid or excessive she appears to outsiders."[10]

While the mechanics of this "excessive control" may vary, when threats occur or are perceived to occur, many women gravitate toward greater *connection* with their children.[11]

Shirley was in New York City on September 11, 2001, and is currently living on the opposite coast. Due to her fears of terrorism and crime, she says she and her son now spend a lot of time nesting at home together, away from the hazards of the world at large. Additionally, she actively tries to postpone her son's entry into the world, slow things down for him, and "let him be *a child*, without worries . . . a carefree existence."

Shirley is using what I call the *shielding* security strategy: a strategy in which mother-child connection serves as a barrier between children and the world's ills. Shirley protects her son both from contact with life's potentially harmful elements (by habitually keeping him home) and from worry about these things (by slowing down his exposure to potentially frightening information). This strategy is widely recognized and has been referred to in the scholarly literature and popular press by various names including "helicopter parenting," "hyper-parenting," or simply "overprotective parenting."[12]

Mothers themselves do not often see their parenting as overprotective. For example, Pat, the mother of four-year-old twins highlighted earlier, says, "I'm more concerned than most people [about threats to my children] because I'm better *educated* than most and have a better understanding of things." Likewise, Shirley says:

SM: I'm not overprotective. The protectiveness level is warranted for
   the world I'm living in. All these playdates and structured activities
   are warranted now.

AV: What's different now than in the past?

SM: I'm not scientific, and you'll hear people say, "These crimes have been around for many years," but I think that as a society, there is an increase in sexualizing children, and it puts them in a vulnerable position. And I think the Internet has given anonymity to perversions, and that's different. People are able to act on impulses . . . and that's a riskier society. That's why I'm consciously *not* trying to push an independence agenda with my son. I err on the side of protection and wanting him to be innocent, and I'll give him information and send him out there when he *wants* to go, when he *asks* for it.

Shirley not only sees the world around her as increasingly risky, thus warranting her type of mothering, but she also frames her anxiety and fears as constructive.

My fears began postpartum, like the first three months . . . gearing up to be a protective mom. You'll hear stories of a mom jumping in front of a car to protect her kids, but that has to come from something, some kind of re-hearsal. So these thoughts were me rehearsing and getting programmed for that kind of thing. . . . I started having fears, and it was my mind exer-cising itself to say: "You're responsible for more than yourself now." I'm pushing a stroller—so what if a car jumps the curb and hits us? Before kids, I didn't have these fears . . . I wasn't thinking about bad things happening. Now that I'm a mom, I do.

Shirley believes her fears, which motherhood intensified, help her to keep her son away from those dangers and also create a difference within *her* so she will be prepared to aid her child should he ever be in mortal danger. Seeing terrorism, perversions, and crime as ever encroaching, she believes it is her responsibility as a mother to somehow, even if by throw-ing herself in front of a vehicle, keep her child safe from all that.

The shielding strategy she uses, like all the security strategies I describe in this book, is associated with particular insecurities. There are two types of insecurity most salient for Shirley, with salience indicated by her frequency of mention and the intensity with which she speaks. One is, not surprisingly, her fear of physical danger, namely from crime, natural disasters, terrorism, and accidents. This is the type of insecurity she presents as most influencing her parenting actions.

The other type of insecurity, however, does not appear to logically relate to her focus on physical protectiveness. This is Shirley's economic insecurity, specifically regarding her job prospects. "There's financial worries that I never had before I was married and had kids. I moved to California, and the housing and economy—everything is so different [than on the East Coast]." Not currently employed, she hopes to start her own baby massage business when her son starts school. "Regarding my career, I'm *terrified*. I'm doing the prework and networking now, and it's really scary."

She does not frame her parenting as addressing this job and economic insecurity, however. Unlike her fear of physical danger, which elicits a strategy of protection from physical harm, her financial and career-focused worries do not elicit a parallel strategy of protection from economic harm, at least not in these early years. We see only the shielding strategy with its focus on mother-child togetherness as a weapon against threats to the body.

DISPLACED INSECURITY

Job insecurity is absolutely typical of mothers who shield. In fact, most mothers using *any* of the connection-oriented strategies enter pregnancy unemployed, self-employed, working less than ten hours a week, or doing only occasional work paid by the job. They rarely have nine-to-five jobs and might teach occasional SAT-prep courses, do on-and-off residential gardening, babysit, or be temporary workers without set schedules.

By contrast, most of the independence-oriented mothers, discussed in the latter half of this book, could be classified as career women with jobs in the same workplace for at least a year prior to pregnancy. These jobs, such as scientist, secretary, shop manager, and lawyer, often have a set schedule, and most independence-oriented women work at least thirty hours a week. These women also have higher degrees of financial security than most connection-oriented mothers, due to often living in two-income households, working longer hours, and holding more financially lucrative positions.

Regarding connection-oriented mothers, why would minimal or inse-cure work translate into such an orientation in child rearing? One possi-ble explanation is that these mothers' valuing continuous physical close-ness with their children requires they spend a lot of *time* together. So perhaps these women were gearing up for stay-at-home motherhood and already backing off from paid careers before the children were born. However, these women's job histories generally reflect life-long insecurity and low or intermittent work hours far preceding pregnancy.[13]

There are other possible explanations for the discrepancy between the work histories of independence- and connection-oriented mothers. For example, full-time working women who expect to be away from their chil-dren much of the day may seek ways to frame their absence as a positive. Thus, their focus on independence ideals as a valuable gift to children may give them an avenue to provide security even while they are away.[14] By contrast, women with weak or insecure ties to paid work may have less to lose in the labor market and more to gain from framing the mother-child relationship as *requiring* an intense outpouring of a mother's time, thus creating greater value in what they hope to do with their time.

Many explanations are plausible and I discuss these in greater length in chapter 3. For now, however, I simply want to point out that among these women there *is* a relationship between their work histories and their philosophical orientations toward motherhood. Specifically, women who enter pregnancy working few hours, women with insecure jobs, or women with little identification with their work lives are the most likely to become connection-oriented mothers during the first three years of their children's lives. These findings are relevant to the current discus-sion of displaced insecurity.

Shirley is networking but is not currently employed and is terrified about her own future career trajectory. With so much anxiety tied up in work, one might expect her parenting strategy to attempt to solve that problem in the next generation by focusing on her child's future career success. For example, she might foster early academic learning, indepen-dence, or confidence in order to make her child more competitive in a shift-ing economy. However, in keeping with prior research, ironically it is "career women"—who already have relatively secure jobs as they enter pregnancy—that voice the greatest concern about their children's economic or professional futures.[15] For example, Maria Castillo, a devoted hospice manager who immigrated from Guatemala as an adolescent, says during pregnancy: "[There are m]any, many, many things that I wish my baby could do: [go] to a certain university, or becom[e] a certain person, becom[e] a politician as opposed to becoming a model or things like that." Deb Feldman, a white former business manager and self-professed workaholic, says her goal for her infant son is for him "to find something that he really loves doing in life and meet his potential somehow . . . I want him to follow his dreams and his skills." And Vivian Yee, a Chinese American research scientist, says independence and self-reliance are vital for her to foster in her baby daughter because they are "important for her confidence level. To become an adult and a contributing member of society, you have to have confidence in yourself. . . . Boys get different cultural messages [than girls]: be strong and make money. I want my daughter to get those same messages." These sorts of statements reflecting a concern about their babies' future careers emerged almost exclusively from women with strong career histories.

By contrast, women who have historically struggled with insecure work voice far *less* concern about their children's future employment and economic security, at least during these first three years of their children's lives. In fact, unlike the career women, women who enter pregnancy working minimal hours or with insecure work situations may be anxious about this for themselves, yet rarely mention anything related to their children's acquisition of skills or to hopes or fears regarding their children's future employment. Instead, they focus their protectiveness of their children on something entirely different. The cure does not match the malady. In a similar dynamic to pouring all of one's insecurities into *the germ*, another common symbolic repository of fear, Shirley's fears flow toward child abduction, terrorism, and accidents. Job insecurity is displaced, while health and safety issues become inflated, like a lightning rod drawing the anxiety storm toward a single point of preoccupation. One possible interpretation of this finding is that a focus on health and safety, whether it is warranted by dangerous neighborhoods or medical problems or seemingly unwarranted, may allow mothers to direct their efforts toward problems over which they feel they can at least *try* to exert control through protective actions.

Displacement of insecurity from work to other realms may be particularly relevant in an era in which so many parents recognize their lack of knowledge about the world of work in which their children will someday seek their places. It is a vast unknown, and for some women this may create feelings of confusion or helplessness regarding how to prepare and protect children. In contrast with this helplessness, Shirley believes she can indeed protect her son from physical threats, and she knows just how: by keeping him home. Avoiding crime, accidents, and other physical catastrophes thus gives her at least one way to make everything better for him. And, as an added incentive, it may also divert her from being terrified about her own job prospects.

WHERE ARE ALL THE HELICOPTER MOTHERS?

The primary safety concerns expressed by shielding mothers are less about falling down the stairs and more about unlikely events such as terrorism and child abduction, reflective of our risk society. While the object of concern is improbable, the horror and dread it inspires seems to justify the level of concern.

Yet, I found Shirley's security strategy is actually an exception, not the rule. Helicopter mothers abound in the popular press, making this form of protective parenting appear to be of epidemic proportions. Shielding is likewise the classic image of overprotective mothering most commonly discussed in the scholarly literature.[16] Yet surprisingly, I did not find this strategy common when talking to today's actual mothers. Even among those who *do* express fears of child abduction, terrorism, or a random car colliding with their child, I found shielding by sequestering or hovering to be rare. Particularly among full-time working women who express such fears, the more common response is to intentionally *expose* their children to risky, unpleasant, or difficult situations. In chapter 5 on the *inoculation* security strategy, I investigate these women who champion independence rather than connection as the best way to equip a child for survival in today's uncertain world.

But even among connection-oriented mothers, I found another strategy of child protection more common than shielding, with the target worry less about harms to the child's body and more about harms to the soul. In the narratives of these mothers, impersonal fears of crime or accidents are conspicuously absent. Instead, they emphasize fears of a more personal nature, with the greatest being that the child will not feel fully loved. Against that threat, the mother-child relationship is held up as such powerful medicine that, as long as *that* is done well, the child's security will be internalized and thereby assured in any setting. I call this the *antidote strategy* because the mother-child connection is drawn upon not as a barrier to particular threats, as with shielding, but rather as an internalized antidote to threats that are assumed to be ubiquitous.

Like mothers who shield, mothers who use the antidote strategy share the job insecurity common to the connection-seeking strategies. Yet the women who use the antidote strategy likewise do not put their mothering anxiety into the realms of work or economic insecurity but rather focus elsewhere: in these cases, on their own experiences of personal loss. These women bring up their own childhood distresses repeatedly in interviews and frame their mothering as an attempt to provide their children with what they wish they had experienced themselves as children.

Thus, both the shielding and the antidote strategies minimize a mother's anxieties about present concerns and focus her energies on either the future (the potential physical threats to the child) or the past (prior emotional harm to the mother). Regarding her child, the mother using the antidote strategy focuses neither on the child's economic security nor his physical safety but rather on his subjective sense of security. This may be because it is easier for her to provide a subjective feeling of emotional safety than to provide other more elusive forms of security, particularly when she sees herself as the primary source of such emotional safety.

One in six women in this study uses the antidote mothering strategy, either exclusively or as one of two primary strategies, whereas only a third as many use the shielding strategy.[17] Both strategies use connection to provide the child with security, but as antidote mothering appears to be more common than shielding and has certainly been far less discussed as a form of intensive mothering, I will focus the remainder of the chapter on this strategy.

ANTIDOTE MOTHERING

The antidote security strategy could almost be called "love therapy." It is the concerted attempt to fill up babies or young children with such profuse quantities of affection, attention, and emotional safety that they will have a secure core—no matter *what* befalls them. The presumed security effect of the mother-child relationship is so absolute that it simply eclipses external threats, and if one engages in correct mothering, children will somehow have all of their security needs met *right there* in that relationship.

This strategy's very heavy motherload—placing the entire onus of the child's security onto the mother—tends to stem from a sense of *insecurity* in the mother's own life. For example, thirty-six-year-old Samantha Pritikin is a white former securities trader who "decided the fast lane was not for me" and now lives off of rental income from a townhouse she bought when she was a trader. She is a single, stay-at-home mother of a four-year-old daughter whom she is raising in the *attachment parenting* style of continuous holding, co-sleeping, and extended nursing (beyond the child's first year).[18] She is currently pregnant with her second child. Samantha is not divorced or separated, nor did she get pregnant by accident. She is a single mother by choice.[19] Single mothers by choice find themselves unpartnered, yet desire a child and thus use either donor sperm or sex to become pregnant on their own. Samantha conceived her child with a married male friend who lives upstate from her and with whom she occasionally has sex. She says that he agreed to unprotected sex with her so that she could have a child on her own and that he sees their firstborn, Chloe, once a year near her birthday. Samantha held Chloe continuously for the first several months of her life and nursed her for three years; at four years of age, Chloe is still sleeping with Samantha.

AV: Why do you do attachment parenting?

SP: Because my priorities are to instill a sense of security and unconditional love in my children.

AV: Why are those things particularly important?

SP: [*quizzical look*] Well [*pause*], the sense of security is important because it's something I myself *lack* in my current life. And unconditional love is important because in my own childhood, I was "loved" [*spoken with skepticism*] apparently because of my good grades and good behavior, and I always felt that if I didn't perform in that way, I would not be loved. I want to convey to Chloe that I love her no matter what . . .

Notice first that the reason why a sense of security is important to instill in Chloe relates to *Samantha*; she sees herself as lacking security in her *own* life. Also notice that there is little stated concern for threats to her child out in the world. Rather, Samantha's focus is on giving her daughter—within the mother-child relationship—all the things that Samantha herself lacked and longs for in her past and present life. For example, she sees her lack of partner as contributing to the insecurity in her own life, yet the solution she gives for partnership insecurity is to make sure her child receives love and security through the mother-child relationship.

This is typical for a woman who uses the antidote strategy. The child becomes her *healing beneficiary*, and the mother gives profuse amounts of love and security to make up for what is lacking in her own life, though it is intended as a cure for the child. In this form of redress, there is little stated concern for either physical or economic dangers. In fact, in marked contrast with the shielding strategy, mothers who use the antidote strategy rarely mention the world beyond the tightly circumscribed mother-child relationship. Thus, the emphasis of this strategy is neither to avoid external perils the mother fears or foresees (shielding) nor to provide the child tools with which to cope with such perils (inoculation, discussed in chapter 5). Rather, antidote mothering aims to lavish upon the child such enormous quantities of maternal love that all those other dangers or insecurities in life just somehow become okay. The mother offers herself as the magic pill against a nebulous threat and takes responsibility for *personally* providing the child with everything a child could possibly want or need.

I will now lay out some of the dynamics of the antidote security strategy, first more generally, and then through a case study of a mother who illustrates how these dynamics can unfold over time.

A SECOND CHANCE

In sociologist Kimberly DaCosta's study of young heterosexual women's future family aspirations, she finds that "women expect to *receive* nurturance through the act of giving nurturance."[20] Katherine, one of her respondents, says, "I would hope the love with the person you marry is unconditional, but no, I don't think that it always is. . . . But I think with children, absolutely, the love is unconditional. . . . [T]he love I would get in a relationship with a man is—this is going to sound horrible—there's always the chance that it might not always be there, but the love for a child will always be there."[21]

In reading the above quote, notice that Katherine refers to the threatened love she will get in a relationship with a man, whereas the love that "will always be there" in the mother-child relationship is her love *"for* a child" [my emphasis]. This may be one key to unlocking what DaCosta refers to as an "essentialized notion of love between a mother and child" versus the prosaic, contingent love women see with men.[22] With men, the tentative love women describe comes from someone outside themselves, which makes it less reliable or at least less controllable, whereas the unthreatened, unconditional love Katherine describes with a child is her own.

Among women who use antidote mothering, there is likewise a focus on their own love. While some other mothers may dream of a child who totally loves and adores them, these women's focus is definitively on giving love to the child (though this love may ultimately be a remedy for something in the women's own lives). For example, Fran Polokow, a white thirty-one-year-old mother of two, is coping with the loss of her first husband: "I lost my college sweetheart/first husband to a rare form of cancer when we were twenty-five years old. This experience affected me in that I realized at an early age that sometimes terrible things happen to end a life much too early. My goal is to provide my children with an enriching, loving, beautiful childhood as best I can because that is something no one can ever take away from them—and I can't control the future."

Prodded by her own past loss, Fran intends to give her children something that cannot die, a beautiful *memory* of enriching love they can carry within themselves regardless of whatever uncontrollable future events befall them.

Penny Walton, a white twenty-nine-year-old magazine publishing intern, likewise reveals how a child can be born into an already existing story, and how a mother's love can play a part in creating a happier ending. Penny discusses her son, two-year-old Reed: "I'm somewhat overconcerned about Reed for two reasons. First, he was born prematurely at seven months, and he was so fragile. . . . And second, we named him after my little brother who died shortly before [my son] was born. My brother had learning disabilities, drug problems, and was the family's black sheep. Because my son carries that name, I kind of associate him with my brother's difficulties, and also feel this desire to make amends, give my brother the life he never got."

Another chance for love and healing is exactly what some mothers seek for their children (and perhaps vicariously for themselves) through the antidote strategy. Christine, who lost her own mother when she was twenty, views loving a child as a way to heal herself:

> When I think about having a child I think about having a girl. . . . [I]t's my mother, it's me all rolled up into one. It's being able to mother myself. To give back to a smaller younger version of myself what I lost. Or if it's not me, then it's my mother. It's another chance to heal my mother, save my mother, keep my mother alive. [The baby] would get stronger, healthier, bigger, instead of weaker and smaller. . . . [S]he would grow up instead of becoming more of an infant. Because my mother was an infant at the end. Her last words were "I'm tired. The baby is tired." And I was wiping her bottom and feeding her with a spoon. . . . It's like being given another chance.[23]

Given the stories children are sometimes born into and the enormous role maternal love can be intended to play in correcting for past pain, insecurity, or loss, we can see the heavy motherload of the antidote strategy. There is a lot at stake in mothering for these women—even before the birth of their babies.

I will now introduce a case study mother to help illustrate the heavy motherload of the antidote mothering strategy.

HEATHER DOVER

Heather Dover, a white thirty-two-year-old mother of a four-year-old girl, Tara, lives with Tara's father, Julian, in a long-term unmarried partnership. Heather spends a few hours a week managing the small apartment building in which they live, which subsidizes her family's rent there, though the building may be closing soon and her housing situation is therefore uncertain. Heather has coarse, sandy blonde hair and thick glasses, and sits on her Indian-print sofa patting her very pregnant belly. Her six-hundred-square-foot apartment smells of cumin, and she has various loose herbs and teas in canning jars above the stove. Her due date with her second child is tomorrow. She is hoping for a healing birth. She says, "Tara's birth was so traumatic. It became an emergency C-section, and they just whisked her away from me afterwards. My uterus was infected, and the hospital personnel were disrespectful and constantly poking and prodding both Tara and me. She got so many needles in her at such an early age. Because of the infection, they wanted her to have IV antibiotics in five different places, and she had to have blood tests to make sure the antibiotics weren't at toxic levels. It was just a hellish nightmare."

In conscious juxtaposition with that first highly medical birth, Heather would like the next baby to enter the world gently: at home with a midwife attendant. Once thought to be medically dangerous, a vaginal birth after cesarean is a safe option for many women. It is somewhat higher risk than a vaginal birth without a preceding cesarean, particularly an emergency one. Heather has great faith, however, that such a birth will be successful at home. "I think a home birth will help me heal the previous birth trauma and will be such a better way to welcome this new baby to the world." Thus, this rewriting of history, this re-visioned birth, is intended for a double healing. In fact, the healing story into which her second baby is being born reaches even beyond her own and the new baby's experiences: "I have this vision that this baby—this sounds kind of corny and dramatic—that it's a healing opportunity not just for me and birth and Tara's birth and our family but actually broader. . . . I'm here in [my multiethnic neighborhood] and there's all kinds of women from all over the world with all kinds of painful stories, and . . . I feel like there's something about this baby that's coming to *right* some of that . . ."

The day of Jasper's birth arrived three days later. Heather's water broke in the morning, and as with Tara's ill-fated birth, the fluid contained meconium (babies' first tar-like excrement), meaning there was once again an elevated risk of infection. Heather remained relaxed and optimistic and drank castor oil to try to bring on her labor, which had yet to begin. Most hospitals allow twenty-four hours after one's water breaks before they induce labor in order to prevent infection; given meconium in the amniotic fluid, this birth would now be classified as high risk.

Heather's contractions began that evening, and six hours after labor began, in her own bed at home, Heather pushed out her healthy eight-pound, twenty-two-inch-long baby boy, Jasper.

Heather is an adoptee, and she says the moment right after birth is "the scariest part given my adoption experience [of being separated from my birth mother]. And it was the scariest part with Tara that she was separated from me after the birth—which was torture." Thus, Jasper's birth was the first time she was able to live her dream of continuous mother-newborn contact. Heather was also not breast-fed as a child and says in a shocked and upset tone that her parents "started [feeding me] solids *really early*. There was this little booklet that they gave my parents [when they adopted me], and I was eating, like, jar food already in that first three months. It's really intense."

Heather's experience as an adoptee is a theme that recurs in each of her interviews. "I don't really know much about the time before my parents adopted me. There was like this gap of—I was supposedly in foster care [for a month]. I don't know what that woman was like. She died before I found my birth mother."

AV: Do you have any gut feelings about your babyhood?

HD: Um, there's, I think there's a piece where there was, like, joy and comfort to find this, these parents who wanted to really love me, and I still feel this deep gratitude and just squishy love. [*laughs*] But there's this other part . . . this deep scream in me of this lonely baby . . . with a deep core belief in my own aloneness that no amount of love can fill. . . . I've had abandonment issues all my life. [As a child,] anytime I went to camp or visited people and had to leave [my parents], I was always a wreck, but it took me years to figure out why because that whole thing is such a crime, the way they do adoption and have the foster care.

Heather attributes her lifelong abandonment issues to her experiences of rejection by her birth mother and to her month in foster care as an infant, placing great determinative power in these early experiences. She also describes later abandonment by her parents.

They both sort of abandoned me as a child, too, since my dad was a community advocate and was just *gone*, always taking care of other people, and my mom was a teacher. Both of my parents were people other people went to for help. So I always had to share my parents with others . . . and I always felt like my parents didn't get it when I started to realize my adoption stuff. My mom would always say, "You stink, you should wash your armpits," and I read somewhere that adoptive parents have different smells. And they were always trying to make my hair different. I always felt this aberrance—you are not my people. We would try to get closer, but we'd shoot past each other.

Heather's narrative returns again and again to her past abandonment experiences. In chapter 3 I will analyze the tendency among connection-oriented mothers (in contrast to independence-oriented mothers) to explain their lives and their parenting actions through repeated mention of distress in their own childhoods, particularly related to how they were *mothered*. That is, I explore variation in the degree to which people draw on psychotherapeutic framings to make sense of their actions, and show how this relates to how they parent their own children.

For now, I simply note that women using connection-oriented strategies focus far more on how they were mothered as children than women using independence-oriented strategies. Given Heather's belief that her lifelong sense of aloneness stems from a lack of good mothering in her own first month of life, it is a short leap to the belief that she must get it right as a mother or her own children will suffer permanent damage. She sees her children's security in emotional terms and as hinging almost exclusively on the mother-child relationship. That is, she carries a very heavy motherload.

CHILD FIRST

Heather and her partner, Julian, have chosen to parent both of their children in the attachment style of holding them the vast majority of the time and sleeping with them in the early years. Heather also nurses on demand into the children's third years, both during the day and at night.

AV: What do you see as a baby's greatest needs?

HD: I think they just really need to know that they're connected. Um, maybe that's *my* need! [*laughs*] But . . . I mean, nursing is all about that. You're close, you're getting this nurturing that's physical food, whatever, but then you're also getting that touch . . .

AV: So was attachment parenting just something you always knew you'd do, or was there some point when you thought about it and thought, "When I have [kids], I want to have them against my body a lot"?

HD: It just felt knee-jerk, like, of *course*. But it wasn't enforced in my upbringing. . . . I certainly didn't nurse [as a baby], so that was a whole other world. So it felt like *How do I know this?* because I didn't really experience this.

AV: And did you ever come up with an answer?

HD: Well, I think one of the reasons I know it is *because* I didn't experience it, so that I feel like there's a deficit there. And I think that's why I'm so physical in my life.

Again we see the healing beneficiary: giving to a child to make up for a deficit in one's own life. On the one hand, Heather believes her internal clamor for touch gives her insights and information about what was missing and what she should therefore provide for her own children. On the other hand, in acknowledging that her physicality may be partly a reaction to a childhood deficit, she implicitly acknowledges that her strong need for touch may be an amplified need (which she then projects onto her children).

One reason for this projection may be her identification with them. For example, Heather identifies with Tara as the firstborn, and when she and Julian need to push Tara aside to keep the baby safe, this brings up her own sense of being pushed aside when her little brother was born. She also identifies with Jasper: "I feel like he's an extension of me. He's even more like me than Tara is . . . [and] I can relate more to Jasper's mannerisms and what he's trying to do. It's really sweet, and makes me almost feel like I can look at myself as a child."

This identity blur may make it difficult to distinguish between the children's needs and her own need to fulfill them. In fact, when Jasper turns out to be an easier, less needy baby than Tara was, Heather finds this a bit unnerving. She says, "He's pretty adaptable. I've almost been anxious. Tara, you know, needed me a lot, needed things from me. And Jasper is like, 'Whatever. You're not going to nurse me? Okay, I'll just fall asleep. Okay, well, whatever. I'll just hang.' You know, he seems to just work it out for himself . . . I've been almost *worried* about him. Aren't you going to wake up? Don't you *need* something?"

Heather's focus on meeting her children's every need also makes it difficult for her to leave the children with others, such as Julian's parents, who sometimes put their own needs above her children's wishes.

HD: [Julian's] parents were pretty hands off [with him as a child] . . . trying to make him independent. I've even had issues with them with Tara, like [they] stick a video in, or take her somewhere that *they* need to go and not really focus on what *she* wants to do. And it's like, "Whoa, what is *that*?"

AV: So in your parenting, do you sort of follow the child's lead in terms of what they're—

HD: I do often. . . . I think this pregnancy has been really interesting for me because I think there's times when I physically can't go where [Tara] wants to go, or I'm just, like, fed up with playing with dolls or whatever it is [*laughs*], I just don't want to go there. And then I have this struggle; I really have this judgment of myself for not being a good mom, that I'm not going where she's going and following her playing or what she's working on and thinking about . . .

When I ask Heather to clarify what she means by a good mom, she replies:

The good mom is this mom who's like—well, you know, attachment-style parenting was kind of all the vogue when we were having Tara, the idea that kids know exactly what they need and give you the cues, and you follow their lead. And, um, it's not that you don't have any boundaries and don't let them know about your needs, but their needs take major priority. And, so, then I always kind of idealize this mom as not only is she *willing* to, you know, follow the lead, but she does it *enthusiastically.* [*laughs*] She's, like, willing to go *everywhere* with this kid, willing to explore all these places, and not force her agenda. And so I think my lack of enthusiasm these last few months has been the part that I've been like, oh man! Where did my enthusiasm go? Why don't I *want* to play with the Barbies for hours? [*laughs*] Why am I thrilled when her peers come and take over?

It is important to note that Heather's good mother ideals and her feelings of guilt when she fails to live up to them are not shared by all connection-oriented mothers. For example, Lena Wasserman, a twenty-nine-year-old German immigrant who likewise sleeps with her six-month-old baby and carries him the majority of the day, has very different ideals. Lena says a good mother is one who "has *fun* being a mom, puts baby first but doesn't forget about herself and still has a life that includes more than just being a mom. That's really, really important, because if the baby is all you think and talk and care about, you will not be able to let go, ever probably. And the baby will be entirely responsible for how you feel about yourself."

Connection-oriented mothers like Lena who engage in high amounts of physical contact with their children yet have different expectations of themselves or of the security mothers are intended to provide do not find mothering as taxing or guilt producing as Heather does. Heather's attitudes and experiences represent only one strand of connection-oriented mothering, namely the antidote security strategy with its focus on sparing the child from emotional suffering through a life-redeeming and all-consuming mother-child relationship. In other words, Heather's connection-orientation has a heavy motherload, and it is the heavy motherload of antidote mothering, not the high level of physical togetherness, that causes her difficulties.

Despite these difficulties, Heather is, in fact, mostly able to put into practice her model of good mothering through continuous holding early in life, extended breast-feeding, and engaging in whatever activities her children prefer for the duration of their interest. Yet she still feels guilty because she finds these things challenging. She believes, for example, that a good mother would play Barbies with complete joy and enthusiasm rather than with thoughts of what she would prefer to be doing. She thinks following the child's lead should be personally fulfilling and should not be experienced as a sacrifice. However, this belief about correct mothering and sacrifice that is not a sacrifice prevents her from lowering her expectations of herself and causes her further guilt and emotional strain.

THE ATTACHMENT GESTAPO

As with many women, Heather's sense of right and wrong in mothering is somewhat a result of expert advice.[24] The most oft-cited expert of attachment parenting, referred to by many as the father of the movement, is Dr. William Sears, a pediatrician, who cowrote *The Baby Book* with his wife, Martha Sears. Heather says, "*The Baby Book* was our little bible [when Tara was young]." *The Baby Book* promotes wearing the baby (rather than the more typical modern Western practice of carrying the baby for short periods between intervals when the baby is set down). Sears and Sears write that "[continuously] carried babies develop better, possibly because the energy they would have wasted on crying [if they were not being held] is diverted into growth."[25] The message is that *not* practicing attachment parenting therefore causes excess crying and stunts a baby's growth. Furthermore, the book claims, the more typical US practice of training a baby to sleep on her own, to get onto a schedule, or to accept not being continuously held requires insensitivity and can result in a distance developing between baby and parent. It adds that "while attachment parenting is not the easiest style of parenting, if practiced properly it should be the most joyful one."[26] That is, if one mothers properly it *should not* be experienced as a sacrifice. By extension, if it *is* a struggle to hold one's baby continuously and to breast-feed several times a night, as it sometimes is for Heather, one may be *improperly* executing this form of mothering. Hence, Heather experiences the guilt of improper mothering along with her already difficult struggles to do right by her children.

The second most oft-cited book from which the attachment mothers in this study draw inspiration is *The Continuum Concept*, written by Jean Liedloff in 1977, which characterizes mainstream modern Western parenting as going far beyond insensitivity and distance. Liedloff chronicles her experiences with the indigenous Yequana people of Venezuela who had had very little contact with modern Western culture at the point of her observations. She compares the contented, noncrying Yequana babies who co-sleep, breast-feed frequently, and are held continuously with the typical US baby, who is whisked away from the mother at birth for weighing and washing. Referencing the highly contested early bonding research of the 1970s,[27] Liedloff warns that if this whisking occurs, or "if the mother is too drugged to experience the bonding fully," then this "gives way to a state of grief."[28] When the baby is returned to her "even minutes after the mother has gone into a physiological state of mourning, the result is often that she feels guilty about not being able 'to turn on mothering,' or 'to love the baby very much'" and she may be catapulted into "the classic civilized tragedy called normal postpartum depression."[29]

Liedloff also describes the typical US parenting scenario of a baby being left to sleep alone, uncradled, by a mother who, with the best intentions, "puts him gently in his crib, which is decorated with yellow ducklings" and "straightens baby's undershirt and covers him with an embroidered sheet and a blanket bearing his initials. She bends to kiss the infant's silky cheek and moves toward the door as the first agonized shriek shakes his body. . . . The mother hesitates, her heart pulled toward him, but resists and goes on her way. He has just been changed and fed. She is sure he does not *really* need anything . . ."[30]

Liedloff ventures an interpretation of the experience of being left to sleep alone from the baby's perspective.

> The newborn infant, with his skin crying out for the ancient touch of smooth, warmth-radiating, living flesh, is wrapped in dry, lifeless cloth. He is put in a box where he is left, no matter how he weeps, in a limbo that is utterly motionless. . . . Eventually, a timeless lifetime later, he falls asleep exhausted.
>
> He awakes in a mindless terror of the silence, the motionlessness. . . . He screams until his chest aches, until his throat is sore. He can bear the pain no more and his sobs weaken and subside. He listens. . . . He rolls his head from side to side. Nothing helps. It is unbearable. He begins to cry again, but it is too much for his strained throat; he soon stops . . . unable to think, unable to hope. He listens. Then he falls asleep again.[31]

The stakes could not be higher for a mother invested in her baby's well-being where even the pain of a vaccination shot may cause her agony. The message is that mainstream (nonattachment) mothering is akin to the child "being tortured."[32]

Although the influence of attachment experts and commentators may not be the complete or even a primary explanation for Heather's beliefs that she should practice a particular type of mothering, her viewing the Sears' book as her little bible certainly reinforces those beliefs.

In addition to the messages of experts, Heather has received messages about correct mothering from the formal and informal social networks in which she has participated. Recall she saw attachment mothering as in vogue when her first child was born. This perception was reinforced by her participation in a women's birthing circle that met weekly begin-ning in pregnancy in anticipation of these women's home births. They discussed the process of birthing with each other and with various mid-wives who were invited to attend and continued meeting after their chil-dren were born to discuss mothering.

AV: Was this birthing circle pretty attachment oriented?

HD: Oh yeah, it was all about slings and people would come in, "Oh look, I made my own sling," and blah, blah, blah, and nursing, and it was like, "Oh, you have a *bottle* in your house—*oh my GOD!*" You know, it was kind of the opposite hazing [from more mainstream pressures]. And after I had my [emergency] C-section, it was this weird kind of, like, "Oh, I didn't have the [right] birth, I can't go, I can't talk about this." So I didn't feel completely pressed out [of that group], but it was, like, a while that I didn't talk with other people about their births, and they didn't talk with me so much about mine 'cuz of the weirdness of that.

In addition to feeling weirdness because she did not have the right type of birth experience, Heather also had difficulties with the group when she went back to work when her first child was still a baby. Whereas during Jasper's early years, Heather came up with a work solution (as an apartment manager) wherein she could both keep a roof over the family's head *and* spend her days with the baby, for her first child, her sense of financial responsibility put her back in her full-time job at an environ-mental advocacy organization as soon as her maternity leave ran out. She expresses deep regrets about this: "I went back to work when Tara was three months old, and it was all because of my perception that we needed to have my income to pay the rent—which probably was some-what realistic, but it wasn't necessarily the only solution. . . . It felt way too soon. I would cry each day. Julian would bring Tara at lunch and I would nurse, but it was hard. So I felt, like, because of that, I missed some of that intense bonding, so I always felt like I was compensating for that."

Full-time work outside the home is an extreme rarity among the at-tachment mothers in this study. In fact, Heather is the only self-professed attachment mother who did full-time work outside the home during her child's first year, though this was only with the first child, and I met her after she had already created an alternative for her second. However, with that first child, Heather felt she had no choice since Julian was a student and she was the primary earner in the family. Furthermore, Julian was both able and willing to spend his days with the baby practicing attachment fathering.

Tara continued to require care at night through age six, and during her first year, there were hard, long nights because she was colicky and breast-fed numerous times each night. "I was stretched, you know. I remember sleepless nights, and then waking up and having to go to work. . . . [T]hat was hard."

Yet despite her emotionally and physically difficult plight as a working mother committed to attachment parenting, Heather did not experience a supportive environment for this in her mothers' group: "Some people in the group worked out really cool arrangements where they weren't having to go back to work, and I was one of the few people that was trying to juggle work and being a mom and nursing still and pumping. So that was kind of weird because there were some people who just didn't *get* that part. . . . I didn't feel supported as a working person."

Heather says her impression of attachment mothering is that "It seems like only privileged people get to do it. Not your everyday privileged suspects, more like artists . . . but I don't see many people who have 'regular jobs' doing this kind of parenting."

In addition to her support group's lack of support for her as a working person, she felt unsupported for her family's use of bottles to feed the baby expressed breast milk, and for the cesarean birth of her daughter.

> [Julian and I] would kind of talk about, you know, the "Attachment Gestapo," [*laughs*] people who would come in and go, "*Uh!*" [*gasps in shock*]. . . . That stressed me out. I definitely had some stress around how do I talk to my kids the right way. And Tara for a while had a conflict because she was biting her friends. She bit her best friend . . . three times in the face, and, um, oh my gosh, dealing with another parent and their judgment, and me trying to like help figure out what's going on with her without coming down on her too hard, you know, that whole thing. I think in

some ways because of the attachment thing, I was afraid to say no, or say, um, to set boundaries in a more firm way with her. And, um, I sometimes wonder about that impact. [But] I was so worried about saying things that would make her feel that she wasn't loved.

Heather fears her children will feel unloved unless she faithfully adheres to her correct mothering model, so there is a lot at stake for her in staying true to it. At the same time, Heather's need to fulfill this model, to *make* her children feel loved, sometimes appears to exceed her children's actual need for it, such as we saw when Jasper's ability to sooth himself created anxiety in Heather and a degree of further worry. Despite sleeping with her baby, breast-feeding multiple times every night, feeding her baby exclusively breast milk, and wearing the baby on one of the parents' bodies at all times, she sees her prior status as a working mother as having created a deficit of bonding for her child that, particularly when paired with what her support group saw as the wrong kind of birth, leaves Heather feeling she must compensate.

THE PRICE OF LOVE

Heather's own physical and emotional limits also create dilemmas for her in her desire to provide optimal nurturance to her children. In the pregnancy interview, I ask how much Heather plans on holding the new baby. She replies: "When the baby's asleep, I might put the baby down so I can take a shower or go poop or something. [*laughs*] 'Can't I go poop *alone*?' That was really hard the first time. 'Can't I take a *shower*?'" Finding time alone is among her greatest challenges as a mother, and with the addition of baby Jasper, it becomes more difficult still, especially since Tara continues to exhibit great needs for Heather.

> She's on the border of being older, but she still needs me so much. So it's a balance of when to give her a push. When she was turning six, she asked me to come in and wipe her butt, and I decided it was time that *she* wipe her own butt. I'm not sure what she gets out of that except for attention. . . . Her teacher says she's adult dependent, which is a word she uses to describe *most* of the kids who get a lot of attention at home. She doesn't say that to the working parents. . . . [33]

Tara's desires for adult assistance appear to be mother specific, and again reflecting Heather's belief in the determinative nature of early experiences with the mother, Heather attributes this to Tara's difficult birth. "[A] lot of things kind of stem back to that, like her needing me. Tara for *years* could only have me to sleep, and [Julian and I] didn't start switching up bedtimes until she was well weaned, which was just before three. Julian would read *with* us, but I was the bedtime person for a long time."

Regarding how much she read to Tara at bedtime, she says, "I've heard of parents making a three-book rule, but I didn't set any limits." And while Julian can now put Tara to bed at six years of age, "Tara still night wakes" and at bedtime she "needs us to be with her until she falls asleep."

Heather's commitment to having her children in arms nearly continuously early in life is not always physically easy for her. She says, "I'm having a lot of trouble with my lower back. I still carry [Jasper] in the sling, which is probably really bad [for my back]. And I still carried Tara when she was three years old."

Extended breast-feeding also poses certain difficulties for her: "With Tara, I nursed about three years. . . . The last year was hard. I'm chronically underweight, so it was hard to eat enough. We also had yeast infections, in her mouth and my breasts. . . . [With Jasper, too,] nursing has sometimes been exasperating, particularly when I have mastitis [a breast infection usually accompanied by severe pain and fever] and I'm tired. I wouldn't want to stop because of that, but it hasn't been all easy."

In addition, there are costs to the rest of the family, such as to Heather's relationship with Julian.

AV: So you sleep in here with Jasper? [*referring to the queen-sized bed she and I are sitting on with the baby*]

HD: Yeah, this is my bed and Jasper's bed, and Julian sleeps in with Tara in the bunk bed [in the other bedroom]. They've been switching who's on top and who's on bottom. . . .

AV: So you and Julian don't sleep together at all?

HD: No. Julian's really bummed about that, but I have to say there's the quality [that] I'm constantly intimate with Jasper, and I don't mind. . . .

Finally, Heather's parenting choices interfere with her sleep. Babies that co-sleep generally continue to wake and require assistance at night for several years rather than the several months more typical of babies who sleep separately.[34] Regarding Tara's babyhood, Heather recalls: "The sleep deprivation was really hard. . . . We had these hard, long nights; like, I remember one night just banging my head on the bed going, "I want to sleep!" [*laughs*] You know, just really losing it. . . . It feels like way more than you can handle."

The idea of more than one can handle relentlessly presses in on Heather's mood. She says, "Some mornings I wake up really cranky, struggling with Tara, then struggling with Julian, and going back to bed and crying, 'I don't want to be this cranky person!' Then there's this better person developing in me of setting better boundaries with family and other people, and I like that part, but I don't like the 'lose it' part, like yelling and being bitchy and mean in a way that isn't how I ordinarily do things. And sometimes I just burst into tears . . . [and have] these periods of, 'Oh my god, can I handle this?'"

Pushing through the physical and emotional difficulties, Heather remains steadfast that her mothering style is the best way to love her children and give them what they deserve, regardless of the costs to her body, her uncertainty as to whether she can handle it emotionally, or the possibility that she will lose it and become bitchy and mean if she cannot. Although Heather is an extreme case, sacrifice for the sake of the child followed by emotional volatility on the part of the mother is a repeated theme among mothers who believe children *deserve* connection-oriented parenting, but who themselves would enjoy a bit more space. For example, a thirty-six-year-old white mother, Ellie Ryder, feels burdened by attachment mothering and is "just *dying* for a weekend away" from her four-month-old daughter. She says, "One of the things that is hard for me is the 'beck and call,' losing my own person, like [when she was born] I felt like, uh, I felt like my needs suddenly became second to this other little creature who I didn't even know, I'd just met." Ellie does not always enjoy the constant holding and frequent breast-feeding of her chosen parenting style. She says when her daughter was a newborn, she was "in body contact, like, 99 percent of the time," a degree of holding that "was a drag." Likewise, she says, "I resented breast-feeding and wished someone else could do it, though I stuck with it since I'm a committed breast feeder." In fact, Ellie likens mothering to servitude. "[B]eing a mother is like being a servant. They're like your little slave master. . . . You don't own your own schedule, your own time, and you keep that up 100 percent . . ." Despite the difficulties of this level of experienced enslavement, Ellie says she does it for her daughter, "to make her feel safe and secure."

Sociologist Chris Bobel likewise finds a high level of sacrifice among the natural mothers she studies through her research of La Leche League attendees (a group that promotes breast-feeding beyond infancy and whose members often practice attachment parenting). Bobel writes that in this population of mothers, "maternal needs tend to fall last."[35] For example: "Nursing 'on demand' is an around-the-clock responsibility. Many League mothers sleep with their babies to facilitate frequent nighttime nursings but complain of relentless fatigue. Husbands often sleep elsewhere until the baby weans. Katrina, a mother of two, remarked, 'Hal and I haven't slept together in a—well, let's say a long time. But that's okay. It's not forever.'"[36]

Bobel continues:

Excessive sleep deprivation (beyond a child's infancy) . . . is often discussed [at La Leche League meetings] as a mother's fact of life, suggesting that sleep is only for the selfish who subordinate their baby's needs. Sacrifice is at the center of a good mother's role. One gets the sense that motherhood is something to be endured; fulfillment is necessarily postponed until the children wean. Kathy, a leader, explained, "Just the other day I was looking through my three-year-old's baby book and noticed the blank for 'sleeps through the night' is still blank. And I have a feeling it always will be . . . but that's okay."[37]

For Ellie, it is *not* always okay, and she occasionally questions her parenting choices. When her baby is thirteen months old, she says, "[My daughter is] still not a great sleeper, and I wonder if it's because of co-sleeping. You hear about these parents who do the cry-it-out method and their kids sleep through the night after three days. And you think, 'FUCK! Is this attachment parenting *worth* it?' But I can't imagine any other way."

LOVE UNTIL YOU SNAP

With Jasper now a toddler, the family has moved, and as I walk through the front door of Heather's new apartment to complete our third interview, she immediately starts sobbing. She cannot speak words through the tears, and I hold her as she continues to cry for ten minutes. Finally, she wipes her tears and runny nose and begins to speak: "It's just *so hard* sometimes. I feel like I'm carrying this whole thing, and I'm just *fried*. Last night Julian went to a meeting at Tara's school, and so I had to be with both kids by myself after being with both of them for most of the day. And I'm just always caregiving, taking care of another child twice a week . . . and parenting. It's out of balance and I need to refuel, to receive. But there's *no time*."

When Heather is pressed to her limits, she becomes alternately sorrowful and angry. With tears streaming and her head bent toward the floor, she expresses the sorrow of her own needs not mattering. However, she also confesses the times when she has felt not sorrow but rage. "I have pushed Tara away—too hard, like slamming her against the couch—and that's when I know I need to reach out for help." There is a parenting crisis line Heather calls when she feels herself losing it as a mother. Heather says, "You just *never* know, that horrible scene from the *Ya-Ya Sisterhood* where the mother just loses it, and you think, how could anyone do that? On the other hand, how could anyone *not* do that several times a day? It's just so close to yelling or violence all the time."

Heather has stretched her level of sacrifice to the breaking point, and this has become problematic. Specifically, she wants to heal her children (of her own sense of woundedness from being abandoned by her birth mother) by giving those children the sense that they are unquestionably the center of her universe and that her world revolves around them. At the same time, this healing causes Heather's own needs to be pushed aside, so she is once again hit with the pain of not mattering that she felt from childhood. Her next-generation solution to a prior sense of unimportance thus perpetuates it. And that comes at a cost.

One way to view antidote mothering is as a *child*-centered strategy in which the child's primacy overshadows the mother's needs to such a degree that it eventually produces resentment and rage. However, I assert it is actually *mother-child*-centered because mother-love is the assumed cure for all human ails, and the ultimate human need. Mother-love is therefore not given as a way to nurture a child's ability to have good relationships with others throughout her life, to be competent and self-assured in the world, or toward any other end. It is given because it is considered sufficient unto itself, and if it is there, the child's security needs are seen as met *en toto*. The motherload of this strategy is enormous.

Over time, however, Heather's vehemence about correct mothering begins to soften. Eighteen months into parenting Jasper, she says:

> I'm freaked out by my inability to know myself and where my breaking point is. It's much better to pop in a video and not lose it even though I'd rather paint and do creative things with them. . . . [I no longer judge when] I see people who aren't doing cloth diapers. With Tara I was much more righteous with my choices as a parent, but righteousness is for people who don't have kids. If you can't handle cloth, you need to cut corners. If you can't carry your baby because you're protecting your back, do what you can do so you can *be* with your baby.

This trend continues, and three years beyond that, Heather is excited to have discovered a new online community within the attachment parenting movement that values mothers taking care of themselves and keeping themselves happy and fortified, both so they can be better mothers and also for their own sakes so they can be more well-balanced human beings. She says it is meaningful that these advocates of the idea that "mom counts" are emerging *within* the attachment community, and she is excited to be seeking greater balance in her mothering.

CONCLUSION

Whether or not parents are aware of either attachment theory or the concept of "maternal deprivation" by name, the notion that children's security stems from early experiences with their mothers has permeated parenting culture. The genie is out, and even though more recent psychological research casts doubt upon this maternally deterministic model,[38] the woman on the street still echoes prior understandings. Furthermore, as cultural diffusion is not unlike the game of telephone, where words get garbled and misinterpreted as they pass repeatedly through human filters, she may be responding to a twisted version of attachment theory's early claims. Rather than seeing this model as descriptive, she may understand it as proscriptive: a mother *should* be able to create security for her child through responsive (i.e., correct) mothering. This imperative can have consequences, such as guilt, resentment, or even rage. Attachment theory has affected attachment relationships. The experimenter has influenced the experiment.

Having a close physical relationship with her young children does not mean a woman has taken on the imperative of security production or that she carries a heavy motherload. Some extremely connection-oriented mothers carry light motherloads and either do not see the world as particularly threatening or do not frame the mother-child relationship as the cure-all for those threats (discussed in chapter 4). However, the shielding and antidote strategies, two connection-oriented mothering strategies with the aims of producing security in a child's life, both entail very heavy motherloads.

Broadly speaking, if a woman fully embraces the role of security provider for her child, there are three methods she can use. First, she can try to create a secure environment for the child to inhabit (situational security); second, she can try to create an inwardly secure child or a sense of security transportable to any environment (security of the self); or third, she can teach the child how to deflect threat or most securely relate with whatever arises in the environment (responsive security). The shielding and antidote security strategies focus on the first two forms of security, respectively.

The shielding strategy seeks situational security, and the mother uses herself as a barrier between her child and potential physical threats (or information about those threats). It is a variant of what we might call classic protective parenting, in which we envision a mother hovering over a child to make sure the child does not get hurt. However, the dangers most emphasized in the narratives of shielding mothers are not the classic concerns about a child falling down the stairs or putting the wrong things in her mouth. Rather, they are the dangers of risk society involving strangers or environmentally inflicted catastrophes. Furthermore, the mother believes her own vigilant actions can protect her child from such threats.

Shielding, and classic protectiveness more generally, has been discussed at length in the scholarly literature as well as the popular press and is often assumed to be *the* strategy parents use in the face of a seemingly fearsome world.[39]

Yet there is another connection-oriented security strategy, also aimed at keeping a child safe, which is less discussed and, at least in this study, actually more common. It is the antidote strategy, in which the mother fills the child with profuse amounts of love in hopes that he will thereby simply *be* secure. A mother using the antidote strategy does not explain her connection orientation by virtue of the physical dangers of risk society. Instead she emphasizes emotional threats, particularly what she sees as the worst threat of all: maternal deprivation. Her focus is on her own past wounds, which she attempts to reconcile through a healing beneficiary, her child, whom she believes *needs* all the love, comforts, or attention the mother craves for herself.

One could argue that all parents project needs onto their children[40] and that these projected needs will frequently be greater or lesser than the child's actual needs. In looking at mothers using the antidote security strategy, the needs they project onto their children appear extreme and unrealistically high.

There are two different processes we can point to in explaining this amplification of needs. The first relates to the fact that in this study a woman's job insecurity is the single best predictor of a connection orientation to mothering, yet connection-oriented women are conspicuously silent on this as an influence in their parenting. This prompts me to speculate that there may be a displacement of insecurity from the economic realm into the physical or emotional realms for safekeeping. Just as Glassner posits that our society directs its fear toward scapegoated "bogeypeople" to avoid facing the overwhelming hurtfulness built into our current social structures,[41] many connection-oriented mothers direct their fears toward a few particular anxiety hotspots—and away from economic insecurity. This anxiety, detached from its source, might seek a place to land and may be best held at bay by a strong focus on something concrete. This could be a fear, such as of child abduction or of one's child feeling unloved, over which one feels some hope of preventative control. To the outside viewer, the anxiety regarding this fear appears out of proportion with the threat, but that is because the fear provides refuge for far more than the overt threat. It is an insecurity dumping ground, absorbing fears funneled from elsewhere in the woman's life, safekeeping multiple insecurities under one blanket worry.

Maslow's hierarchy of needs may suggest that only those whose physical or economic security needs were met would have the luxury of pursuing emotional security. However, in some cases emotional security may feel like such a more plausible goal than physical or economic security that it may be the emotional solution for which the mother reaches.

Second, the needs projected onto a child in the antidote strategy may be amplified by the mother's own prior experiences of loss. For example, a person whose father died when she was a child has a very different need for fathering than either a person whose father remained living or a person whose father was never a part of her life. Antidote mothering therefore attempts to heal one person (the child) of losses and wounds experienced by another person (the mother) whose needs may have been amplified by the experience of loss. This use of a healing beneficiary creates the conditions under which the mother's needs are projected onto a child and met either unnecessarily or with unnecessary intensity.

There are also effects on the *mother* of using a healing beneficiary. On the one hand, by virtue of giving a child the love, safety, and connection the mother herself longs for, the mother sometimes experiences a healing of her own and a rewriting of history. For example, Heather's separation from her birth mother as a baby, as well as her separation from her first baby after the birth, is to some degree righted by her second child's natural birth in her home and the lack of painful separation afterward. More generally, her fear of abandonment is somewhat assuaged by the certainty of love she experiences with her children. Thus, she is nurtured through the act of nurturing, a phenomenon that is particularly evident because she has a high degree of identification with her child.

On the other hand, the child's extremely primary status in the antidote strategy—and the related secondary status of the mother as a desirous and deserving human being—can re-create for the mother in the current generation the same failure to have her own needs met from childhood that she sees as propelling her to this level of giving in the first place. Thus, by changing history for her child, she repeats it for herself.

There are political ramifications to this dynamic. This chapter discussed the insecurity displacement that occurs when a woman locates a relatively remote realm of life (typically in which harms dwell in the past or future rather than the present) to which she can divert her insecurity from other more threatening or immediate realms. For example, for women using the shielding strategy, concerns over economic uncertainty are funneled into fears of future physical harms due to risk-society threats such as terrorism, pandemics, or child abduction. Such displacements make it less likely people will engage in collective action to bring about greater economic security for all. Among women using the antidote strategy, concern is again diverted from work and economic insecurity, but the receiving realm for that insecurity is emotional dangers. The mother's own family of origin experiences loom large and she sees (typically maternal) deprivation in her own upbringing as the seminal influence on both her own current insecurities and her parenting choices. This privatization of fear again lets society off the hook. It exacerbates the belief that parents—rather than the economy, the lack of social safeguards, or the decline in face-to-face community connections—are responsible for today's insecurity and are likewise almost single-handedly responsible for its remediation. By the same logic, the mother considers *herself* ultimately responsible for her *own* children's security and well-being in the world. She has a mother-centered view of human security and sees the mother-child relationship as *the* determinant of children leading secure lives, which she defines as emotional security.

Carrying this heavy motherload, but having no acceptable models from childhood on which to draw, she may be particularly susceptible to advice literatures as a source of alternative models. These models reify her projections and create a sense of certainty in what she does. Indeed, the *certainty* of much parenting advice—both in written form and in mother-to-mother policing—may itself serve as refuge for some women in the face of uncertainty and insecurity.[42]

However, a mother's adherence to a model of correct mothering may cause her to experience guilt when she fails to live up to this model (which, by implication, would make her mothering incorrect, harmful, and depriving). Furthermore, she does not view the sacrificial nature of her giving as heroic or reflective of her deep goodness and dedication as a mother. Rather, any difficulty in putting the child's needs first produces further guilt as she sees the degree of difficulty and sacrifice as indicating the degree to which her own wants *conflict* with the joy of meeting a child's needs. She believes that it should not hurt so much for a mother to simply give what any child naturally wants and deserves, and her difficulty in giving thus casts into doubt her own sense of naturalness as a mother. She reads her perseverant giving in the face of obstacles not as reflecting an intense will to love but as a sign of her inadequacy, which threatens to deprive the child. Thus, she suffers not only the physical and emotional consequences of giving until it hurts but also a resulting guilt and self-doubt.

As she tries to push through these difficulties and to continue giving despite it all, she sees her own needs as not counting, and there is a resulting pressure buildup that may eventually release through an expression of anger.

Correct mothering hits the wall.

3 Compensatory Connection Strategy

MOTHERING THAT SAVES THE MOTHER

[W]hen you meet someone new and you're dating, you're afraid that maybe they won't love you. With a kid, you don't have to worry about that.

—Daphne Petrolis, thirty-one-year-old mother

Partners come and go, but the child stays. Everything one vainly hoped to find in the relationship with one's partner is sought in or directed to a child . . . The child becomes the final alternative to loneliness, a bastion against the vanishing chances of loving and being loved.

—Ulrich Beck and E. Beck-Gernsheim[1]

When people feel emotionally or physically threatened, a common response is to draw closer to those they trust.[2] A woman may reach automatically for the phone to call a confidante when a romantic relationship begins to falter. A child may preconsciously reach for her security blanket when something scares her.

The question here is: Does a society as a whole respond like an individual when it is under threat? That is, as terrorism, toxins, child abduction, and other dangers are amplified in the public consciousness, and as long-term marriage, long-term jobs, home ownership, and other sources of reliability and life-grounding are seen to be more and more at risk, is there a society-wide gravitation toward some generalized trusted other for solace?

If so, the likeliest place to look is within the family. It has been found that, after a large-scale threat such as a terrorist attack, people tend to spend more time with their families.[3] One possible explanation of this is an urge to protect loved ones. In the last chapter, we saw how mothers' concerns about a variety of threats led them to diligent attempts to provide security, practically at any cost. But there is another reason why a person may gravitate toward her loved ones after frightening occurrences: *she may be frightened.* Togetherness may assuage some of her own fears. Women are not simply security producers providing for the needs of others; they are security consumers with needs of their own. In this chapter, I investigate whether, for some women, children have become a sort of living security blanket to ameliorate the feeling of risk and destabilization in American social, family, and work life.

I use the term *compensatory connection* to refer to one part of life being given exaggerated importance to make up for security deficiencies elsewhere in one's life. I will examine contemporary mothering to see whether compensatory connection is at play in women's relationships with their children and, if so, what dynamics that type of connection produces in these women's families and in their lives as a whole.

Looking at mothers' own stakes in an intensive parent-child relationship offers a necessary corrective to existing understandings that focus disproportionately on how mothers meet the needs of others. For example, in explaining the recent rise of intensive mothering, Sharon Hays provides a social-equilibrium account. She asserts that "the more powerful and all-encompassing the rationalized market becomes, the more powerful becomes its ideological opposition in the logic of intensive mothering."[4] Under this ideology, the pursuit of "self-interested profit maximization" in the marketplace requires a counterbalance that intensive mothering provides through its "unselfish nurturing" and "commitment to the good of others."[5]

Other explanations for the intensification of mothering in the last several decades include economic insecurity, with privileged parents pouring ever-greater resources into their children to keep them from slipping down the class ladder.[6] There is also the "moral panic" explanation for hands-on parenting.[7] This includes worrying about such things as peer pressure, the Internet, drug use, and gangs, as well as risk society fears (highlighted in chapter 2 regarding the shielding strategy), such as child abduction, terrorism, or pandemics. Indeed, the majority of American parents cite "outside influences of society" as the primary culprit making parenting more difficult today.[8]

Each of these explanations captures an important piece of the security story in motherhood, yet what they all have in common is an underlying assumption that intensive mothering exists because society or children *need* it. Motherhood is thus framed as an other-oriented solution to such ills as rampant capitalism, college competition, and crime, and mothers are framed as divided from their own self-interest. We saw in the last chapter how women's adherence to this framing can have its own repercussions.

But the story does not stop there. Whether theory admits it or not, mothers may also be serving their *own* interests through intensive mothering. De Marneffe attempts to correct this blind spot in motherhood studies by introducing a "desire to mother," stemming from the enjoyment, meaning, and other benefits a woman can gain *for herself* from deep engagement with her children.[9] This reuniting of mothers with their own self-interest is, I believe, a crucial step in understanding mothering intensity today. The next step is to examine how the social world affects women's stakes in motherhood in such a way as to specifically make an *intensive* mother-child relationship something many women want.

THE HISTORY OF COMPENSATORY CONNECTION

A society-wide shift in so-called personal relationship dynamics is not historically unprecedented. For example, after a particular type of relationship is diminished or destabilized, culture sometimes shifts in a widespread way and people ascribe more meaning to or derive more security from another type of relationship.

Kin networks once wielded great power in families that relied on them for learning a family trade, making marriage decisions, and transferring property. Kin were part of the fabric of life, the hub of one's social connections. During industrialization, when many nuclear families split away from this hub in order to locate themselves in urban areas near centralized workplaces, the new and smaller family units could no longer rely as heavily on kin. This decline in the influence, support, and stability offered by kin corresponded historically to the blossoming of the companionate marriage. A whole extended family's worth of connection and security was squeezed into a single symbolic repository in the husband-wife dyad, which became more emotionalized. Cultural scholar David Shumway writes that marriage in that time period "came increasingly under the pressure of ever-greater personal expectations. The discourse of romance narrated these expectations, but it was not by itself responsible for their rise. Rather, increasing social fragmentation meant marriage had to fill in the emotional gap left by the demise of other relations. As individuals found themselves ever more alienated from each other and from their work, they made marriage the refuge of human connection."[10]

Shumway describes precisely the dynamics of compensatory connection, as the romantic value ascribed to marriage, to weddings, and to life-long heterosexual love skyrocketed, and there were increased expectations of a powerful and important male-female bond. The "marriage load" became enormous.

Putting such high expectations on a single relationship ultimately destabilized it, and the late twentieth-century breakup of the companionate marriage, along with the simultaneous destabilization of multiple other social and economic life realms, has left another security gap.[11] The current era may therefore be another historical moment in which society shifts its energy to highlight and magnify the perceived significance of one relationship while others wane.

Looking specifically to children for what is lacking elsewhere in one's life also has historical precedent. According to historian John Gillis, in the mid-nineteenth century, when many Evangelicals left the Church, the religious exodus created a type of insecurity as prior forms of grace disappeared. "This crisis of faith produced among them a desperate and creative search of new sources of grace, a quest that ultimately located salvation in the most unexpected places . . . in childhood. In post-Evangelical middle-class consciousness . . . [t]he sacred was displaced from the realm of the supernatural to the family, with the result that . . . children became objects of sentimentalization, bordering on worship."[12]

The loss of religious certainty was thus stabilized by emphasizing the view of one's children as pure and perfect. While Gillis ties these changes in adult-child relations to shifts in religious life, many others point out that the Cult of Domesticity and the middle-class emotionalizing of the mother-child bond arose precisely at that moment in history when middle-class white women ceased to be economically productive.[13] This complementary account suggests that the increase in attention given to mothering in the Victorian era was a form of compensatory connection, creating a new source of life grounding when these women ceased their economically productive labor.

Social psychologist Ilene Philipson applies a similar argument to the 1950s era, during another historical blip in white middle-class women's economic productivity. She argues that women's "involvement with children [during this period was] substituted for meaningful work" as well as for other meaningful relationships.[14] "Children are often used to compensate mothers for the affection that absent or emotionally remote husbands fail to provide, and for the companionship that would have been supplied in other social-historical situations by kin and friends."[15]

Furthermore, she argues that white middle-class women's singularity of focus on motherhood during that era contributed to the rise of narcissism as a social disease among their children.

COMPENSATORY CONNECTION TODAY

While we see that parents and particularly mothers have turned to children during prior historical periods when other forms of security, meaning, and purpose have been threatened, the current era is unique in the *degree* to which mothering has intensified and in the unprecedented emotional absorption in children.[16] We might therefore hypothesize that there is something different or more extreme taking place to propel this intensification.

The current era is also, in contrast to the Victorian era or the 1950s, the first time in history that American mothering has intensified during a period in which the majority of middle-class mothers are economically productive. We can therefore no longer attribute the increased attention to motherhood solely to the curtailment of women's productive energy in other spheres. Indeed, the pronounced existence of intensive mothering among career women suggests that being gainfully employed may no longer be a sufficient basis for maintaining a security equilibrium, at least not in the new economy.[17]

Sociologist Richard Sennett describes how present-day labor market insecurity topples our society's former basis of moral identity in work.[18] The prior axiom, "you are what you do," is decreasingly appropriate in a flexible and constantly shifting labor market, and he argues that people are therefore in search of a new source of lasting identity. In an unfortunate (but not coincidental) synchronicity, just as middle-class women discovered work as a new basis of their security in the 1970s, work destabilized. Women thus had to seek and buttress their security elsewhere.

Some might have sought it in marriage; however, marriage also destabilized at this very same historical moment—as did state protections and community bonds. In this perfect storm, the mother-child relationship was the last one standing, and it is no surprise many women anchored their lives in that relationship.

Unlike a woman's partner who can leave her at will, a child's extreme vulnerability and dependency, as well as federal laws of guardianship, all but guarantee that this little person will stick with her for the better part of two decades, with the emotional bond expected to continue for a lifetime. One can become an ex-wife in our society, but we do not have a term for an ex-mother. And that creates a sense of permanence and security that many women lack elsewhere in their lives.

DaCosta has closely examined the relationship between single heterosexual women's expectations of contingent, possibly expendable relationships with marriage partners and their expectations of enduring unconditional love with their children. She argues that "the negotiated, unstable character of adult love leads women to emphasize the mother-child bond as a more reliable arena in which to fulfill their needs for nurturance and security."[19] This is a compensatory connection argument based on the insecurity of one aspect of these women's lives, namely heterosexual partnerships, propelling them toward a greater focus on the seemingly more secure realm of motherhood. While these women may *wish* for unconditional love with their future partners, they do not *expect* it with partners, only with children. Tiffany, one of DaCosta's respondents, says, "[Y]our husband is not, like, permanent, you know what I'm saying. There's divorce now and, you know, he can leave. Your child can disown you or whatever, but you're still going to be that child's mother. . . . You're always going to have that relationship."[20]

The women DaCosta studies view marriage relationships as contingent. If a particular marriage does not satisfy the parties involved, it will end. Relationships with one's children, by contrast, are not viewed as elective or sized up for satisfaction to determine whether they should continue. Thus, although a husband may be able to provide various forms of security—he may help pay the bills, offer physical comforts, or intimidate the landlord—if a woman does not feel she can fully depend on the marriage continuing, those securities may not feel so secure. A child, by contrast, provides a particular variety of security that may be lacking elsewhere in the woman's life: a sense of permanence. Thus, it is not that she depends on the child's protections per se, but rather that she can depend on the relationship.

Edin and Kefalas show how this occurs among poor, urban young women. Prior to having children, these women's longings for the mainstream middle-class ideal of the white picket fence confront harsh realities of unacceptable prospective husbands and no decent job prospects. This leaves motherhood as the primary path for them to grow up, attain respectability, and accomplish something worthy.[21] "The redemptive stories our mothers tell speak to the primacy of the mothering role, how it can become virtually the only source of identity and meaning in a young woman's life. . . . [T]hey believe motherhood has 'saved' them."[22]

A natural next question is: Does this only happen among poor women? What is striking in my findings is that the married, privileged women in my sample who *have* the white picket fences, the working husbands, and the education and opportunities for meaningful, lucrative careers often likewise express that motherhood has saved them. How can this be? These mothers *appear* not to need saving. They seem to already have ample security. Yet surprisingly many women who on the surface appear to have it all voice tremendous insecurity.[23] Part of this is insecurity about the potential *loss* of it all. What if I lose my job? What if it doesn't work out between me and my husband? What if my child can't get into college or find a decent job? What if something goes terribly wrong—an accident, an illness, a crime—and our world is suddenly turned upside down? To manage that insecurity, many well-off and married mothers, just like financially struggling single mothers, draw upon their children. Again, the type of security a child offers is more a *feeling* of safety than any form of practical security. A child cannot shield one from crime, get one a job, or make it work with a romantic partner, but when these realms of life feel unpredictable, women do not always seek remedy in those same realms. Instead, they often seek a *sense* of security elsewhere.

Attachment researchers have posed the intriguing possibility that the "set goal of the attachment behavioral system [may be] viewed as 'felt security'" rather than some more objective measure of security.[24] That is, people may be motivated to *feel* secure even more than they are motivated to *be* secure through predictable work, a steady marriage, secure finances, or physical safety.

Almost all of the women using compensatory connection began their participation in the study with personal incomes lower than the national average for women, suggesting economics may indeed be a source of insecurity and part of what they are compensating for. Nonetheless, almost half of these women live in middle-class or upper-middle-class households because their partners earn greater incomes. Thus, lifestyle and household income appear less salient to a woman's need for compensatory connection with her children than her own personal earnings. That is, if a woman lives in a large four-bedroom house, drives a minivan, and shops at Whole Foods—all symbols of an upper-middle-class lifestyle—but knows she could not support herself and her children if she were on her own, she may feel economically *comfortable* yet not economically *secure*.[25] And that insecurity prompts her to seek a security solution, sometimes in the relationship with her children.

Compensatory connection is one of the two most prevalent security strategies among the participants in this study as a whole. One in four women uses this strategy either singly or in combination with one other strategy, and one in six women uses it almost exclusively.

In contrast to women who use the antidote and shielding strategies and who view mothering as the end-all of *children's* security, a woman who sees mother-child connection as her *own* ultimate source of security carries a very different type of motherload. The expectation for redemption from this one all-powerful relationship remains, but the focus is on herself and her own needs.

I make no assumption that meeting one's emotional needs through mothering is harmful, selfish, or otherwise problematic. Certainly the resentment resulting from the selfless love of antidote mothering is far less likely to occur if one's own needs are being acknowledged and satisfied through a more self-oriented relationship. However, a whole different set of issues arises when the mother's own security is a primary motivator in her mothering.

To better understand these issues, I present the case study of a mother who is on the extreme end of the compensatory-connection strategy. I use the extreme case so that the dynamics can be most easily seen.

GINA HALEY

When I drove up to Gina Haley's large urban home, there was an SUV out front with bumper stickers saying *Human Milk for Human Babies* and *My Baby Was Born at Home.* Gina is a thirty-three-year-old mother of four who runs an in-home day care three days a week in which she watches two children in addition to her own younger two.[26] She is also a La Leche League leader, a voluntary position aimed at helping women, often in a group setting, to succeed at breast-feeding their children. The group members generally advocate for nursing children beyond the first year.

Gina is a slim, very attractive woman with warm brown eyes, who offers me tea and food whenever I visit. Her baby daughter, Ginny, whose name quite resembles Gina's own, is a chubby, contented baby. She almost never cries, at least not according to Gina's report or during my observations. Gina holds her literally every moment of the day and night and appears highly attuned to her needs. The following are observations from the six-month visit:

> Ginny makes a slight move in her sling, and Gina instantly adjusts her own position, moving the sling slightly back, creating a new position together that Ginny seems happy with, gauging from her settledness. The adjustment is seamless and occurs while Gina is having an adult conversation with me, which continues uninterrupted. These shifts occur every couple minutes, seemingly without distracting Gina at all. Likewise, when Ginny makes light fussing sounds, Gina responds by playing with Ginny's feet, twirling

her fingers in the air for something for Ginny to look at, or handing her a key ring. These interventions are always successful, and the fussing or wriggling ceases as Ginny begins to coo or explore quietly. Typically, Gina doesn't even look down for the intervention but acts as if by instinct, retaining her adult-focused activities while constantly attending to the subtle needs of her baby.

When I draw back from the conversation or need to write something down or remove a teabag from my cup, Gina then switches to face-to-face interactions with Ginny, talking baby talk quietly with her, making faces, or lightly tickling her.

At the same time, Gina's older child, Reggie, who is now five, comes and goes from the interaction. When I arrive, she sets him up with some paints and large paper on an easel. After about twenty minutes, he loses interest in that and begins trying to dislodge a loose board from an archway of their house. She asks, "Do you want to knock that board out?" He seems excited at the prospect of destruction and says yes. She quickly locates a hammer, and for five minutes, he lets loose on the board until it comes off. "Thank you," she says, putting the hammer and board up high, out of his reach, and then she suggests three quiet activities for him to choose from to do next. He chooses a puzzle, and she sets it out for him. All of this occurs with almost no interruption in our interview, and all of it occurs while she continues to attend to Ginny in a sling on her body, almost as if without effort.

I am struck by Gina's ability to attend to our adult-oriented interview while also attending to Ginny's needs as an infant and to Reggie's older boy needs, all without any hint of strain. In many interviews for this study, it appears quite difficult for mothers to deal with an interview if their babies are present. It often seems as if adult interactions and meeting a child's needs are at odds; the mothers wince and apologize as their babies present needs, and they either try to ignore them as long as possible so we can continue or they quit their interaction with me in order to attend to the baby. In the majority of cases, research participants are unable to focus or give extended answers to my questions until their children begin napping or are cared for by a partner or someone else. But Gina manages to juggle multiple interactions with no apparent conflict between them.

Gina's parenting journey began when she was seventeen years old and became pregnant with a daughter. She married her boyfriend, and then became pregnant with a son when she was twenty. She left her husband during the second pregnancy and raised her two children as a single mother, working full-time while putting herself through a high school completion program and then college, and finally she began her career as a child-care provider.

Before the birth of her son, she learned about attachment parenting and radically changed her parenting style. Whereas she rarely held her first child, who spent most of her babyhood untouched in an infant seat or in a crib in a separate room, with the departure of her husband, Gina began sleeping with her second baby. She also began to hold him nearly continuously during the day.

It is worth noting that this shift in parenting style after a divorce is not unique to Gina. J. T., another study participant, interprets her own mother's actions after her parents' divorce, saying, "My mom connects emotionally only when *she* needs it. Like, my sister slept in her bed after the divorce, but this was totally for my mom, not for my sister."

Gina's family members cast judgment upon her radically altered style of parenting after the divorce, deeming it overly indulgent and coddling, but it felt intuitively right to Gina, and she reports becoming a much happier mother. Gina believes a baby's greatest needs are "constant holding, just never being put down . . . to be breast-fed and never left." The constant holding and frequent breast-feeding also make *her* feel cozy and whole, so she sees it as meeting both her own and her children's needs.

Eight years after the divorce, she married Stuart, a much older man whom she characterizes as a somewhat conservative businessman with whom she has a tumultuous hot-and-cold relationship. "When my husband and I *talk*, we end up in an argument mode. So I keep it superficial to keep it from erupting." His condom broke during their engagement period and she became pregnant. Since they both already had children from previous relationships and he had made clear he was done having children, he encouraged her to have an abortion. She chose to have the baby, Reggie, and remains resentful of Stuart for wanting her to terminate the pregnancy.

After Reggie's birth, Stuart was ardent about wanting no more children and Gina "acted like I was kind of going along with it, but internally, I knew I wanted more." Four years later, she secretly stopped taking her birth control pills and planned the exact night of the conception. She got pregnant and made it appear accidental (the baby fusses in her arms as she says this). This time, he *insisted* she have an abortion and his *mother* insisted she have an abortion; the family went through several weeks of "utter hell" as Gina proclaimed she was keeping the baby. Finally, her husband relented, he had a vasectomy, and they had another child, a daughter, Ginny.

While Gina's first two children were born in the hospital, the most recent two were born at home with very minimal midwife assistance, and both currently sleep with her and Stuart.

When Ginny was born, Gina cuddled with her continuously in bed and had one of her other children hold Ginny only for several minutes once every few days when Gina took showers. After the first two weeks, however, Gina decided those moments of mother-child separation during showers were unacceptable and she bought a water sling so she could continue to hold Ginny while she bathed. At the time of the six-month interview, she has still never put her baby down except for during an occasional messy diaper change and a very occasional car ride (Gina changed her lifestyle after Ginny's birth and almost never drives at this point—a challenge as a mother of young teens—in order not to have to put Ginny down).

Gina nurses preemptively, offering the breast before the baby asks for it. At the time of the six-month interview, she offers the breast four or five times an hour during my observations, and according to Gina's estimates, she breast-feeds "about fifty times in a twenty-four hour period." Gina characterizes her current level of closeness with her baby as "complete enmeshment," which she says with a sigh, using the term positively.

Like many connection-oriented women in this study, Gina repeatedly refers to her own family history in her narrative. Gina is the youngest of her parents' three children. She characterizes her mother as an unaffectionate person who, according to the family talk, had an affair, which is how Gina was actually conceived. Gina's aunt told her that her mother did not want to be pregnant, but abortion was illegal and so, according to the aunt, she simply did vigorous exercise that she was told not to do during pregnancy and smoked a lot to try to lose the baby. Gina survived, but was born prematurely. She was kept in a hospital incubator in the neonatal intensive care unit for a month and a half, during which time she believes she was not touched at all. She was also not breast-fed.

When Gina was two, her mother left the family, gave custody of the children to Gina's father, and moved to another city six hours away. Gina's father was playful when he was around, but he was working two jobs and putting himself through school, so she was in full-time day care during the day and was raised by a housekeeper during the evenings. Gina would cry, "Why did my Mommy leave me?" and reports that she began having abandonment issues. An intensive relationship with her children helped assuage these issues. "I realized in therapy as an adult that I didn't want my kids to abandon me, to make up for how I was left as a child, so it impacted how I parented."

If having a child lessens the sting of abandonment from childhood or fills a security void left by a tenuous work or social life through a beautiful and loving present-day connection with another human being, this is not necessarily problematic. Gina has certainly enjoyed early intimacy with all of her children, including the present one. She says, "I'm completely enamored of her and spend all of my time when I'm not doing other things either nursing or giving her direct face-to-face attention. I just love cuddling her and snuggling her, and feel such complete and utter gratitude. Every night I tell her, 'Thank you so much for being here.' I realize this could so easily *not* have happened."

Many other mothers, such as Heather highlighted in the prior chapter, might *want* to give their children an extended womb period of total comfort and connection, but giving so much poses a challenge to them and can lead to burnout, anger, or frustration with the babies for having so many needs. Many would see what Gina is doing as a noble *sacrifice* for the sake of the child, yet for Gina, this level of giving (which she does not see as giving at all) fortifies *her*. She is in baby bliss.

Gina's daughter also seems quite content with the situation. She is held, fed, played with, and engaged with as much as any baby could desire, and her cues are responded to instantly. While some schools of thought, such as expressed by Gina's extended family, claim that constant holding and round-the-clock nursing is overly indulgent of the baby, the vast majority of pediatricians and parenting advice books state that one cannot spoil young babies by holding them too much, and that doing so is in perfect accord with babies' needs.[27]

In studying Gina and other women whose parenting is particularly driven by compensatory connection, however, I find several unintended consequences emerging from the strategy alongside the tenderness and physical warmth. Before analyzing these, let me clarify that the repercussions I will discuss are not due to attachment parenting. Indeed, many women in this study practice attachment parenting and do not encounter the problems that I will elaborate in Gina's case. Her difficulties, like Heather's, stem not from her mothering style but from the insecurity that prompts it, not from attachment parenting but from a heavy motherload.

Gina's Attachment-scape

We have already seen that Gina's past attachments in her family of origin were not reliable as her mother abandoned the family and her father was largely absent due to work and schooling.

In her present life, Gina's web of attachments—what I will call her attachment-scape—is likewise weak. For example, she does not have close friends: "My two best friends from high school [live elsewhere in the state], but as happens, you kind of drift apart when you live apart. . . . I don't have any super close friends . . . [and] friendship in general is not super important to me. . . . Mostly short-term connections meet my friendship needs, and I just find it's draining to be with other people too long."

Regarding a career, Gina applied to a master's program in social work seven years ago and found out she was pregnant with Reggie the same week she found out she was not accepted to the program. "So I thought, '*Perfect!*'" She would embark on this new project of parenting instead. Motherhood then substituted for advancing her career, though in a dynamic similar to that of her friendships, she was never terribly motivated in the career realm anyway, so children only removed her from attachments in which she was already not highly invested.

AV: Is a paid career something that has mattered to you throughout your life?

GH: See that's the thing. I feel like it *should*, in this day and age. And once the kids are older I wouldn't want to not have anything in my life. But right now, my self-esteem comes entirely from the kids.

AV: How much security have you received from your job at different points in your life?

GH: I never really got much security from a job. The most *esteem* I've gotten from anything outside the kids was in college when I was single and I graduated *cum laude*. That added a lot of self-esteem to my life. But it didn't go on, so then it lost its meaning. Bachelors are a dime a dozen. Without a career, though, my parents worry about me relying on a man since he could die or leave. And my husband's parents see me as a leech.

Her parents' concern about her vulnerability in case Stuart is no longer there to provide for her shows the financial insecurity stemming from her lack of a well-paying job.[28] Yet ironically, Gina's financial dependence on her husband is part of what she sees as stabilizing that relationship. In answering what draws her to Stuart, she says, "To be totally coldhearted sounding, of course there's a big part of it that's just the sheer fact that we do own a home together and have two kids together." She later adds: "Sometimes, I think, well, what if I won the lottery, you know, would I be tempted to be on my own [i.e., leave my husband]? And sometimes the answer is definitely yes, but more often, no, because I don't want to lose the kids to [him]. . . ."

She is bound to Stuart by virtue of both her financial dependence on him and her fears that he might be awarded custody of the children were they to divorce. Despite these ties to him, on an emotional level Gina voices a very expendable view of their partnership: "I've always been: 'Yeah, this may or may not work out,' and when there's a fight, I'm just: 'Well, we just won't be together,' whereas he's hurt and wants us to be together. I still sometimes want to run away because I can't handle it."

We might wonder if Gina is so emotionally absorbed in her baby that there is simply no room for other attachments and therefore her blasé attitude toward the partnership is an *outcome* of her intensive mother-child relationship. However, Gina states that her ambivalence in her relationship with her husband predates their having children together. Her deception with Stuart about being on birth control pills and the secret devising of a pregnancy vehemently against his will also suggests that Gina's intimacy with the baby has been at odds with emotional intimacy with her husband since before the baby was even conceived.

Returning to the other elements of her attachment-scape, her tenuous career history as a high school dropout, single mother student, and then part-time child-care provider all predate the pregnancy with Ginny, as does her financial insecurity of near-total dependence on someone else's earnings for her subsistence. Additionally, her sense of abandonment insecurity carried over from childhood, which she herself sees as directly causing her enmeshment with her children. All these elements indicate that her attachment-scape was insecure first, *then* she planned the pregnancy and engaged in her intensive parenting style.

However, as we continue to listen, we find evidence that compensatory connection is not simply an outcome of insecurity in her various life realms but also a *contributor* to that insecurity. For example, regarding friendship, Gina says, "I can be equally happy to be with the kids and can forget to call my friends for weeks at a time." Enthrallment with one's children causing one not to connect with others is common. Even among parents of older children, "the new parenting style consumes the lives of the parents who adopt it, often at the expense of other meaningful relationships."[29]

Examining Gina's marriage, we see how her physical intimacy with the baby interferes with her partnership as well. She discusses the impossibility of sex with Stuart given that she does not put Ginny down, even when asleep: "Needless to say, my husband is going a little crazy. It doesn't bother me as much because I realize this is such a short time in the big scheme of things and that eventually we'll have our love life back. But he is very upset by it, which I understand." It is not simply sex that presents difficulties between her and her husband, however, but rather all forms of physical warmth. "[Affection is] much more important for him. It's a definite issue in our marriage since I give so much touch to the kids, but with him I have a barrier."

In two-parent families, it is not uncommon for the birth of a baby to entail a shift for the parents from the face-to-face relating of courtship to a more side-by-side form of relating, and as we saw in chapter 2, couples may sleep separately during the newborn phase in order to maximize sleep or divide the nighttime parenting labor. Still, the sharing of the epic joint project of parenting can sometimes lead to greater intimacy. Alma Perez, a Chicana mother of a three-month-old boy, says, "I love my husband more now than I ever have. It's incredible to see him with our baby and to see how much love there is between them. And somehow, loving our baby boy and seeing how precious and beautiful he is makes me recognize more the preciousness and beauty of my husband, like I'm seeing our son in him or realizing that at the beginning of his life, he was also just like this . . ."

Likewise, Jordan Cousins, a white stay-at-home father of a five-month-old girl, says having a baby has made his relationship with his wife "a lot deeper because it's another shared incredible experience every day. And also the inevitable fact that most of what we share is private with a baby at three in the morning. There's a certain romance to that that other people aren't in on."

EXCLUSIVITY

While the intimacy generated through the shared incredible experience of parenting can be fulfilling, that is only possible if it is indeed shared. In Gina's case, she does not wish to share it. "[I preferred to have a girl] because my biggest concern was if we had a boy that my husband would take over. I already feel like he's taking Reggie off to do boy things . . . and I didn't want that with the next child."

Gina guards the parenting terrain and does not welcome her husband's participation, a phenomenon known as maternal gatekeeping. While not all women are territorial around parenting, and men often decline their share of the work even when the gates are wide open, gatekeeping is "one important source of men's under-involvement in domestic labor."[30] Gatekeeping has been shown to occur primarily among women for whom the mothering identity is the primary source of self-esteem and satisfaction.[31]

Gina says her son and husband spend time together and "have fun, but that didn't start until Ginny was born and took Reggie's place. Before that, it was too hard for me [to have Reggie be with his dad rather than with me]." Obviously, there are implications to the child from not letting him have a relationship with his father until another baby came along to "take his place." Putting those issues aside for a moment and just looking at the partnership relationship, given that Gina will not leave the children under any circumstance, she and her husband cannot be alone together and cultivate a face-to-face couplehood, nor can they cultivate the intimacy of a side-by-side joint venture since Gina does not welcome him as a coparent.

Gina attributes her unwelcoming attitude partly to the fact that Stuart initially wanted to abort their two pregnancies. Because of that, Gina says, she "hoarded the experience of the pregnancy and birth" from her husband, and did not allow him to be a part of it. "I'm pretty selfish in terms of wanting the whole experience to myself."

Her use of the word "hoard" to describe the experience suggests a view of connection with the baby as a scarce resource, a zero-sum in which anyone else experiencing the baby means she no longer has the whole experience for herself. In a strict zero-sum game, the baby loving her husband means the baby loves her exactly that much less, and conversely Gina loving her husband means she is not loving her baby fully. But if it is husband versus baby for Gina, her relationship with the baby unambiguously wins.

Thus, we see two repercussions of compensatory connection, both related to exclusivity. The first is that the relationship with the baby is so enthralling and all consuming to her that she does not seek to create or nurture other possible realms of security for herself. This negatively affects her friendships, paid work, and connection with her husband—all of which limit *her* experiences. And the second repercussion regards the *baby's* limited experiences. Gina is threatened by the baby having other attachments besides to her: "My most important focus for my youngest . . . has a selfish component, since my goal is to have her really attached to *me*. I'm not encouraging her to be attached to others."

While most mothers' rationales for attachment parenting center on giving their children security and meeting their most basic human need for connection—which includes connection with other caregivers—we see Gina's most important focus is having the baby bonded to *her*.

The exclusive nature of the relationship highlights how her continuous holding is not intended simply to meet her baby's needs for love and affection but also her own. To this end, she restricts the experiences the baby is permitted to have and the cast of characters with whom the baby can have them.

I want to emphasize that Gina's need for the baby's unquestioned attachment to her in order to feel secure and her zero-sum appraisal of that attachment is not typical of attachment parenting, nor is it typical of the indigenous cultures from which many attachment mothers take inspiration. For example, primatologist Sarah Blaffer Hrdy finds that "mothers in virtually every culture . . . allow others to hold their babies from birth onward, to a greater or lesser extent depending on tradition. Among the !Kung foragers of the Kalahari, babies are held by a father, grandmother, older sibling, or some other allomother [approximately] 25 percent of the time. Among the Efe foragers of Central Africa, babies spend 60 percent of their daylight hours being toted around by somebody other than their mother. In 87 percent of foraging societies, mothers sometimes suckle each other's children, another remarkable display of social trust."[32]

Indeed, Hrdy argues that "cooperative breeding," which is sharing the child care and provisioning for one's children with others, is an evolutionary development that ushered the human species beyond the social development of the great apes (who do not share child care with others) and contributed to the development in society of greater cooperative behavior and mutual trust.[33]

With Gina's inability to share child rearing, even with her partner, we see a thwarting of that cooperation and trust.

MATERNAL ATTACHMENT TO CHILDREN

Gina intends for the total enmeshment of the mother-child relationship in the present to make up for her lack of security elsewhere and is upfront about how being near her children quells her anxieties. "I get really anxious . . . and just don't feel quite right out in the world without at least one child next to me; it just feels very abnormal to me. Um, I guess that's kind of surprising . . . at my age—I feel I should be a lot more confident out there in the world and not need a child as almost a crutch, you know."

Chris Bobel finds similarly mother-oriented relationship dynamics in her study of "natural mothers" whose practices resemble Gina's. Bobel writes: "Again and again, I heard women speak of their reluctance to separate from their children, resisting this division for *their own sake* . . ."[34]

While Gina and the women Bobel studies may be extreme in their desires to be with their children, there are less extreme versions of this within many mother-child relationships. Daphne de Marneffe's work addresses the "embodied, aching desire to be with their children that many mothers feel" but which our culture fails to openly acknowledge.[35] Overlooking women's own desires for togetherness and focusing on children's dependency needs only, she claims, we turn children "into the repository of our *mutual* desire for human connection."[36] For example, if "the studies show that children do fine in day care, we independent adults are supposed to go about our business without remorse. . . . [But] adults' desire to nurture their children is much more passionate and complex than the opposition of dependent child and independent adult would have us believe."[37]

Attachment researchers certainly recognize that not only children but also adults experience attachment relationships with people whose presence they seek in order to feel secure. However, "most research on adult attachment in social and clinical psychology has highlighted attachment in romantic relationships."[38] This assumed primacy of the romantic partnership in adult attachment relationships may be misplaced, at least among mothers of young children, as I find partnership among the relationships these mothers speak of with the least emotional intensity. By contrast, they speak of children with the most. (Independence-oriented mothers also speak of work with great emotional intensity.)

Psychologist R. Chris Fraley and his colleagues are currently seeking to correct the romantic relationship bias in adult attachment studies by assessing attachment styles with respect to a variety of people in adults' lives. The broader set of relationships his team is investigating includes relationships with one's mother, father, romantic partner, and friends.[39] However, this still omits from consideration the possibility of a parent's attachment to her own child (as well as to her job). Because of this widespread omission, attachment researchers continue to claim that "parents do not direct attachment behaviors toward their infants."[40] Studies of mother-child attachment security thus typically regard mothers only as attachment objects within the context of this relationship rather than as attachment subjects with their own security needs and attachments to their children.

In contrast with these studies, I find that Gina and the other women who use the compensatory-connection strategy display with their children all three criteria of attachment described by John Bowlby, the founder of attachment theory. These are as follows: (1) *proximity seeking*, wanting to be with the attachment figure (i.e., the child), especially under conditions of threat; (2) *secure base*, deriving comfort and security from the attachment figure; and (3) *separation protest*, protesting when the attachment figure becomes or threatens to become unavailable.[41]

It is important to stay mindful that Gina is an extreme case and her compensatory connection surpasses that of the other women I studied. I nonetheless propose that children are, in some cases, attachment figures for mothers, particularly in those cases where work, partnership, and other forms of meaningful connection are weakest or least reliable.

CONNECTION SEEKING AND INSECURITY

Before continuing with the case study analysis of Gina, I will explore within the broader set of mothers the relationship between the security of various realms of life and connection seeking with a child.

Work

The single clearest distinguishing factor between the women who make the mother-child *connection* the cornerstone of security and those who try harder to foster *independence* is their relationship with work. In chapter 2, we saw that career women with longer work hours prior to pregnancy and more permanent work tend to be more independence oriented regarding their children, whereas women working fewer hours in less permanent work tend to be more connection oriented.

Here, I focus on one interpretation of that finding: some connection-oriented women may be seeking to fill the security gap in their lives left by insecure or minimal work. That is, they may be engaging in the compensatory-connection security strategy. This interpretation finds support in other research that shows how a focus on an exclusive mother-child relationship occurs among those in "low-paying, low-prestige, or unfulfilling jobs with few psychological rewards or prospects for advancement. . . . [This is because unfulfilling work does] not displace women's valued roles as wives and mothers—roles in which they may feel irreplaceable and can exercise significant autonomy and power."[42] That is, if we assume a human need to be valued and to exert influence, then when that need cannot be met in the workplace, women—who have cultural permission to do so more than men—may instead focus their energies on the family. Sociologist Sarah Damaske likewise argues that, in contrast with the "opt-out" rhetoric of professional women leaving high-paying jobs to seek fulfillment in full-time motherhood, it is actually working-class and working-poor women who are more likely to become stay-at-home mothers. This is not merely because their low wages do not offset the costs of child care but also because they are underappreciated for their work. Lacking both economic and social rewards, some women simply withdraw from the labor market and turn their attention more fully to the mother-child relationship.[43]

Insecure work seems to predispose a connection orientation in the women I study as well. For example, Daphne Petrolis, a thirty-one-year-old Greek immigrant, describes how having a child acts as a palliative, distracting her from the insecurity she feels about her work life.

> In a way, [parenting is] like a job and makes me feel good about myself, and it's an excuse not to find a job. I was thinking about why it's hard to put Adrian in a day care, and it's kind of like [parenting is] a way for me not to deal with issues of finding work. It's as if my life were on hold . . . [and I] wasn't doing anything fulfilling, so then I had Adrian and that was a good excuse for me not to do anything for a career. But now I have two days available [when he is in day care] and I need to figure out what to do with them. So the issue is open again and it's scary. Dealing with Adrian, it's very convenient not to deal with these issues.

With great candor, Daphne acknowledges how parenting allows her to avoid anxiety about her career by temporarily taking the place of a paid job in her life. Motherhood certainly possesses an advantage over most careers in the new economy where job security is rare. Motherhood has job security (even if it comes at the cost of financial security). Motherhood also does not require a job search where one puts one's skills, talents, and even personhood out for the world to judge (and in most cases reject), which is an act of extreme vulnerability many people might prefer to avoid.[44]

Notice in Daphne's case that by motherhood distracting her from worry about her less secure realms, it allows that insecurity to continue. This

cycle, from insecurity to involvement with a child and from involvement with a child to exacerbated insecurity, is similar to the dynamic
with Gina. However, this is only one way motherhood can relate with
career insecurity, and it is not the case for all women.

Deb Feldman is likewise unemployed but her fifteen-month-old son
does *not* give her an out or distract her from pursuing a career path. She
is actively applying for jobs. Her son, however, does ease the emotional
toll of unemployment and an otherwise harrowing job search. She says,
[*eyes welling up*] "Isaac is so compassionate toward others and feels such
empathy. I was really upset a week ago about a job [I had applied to] being filled [by someone else], and I was at the computer reading this rejection . . . and Isaac came up and gave me a big hug, and I thought, 'How
does he *know*?'" [*fully in tears*].

Deb reveals a second way motherhood can relate with job insecurity:
motherhood can offer such love that even as one struggles to increase security in one's career (or partnership or elsewhere), the joy of motherhood
softens the pain and anxiety of that struggle.

A third mother, Ignacia Cruz, an unmarried black Filipina teenager
whose clinical depression caused her to lose her factory job just prior to
becoming pregnant, also finds great solace in difficult times through her
relationship with her child. Despite living off her disability checks and
being unmarried and unemployed, having a child gives her a continuous
loving presence in her life that she believes is helping her emerge from
her depression. She says, "It's just the biggest love I could ever imagine. I
love talking with him all day, carrying him outside and telling him about
what we see, about the trees and the sky." During pregnancy, she created
a baby book for him, to which she continues to add pages. It is not a com-
mercially produced fill-in-the-blanks book but simply a plain notebook
into which she pastes images, such as a printout of his ultrasound picture
with little arrows and text saying, "This is your sweet little nose," and "I
can't wait to meet you."

Rather than the love and emotional security with her son distracting
her from other less secure elements of her life, it fortifies her to repair
them. "I want to give him a good life, so I cleaned up my act, turned off
the TV, and got my [high school] diploma." Her love is a motivator to
improve her circumstances and create greater security in her life. Even

before he was born, simply being pregnant helped her improve her life: "It totally made me quit smoking, and I stopped eating junk food since I don't want *him* to eat that kind of crap. I want him to eat carrot sticks and bananas." So while her son may fill an emotional vacancy in her life, their relationship does not mollify or distract her from insecurity elsewhere or allow her to avoid dealing with those issues, as in Daphne's case. Nor does it make her feel less bad about that insecurity, as in Deb's case. Rather, motherhood magnifies the unacceptability of insecurity in Ignacia's life and motivates her to *do* something about it.

Thus, while Daphne, Deb, and Ignacia to some degree all experience their children as compensating for their lacking careers and for other insecurities in their lives, we see three models for how motherhood can prompt one to respond to that insecurity. Motherhood can *distract* from one's insecurity (allowing it to continue), *ease the pain* of that insecurity (making correction less urgent but possibly more likely to occur as one's attempts at remedy carry less emotional sting), or highlight the *unacceptability* of that insecurity (which directly propels one to remedy it).

It is only the first of these—distraction—that places security with one's child at odds with security in other life realms, making a repaired attachment-scape difficult to accomplish. Notice it is Daphne who experiences this distraction and also she who describes her relationship with her son as pacifying *her* insecurity, the clearest case of compensatory connection. Ignacia, an unemployed teen mother whose son is likewise the greatest source of her own security, has the additional element of a strong desire to bring security to her *son*. His presence brings her life's insecurity into high relief, causes a new sense of alarm, and drives her to repair it. The distinction between Daphne's distraction and Ignacia's drive to healing suggests that a disproportional focus on a child as a way to meet one's own security needs may put that relationship at risk of distracting from—rather than helping to heal or repair—the insecurity in the rest of one's life.

Partnership

There is also an interesting relationship between insecurity in one's partnership and a connection orientation with one's child. During pregnancy, almost half of connection-oriented women either expressed the possibility of leaving their partners or concern that their partners might leave them—or they were single mothers wishing to be partnered. By contrast, only a fourth of independence-oriented women voiced these concerns. Thus, the women who most frequently shared one of these forms of insecurity in their partnerships were those who sought intense relationships with their children. Although we may not generalize from a sample of this size, this is consistent with and lends preliminary support to a compensatory-connection argument.

We see additional clues pointing to compensatory connection in how mothers frame their relationships. For example, Deb Feldman, whose fifteen-month-old son, Isaac, gave her that comforting hug after she read her job rejection e-mail, also experiences communication barriers and other marital difficulties with her husband. She feels her son ameliorates these difficulties as well: "[My emotional response to having a baby is] happiness pretty much all the time. Things could be going really bad with [me and my husband], but if I'm spending the day with Isaac, I forget all about that. . . . Ever since he was two months old, he's smiled all the time, with those big dimples, so it doesn't matter what's going on with me, I still am happy when I'm with him."

One's child relieving the emotional stress of a difficult partnership does not indicate that one is amplifying the mother-child realm to compensate for problems in the marriage, yet it is noteworthy that talk of children emotionally easing difficulties in one's life is commonplace among connection-oriented mothers in this study and far less common among those oriented toward independence.

The greater divide between connection- and independence-oriented mothers regarding their partnerships, however, is not so much differences in divorce expectations as differences in attention and prioritization. Connection-oriented women put less narrative emphasis on their partners, speak less frequently of efforts made to strengthen and maintain their partnership relationships, seldom mention their partners' needs, and speak almost exclusively of the mother-child relationship versus discussing the family as a unit. By contrast, mothers who prioritize autonomy with their children frequently refer to their whole families, spontaneously bring up their partners more, and specifically discuss concessions to their partners, such as letting them name their babies or regularly keeping the babies up late in order to attend events the partners enjoy. For example, Maria Castillo, a Guatemalan immigrant and full-time working mother of a two-year-old, says, "I don't think [having a child] had a major change, like, in my whole life, only my relationship with [my husband]. . . . I was used to taking care of him, and with a baby, I think he's the one who has suffered. So I always try to see how he's doing and to prepare his favorite foods. . . ."

She not only articulates that her husband has needs but also expresses compassion for him and attempts to meet some of those needs both before and after having a child. Voicing this consideration of a partner's needs is not common in the narratives of connection-oriented women. We might surmise that a connection-oriented woman's child-first ideology puts her child's needs above her own as well as above her partner's, yet the infrequent mention of the partner, his emotional needs, or her emotional needs of *him* in the pregnancy narratives suggests this low partner salience predates the birth of the child.

In addition, independence-oriented women prioritize time alone with their partners without children present and schedule regular dates with their partners. Amira Blankenship, one such mother with a full-time career, says, "We *like* to have family time and do things with [our baby] on the weekend [since he is in paid care fifty hours during the week], but it's also important for [my husband] and me to do things just us on the weekends, do adult things."

By contrast, Gina, clearly a connection-oriented mother, says, "People say, 'You need dates with your husband!' But you can go out with your baby *and* your husband. . . . I'm not willing to leave the kids to do things just the two of us."

Reluctance to leave the baby, even with trusted caregivers, is not uncommon among connection-oriented mothers. This exclusivity, possibly born of the presumed importance of the mother-child bond, can end up pitting the relationship with one's child against one's other relationships, such as one's partnership. Thus, a relationship with the child intended to compensate for insecurity elsewhere in one's life can at times exacerbate that insecurity.

Another notable difference between connection- and independence-oriented mothers is that when speaking about their children, independence-oriented mothers frequently use the word "we" to refer to themselves and their partners, such as, "We want a nanny for our son rather than day care." This differs from connection-oriented mothers who generally use the singular first person when referring to parenting decisions, such as, "I don't want the baby to sleep in another room."

We therefore see that an independence-oriented approach with a child does not necessarily indicate independence seeking with a partner. In fact, part of the impetus for seeking an independent child may be in order to better accommodate a spouse's needs and to maintain a couple-hood beyond parenthood, which autonomy seekers prioritize. Likewise, a connection orientation with a child does not necessarily indicate a person who seeks an intensely connected partnership. Indeed, these intensities seem inversely related, with connection-oriented mothers being the least prioritizing of the couple relationship. This is consistent with a compensatory-connection argument, although the partnership deficit that children fill may be less one of security and more one of salience or prioritization.

The Use of Psychotherapeutic Framings

Insecurity stemming from childhood distress is difficult to quantify, since what one person experiences as hurtful might be less so for another person. Therefore, rather than impose a subjective judgment on how distressing, say, the death of a parent might be versus having a mean second-grade teacher, I look at a woman's *expression* of the childhood occurrences she describes and how salient they appear to be for her. That is, if the mean second-grade teacher is mentioned over and over in the narrative and described as distressing and as highly influential in her later life, then I classify it as salient.

Framing insecurity from childhood distress exclusively based on self-report is imperfect, leaving out people who cope with distressing events by denial or downplaying. Thus, what I can discern from the narratives might more aptly be called "emphasis on childhood pain" or the level to which women draw on painful childhood experiences to explain their emotional (or other forms of) insecurity as adults.

While the rate of reporting a distressing childhood event is about the same for connection- and independence-oriented mothers, with about half of the mothers in each group volunteering a distressing childhood event in their interviews, the expressed salience of that distress is far higher for connection-oriented mothers. These mothers talk more frequently and at greater length about their suffering as children, particularly at the hands of their mothers, and they attribute more of their current emotional states, life circumstances, and parenting choices to how they themselves were (inadequately) parented. Many of these women refer to themselves as having developed abandonment issues.

Independence-oriented mothers also share stories of childhood distress, including abuse, poverty, intrusive parenting, inadequate attention, or parental abandonment. However, these experiences do not repeatedly surface in the narratives, and the mothers refer to them far less often in explaining the rest of their life stories.

This is not to suggest that people who are more deeply wounded in childhood seek greater attachment with their own children. I have no way of determining the unspoken wounds of those who do not to share them with me, and the degree of articulation does not necessarily relate to the degree of suffering. However, it is not unreasonable to suggest that those women whose life narratives are most self-consciously framed by childhood distress, particularly what they interpret as some form of parental abandonment, do have a more connection-seeking philosophical strategy. The women may frame their connection seeking as occurring for their children's sakes, such as occurs in the antidote or shielding strategies, or for their own sakes, as in the compensatory-connection strategy. In either case, the emphasis on past hurts seems to increase women's expectations that the mother-child relationship in the current generation will resolve those hurts, either for themselves or for their children, through an intensely connected relationship.

Heather Dover, highlighted in chapter 2, whose narrative returns repeatedly to being adopted as a baby, explains her nearly continuous baby holding by saying, "My own early experience of mother abandonment probably has something to do with it." Likewise Beck Farrow, a white middle-class lesbian, connects the intensity of her drive toward mother-child togetherness to her experiences of childhood abandonment: "When Dakota was first born, she was *everything*. . . . I preferred to be at home with the three of us, whereas [my wife] wanted to go have more couple time, but that brought up my abandonment issues, and I didn't want to leave Dakota with another person."

Nelson likewise finds that a connection orientation with one's children is "at least in part driven by a drive for connection across generations, especially when upward ties have been frayed. . . ."[45] For example, her respondent Anna Benton, a white upper-middle-class mother, explains her own intimacy seeking with her children by saying, "I'm sure it's more for my own need to be intimate and close because I wasn't that close with my parents."[46]

Women vary in the degree to which they believe their own upbringings have defined their lives. My argument regarding this follows a straightforward logic: If a woman views her own childhood as decisive in her life, she generalizes this and imbues the institution of motherhood more broadly with a high degree of determining power. Then when she has her own child, she maintains this maternally deterministic view, adding weight to her motherload.

This is different than a purely psychological theory such as "the repetition compulsion" wherein a mother's childhood wounds cause her to inadvertently wound her children, even when striving to do otherwise. Rather, this more sociological understanding draws a connection between the degree to which one assigns shaping influence to one's own childhood experiences—which could relate to cultural or structural factors—and the high expectation that one is responsible for one's children's security.[47] This maternally deterministic view and the related heavy motherload then bring about their own issues.[48]

The life elements discussed above—paid work, the partner relationship, and (one's framing of) one's childhood experiences—are three key realms of a woman's attachment-scape from which her sense of security or insecurity emerges as she begins the mothering journey with a new child. We have seen that the woman's degree of connection seeking with her child relates to weak, nonprioritized, or insecure ties in all three realms. Looking at these trends collectively, I am able to conclude the following: in this research, women entering motherhood with insecure attachment-scapes are more prone to seek intensely connected relationships with their children than women with secure attachment-scapes. This suggests the existence of compensatory connection.

REJECTION OF INDEPENDENCE

Of course, most mothers seek at least somewhat connected relationships with their children. Most also enjoy certain security benefits from motherhood (even as they also incur numerous economic and other security costs). In most cases, this is unproblematic. However, Gina's zealous seeking of those security benefits through her parenting goal of having her baby attached only to her has ramifications. We have already seen some of those ramifications through Gina's limitation of both other sources of security in her own life and the baby's experiences with other caring people. That is, Gina's need for exclusivity prevents both her and Ginny from developing relationships beyond the mother-child cocoon. But such extreme mother-driven connection seeking also has effects on Gina and Ginny's relationship with *each other*.

Gina believes parents these days push their kids hard "toward independence, and that just seems wrong and so unhealthy." She says, "Mainstream parents [i.e., those who do not practice attachment parenting] seem to work hard to *detach* from their kids at a really early age. People seem in such a rush. . . . I was telling my fifteen-year-old how when she was little and I left, she'd cry and cry, and she told me kind of tongue-in-cheek that now when I come *in* the room she cries! But we have so much time ahead of us, so long when our children will *not* want to be with us, that it seems crazy to be encouraging that when they're little."

She sees mainstream parents' rush to foster independence in their babies as denying the developmental appropriateness of deep dependency during babyhood. Yet Gina's desire to *prolong* that dependency may likewise fail to embrace appropriate child development at the point when the baby is ready to move on to the next step. At six months, she says, "I have some fears of her independence. For now, it's totally perfect because she has no desire for independence. And it will be okay when she does—it's somehow worked out with the older kids—but for now, she never wants to get down and that's perfect. With my second-born, he screamed to be put down at five or six months, but this one hasn't. I think it will be hard when she wants that, hard in terms of the emotional response. But I hope I don't convey that to her."

While Gina hopes her distress won't show when Ginny wants to explore the world beyond her arms, the perfection of Ginny's lack of interest in getting down indicates that at some point things will be less perfect. This is at odds with other aspects of Gina's parenting. Gina would undoubtedly be horrified if a child ever had to reach the point of *screaming* to be fed. She tries to avoid Ginny having to so much as whimper by anticipating and meeting her needs before they even arise (such as by offering the breast before Ginny asks for it). Yet it is evident that this philosophy applies only to meeting dependency needs, not needs for differentiation. If she anticipated these needs, she might offer her child floor time before the child demanded it, and the fact that her second child had to scream to be put down indicates this was not the case.

In addition to her gratitude that Ginny is still content in her arms, Gina considers it lucky that her younger son, Reggie, still wanted to be held in the sling many hours each day even after he was walking and that he continued to want to nurse even after her supply dried up during her next pregnancy when he was four. "Even if [nursing an older child] is selfish, it's still doing the babies a lot of good. People say, 'You're doing extended nursing for your own needs, not theirs,' but you can't force a baby to nurse!"

With Reggie now five years old, having finally weaned, Gina says, "I'm keeping Reggie out of kindergarten because I want him home with me one more year. I knew we never would have this time again. That's how it was with the older girls; once they started school, that was the breaking point in the relationship. They say 'Once you leave your baby, it's easier to leave them.' So I want to be with [these younger kids] full-time at least the first five years."

Kim Monroe, one of the "natural mothers" Bobel studies, likewise kept her son home when he reached kindergarten age. Kim says, "[A]t the time when Michael became school-age, it just didn't feel right to send a child that young off to school. . . . My *child* might have been ready to go to school, but *I* wasn't ready."[49]

Insofar as compensatory connection fosters intense mother-child attachment primarily to meet the mother's needs rather than the child's, it may make it difficult for the mother to recognize the child's developmentally changing needs and the independence overtures he makes, and therefore to appropriately respond to his signals.

Philipson argues that when motherhood takes the place of "meaningful work and satisfying emotional relationships with other adults, children's own needs can easily be ignored or misperceived. When the rearing of children justifies a woman's existence and is constitutive of her identity, the movement of those children toward autonomy can logically be seen as a threatening and frightening occurrence."[50]

GROWTH AS ABANDONMENT

We have seen how compensatory connection may thwart the mother's development of a more secure attachment-scape beyond the mother-child relationship. However, with someone like Gina for whom the mother-child relationship is so all consuming, we have to ask whether her needs perhaps *could* indeed be met through this single intense relationship. Is it possible that the benefits to her of love and closeness with her child are so fulfilling as to be worth the security costs in the rest of her life? Even if Gina's own answer to this question were yes—and even putting the child's well-being completely aside for a moment—there is still another issue with compensatory connection built into the mother-child relationship itself: the passage of time. When a child's growth and increasing independence over time destabilizes the basis of connection, the relationship is inherently insecure. Children do grow. And this has ramifications on both the child's *and* Gina's well-being.

Gina's children's growing independence creates a rupture as they age. Touch is difficult for her with nonbabies. She says that much as she has a barrier around touch with her husband, "even with the older kids, it doesn't come naturally. I don't know why." Recall her earlier statement that once her older children started school, "that was the breaking point in the relationship." It wasn't just that they needed her less or wanted less affection. It was also that *she* felt less affection toward *them*. "With each subsequent child that comes along, they replace the others, so all of my affection goes to the new one. Once they get older, maybe nine or ten, I lose the ability to be affectionate. I want to try to guard against that with these two."

In the name of love, she is actively struggling against this tendency. It is important for her to remain affectionate with her younger children even as they age, just as it is important for her not to convey her emotional distress when Ginny eventually wants to get down to crawl or play on the floor. She wants to love all her children equally and in all phases of their development. But it is difficult for her since her own sense of abandonment is triggered by her baby's growth, and her one pillar of security in life is destined to grow up and leave her.

GINA: TWO YEARS LATER

Fast-forward to Ginny's toddlerhood: Gina is now living in a large suburban home an hour from the city where she previously lived. She is still married to Stuart, still offering part-time day care out of her home, and still offering me tea and muffins upon arrival. Ginny, now almost three years old, and Reggie, seven, are both drawing with crayons at the kitchen counter when I enter. Reggie is being homeschooled.

Whereas her prior house was an example of relaxed housekeeping, with laundry out, frozen pizza for dinner, and a charming proliferation of clutter, this home appears perfectly kept and decidedly adult. Children's games and toys are brought out only when in use and are then returned to closets, the bathroom is pristine, and the floors lack the crumbs and smudges characteristic of a home with young children. Since they moved into the new home, Gina says she has been motivated to keep the place looking nice.

Gina and I sit down at a sofa near the children, and she speaks in front of them without concern for them overhearing sensitive topics.

She describes her relationship with Ginny as primarily physical.

> As bad as I feel about this, I don't sit down and actively play with her or Reggie. I get things set up, put out toys or paper and crayons, then I cook and clean. I feel I should be doing more one-on-one, quality time, actively playing. A whole day may go by and she says, 'Read to me,' and by the end of the day, it still hasn't happened because the phone rings and I'm driving kids around, dealing with teen issues, and I'm distracted. So a lot of times, our main connection is through nursing and holding, not so much direct contact. She gets touch, but she doesn't get a lot of emotional connection.

Despite claiming that Ginny does not get much emotional connection, Gina herself feels emotional connection with Ginny and expresses this elsewhere in the interview. "I feel very, very connected [with her] . . . physically very close, emotionally very close. It's just one of those things where I love the feel of her skin, I love the way she smells, I love having her cuddled up next to me. It's still kind of a very magical thing—like the newborn period where you can't imagine not being with that baby or not smelling that baby and you're so close—it's very similar to that."

Gina has still never been away from Ginny, never stepped out to the grocery store for a half hour while Ginny's father watches her, never worked out at a gym, or never had dinner out alone with her husband or a friend. Gina says, "At this point, Ginny could handle more separation than I could." They are, however, occasionally in separate rooms now, and most frequently not in direct physical contact.

Ginny bypassed the crawling phase almost entirely and walked at twelve months once Gina let her down. Floor time remained rare, however, for another six months beyond that. Gina says, "One and a half was about the time she started having more separation from me. She always adored her dad and her siblings, but that was the point where I wasn't holding her all the time in the sling, keeping her in one place, so she could actually walk off and do her own thing."

Though Gina remains effusive about her love of her daughter, something has changed. Whereas she used to speak in fairly neutral tones about such things as hoarding her children from her husband, as if she may or may not see such things as problematic, this time, she seems decidedly humbled. She uses words like "bad" and "unhealthy" to describe some of her actions and wonders if they may be causing ill effects in the children.

This new level of self-questioning is evident as she shares some motivations behind her parenting, starting from her first "accidentally on purpose" pregnancy when she was a teenager.

[I was] extremely needy in my teen years, so I sought solace in boys and somewhat in drugs. . . . [E]ven when I was very young, I was always attracted to babysitting and day camps for kids and things like that. And so I think that, through nurturing children, it was filling some of my needs for nurturing. But on the flip side, I think it was really bad because, um, then I got pregnant at that age [seventeen] because, you know—I'm quite sure it was subconsciously planned, and that was a really negative way to act out on trying to meet my needs.

Seeing her first pregnancy as a really negative way to meet her needs shows that she is not only aware of the compensatory connection driving her urge for a baby but also views that as bad.

Furthermore, she recognizes how she is different from her fellow attachment parents by virtue of her unmet needs being projected onto her children.

GH: [I]f you came from a very normal, healthy upbringing and do attachment parenting, then it looks normal and healthy. But if you come from a slightly warped beginning, as I did, then it looks like you are just doing it for your own reasons and you worry about the children, like, "Oh, are you actually *harming* these children because you're doing it for your own reasons and not just for their sake?" It's not altruistic; it's, you know, selfish, so I kind of struggle with that. But I also know that if I go against my feelings, even if they're unhealthy and whacked out and warped, if I go against them and, like, say, "Okay, I *should* leave my children with my husband or with my in-laws or whatever just because it's good for them," I can't do it. . . . But I also then worry that once they get a little older that I become more detached. Like from the teens . . . once the other kids came along, I think I really, in a very negative way, drew back.

AV: Do you think that will happen with these younger two since there aren't going to be any more children?

GH: I've noticed it with Reggie. I don't know if it's just a result of having another child, but I actually have to consciously show affection. And I think, *What kind of mother has to remind herself to hug her son?* . . . I think my husband is actually more affectionate with Reggie than I am. That doesn't fit my self-image as a nurturing stay-at-home mom.

Part of the reason for Gina's new focus on the unhealthy aspects of her parenting may relate to her older son, Reggie. Reggie continues to sleep with his parents and Ginny despite Gina and Stuart's best efforts to move him to a twin-size bed directly abutting their king-size bed. Even if they move him there in his sleep, he sleepwalks back to Gina's side, and Stuart inevitably ends up in the twin. "I'm concerned because he can't be alone, can't go across the house by himself. And having him in bed is just starting not to feel good anymore." Reggie's fears of being alone include an inability even to step into another room. I observed the following on a visit to their home:

> *Reggie wants LEGOs, which are in the next room. Since Gina does not want to stop the interview to accompany him, she asks Ginny if she'll go (he can go to another room without Gina so long as someone else goes with him). Ginny, who is in Gina's lap nursing, refuses to go because she wants to continue nursing. Gina tries setting up a race to see if the kids can get the LEGOs in less than thirty seconds. After a bit of further prodding, Ginny relents and the kids finally go off for several seconds to the other room and return with the LEGOs.*

Reggie's needs emerge several other times over the course of the interview. At another point, he needs to go to the bathroom and wants Gina to go with him. Gina asks Ginny to accompany him instead so the interview can continue. His inability to go to the bathroom or fetch nearby toys without accompaniment is in marked contrast to Ginny, whom Gina describes as "pretty darn self-sufficient." Several times during the interview, Ginny (who, though not yet three, is fully potty trained) self-initiates trips to the bathroom, skips off alone, then comes back and gets involved in some activity on her own.

In attempts to help Reggie learn to be alone for brief periods, Gina enrolled him in an hour-long art class once a week. The first few class meetings, Gina (and therefore Ginny) stayed. Then she and Ginny stood further back for several weeks, then at the door for a couple class meetings, then a bit down the hall. Finally—"not that he was happy about it"— Reggie let her and Ginny go down the block to a park during the hour. This has only been a recent development.

> Sometimes I think [Reggie's separation anxiety] is innate, and he would be this way regardless, but other times I feel like I'm *totally* responsible for it. . . . There should definitely be more of a balance than I've allowed. . . .

For most kids, if they are totally healthy kids, all else being equal, attachment parenting is the best thing in the world for them. But . . . maybe the way I've done it—and also having a strained relationship with my husband and with his family—I think those things combine to create a lot of separation anxiety that doesn't seem quite right. . . . I kind of feel like it's a bit over the top.

Despite Ginny presenting as a developmentally normal, independent, and spirited toddler, Gina's concern for Reggie's separation anxiety has made her question her parenting style, at least when applied to children older than three (before then, she is unambiguous that a child needs the love and security brought by the continuous physical presence of his mother).

INDEPENDENCE-CONNECTION DYNAMICS

Fear of losing the children appears to be part of what propels Gina's continued discomfort with Stuart spending time with them.

GH: I can't explain this, but I have zero issues with [Ginny] going off with her siblings, but when she wants to go off with my husband, I have a lot more insecurity with that. . . . Of course, intellectually, I know it's healthy and great that she has a relationship with her dad and if anything ever happened to me, she'd need him, so it's reassuring on the one hand. But there's an emotional part of it that's, like, well, I may try to hurry through something more quickly if she's with my husband. . . .

AV: I wish we could figure out this whole husband dynamic.

GH: Yeah. Why I don't feel comfortable with my husband being close to the kids is a strange thing. Possibly because he has such close ties with his family [of origin], and they've been very pushy with his kids from the previous marriage—they've been parental figures in some ways—so it's made me really leery; I never want that to happen. . . . [H]aving the kids go off with him, it makes me a bit concerned that eventually he'll just leave me behind all together and he'll go off with his family, and I don't want that ever to happen. I know it's totally warped and totally wrong, but I'm adamant that they not take over because I have these concerns that they could end up taking my family away.

We finally get a glimpse at what is propelling Gina's fear of her children spending time with their father. She believes the time may make it more likely he would take custody of the children if the marriage were to dissolve. She thus appears to be protecting her most prized mother-child bond by severing all other connections that might encroach upon it, and the closer he is with the children, the more her relationship with them feels threatened.

This explains why she isn't comfortable with the children being close with him. A remaining mystery is why *she* isn't comfortable being close with him. Why would Gina, who purports to be carrying such anxiety and fear of abandonment, not seek comfort in her partner? She says that Stuart is verbally and physically affectionate, he 100 percent accepts her with all her flaws, he's crazy in love with her, physically and emotionally, and he feels like she's his soul mate. Sometimes, she adds, she feels fake because she doesn't feel that way.

Her own lack of heartfelt connection with him is finally explained, below:

AV: Why do you say you feel fake?

GH: There are so many times that I wouldn't ever say my deep-seated feelings. He'll ask me a point blank question: "Do you ever feel your emotional needs aren't met in the relationship?" and I'll say no—even though it's a total lie! And he'll always talk about how he fell in love with me when he first saw me, and he never felt that way before. I will never say anything like, "Well, Honey, I never felt that way about you but I went out with you anyway!" That just wouldn't seem right. So sometimes I just don't feel like I'm emotionally honest. . . .

AV: Why do you think your emotional needs are not met with him?

GH: I think a lot of it is my fault, that I put up an emotional barrier a lot of the time. . . . I just get too into my head, and, I just don't, I don't know. I think it probably comes down to my abandonment issue, and I feel like, if I were the one to care too much, that would be a bad, dangerous thing, so I make sure whoever I'm with is the one who cares more. I'm not used to this long-term thing because I always had short-term relationships, and I'd always be the one to end them, and I'd always have someone else waiting before I ended that one—it was just always that way. So it's been, like, a really kind of nerve-wracking experience [to stay with Stuart], and I've been really tempted to . . . I don't know . . . I think I just don't allow myself to be more open to him.

The key statement here is that if she were the one to care too much, that would be a bad, dangerous thing. That is, given the possibility that relationships may not last, her security comes from *not* caring. This may explain why she has not developed close friendships, has not invested herself in a career, and has not fully embraced a romantic partner. To avoid the dangers of emotionally connecting, she keeps all relationships short-term and expendable, and maintains the upper hand by being the object of adoration who remains indifferent.

In this way, Gina's story lends support to Robert Bellah, Margaret Mead, and others in the theoretical tradition claiming that increasing societal uncertainty propels people toward greater independence.[51] In this tradition, sociologist Iain Wilkinson writes, "[W]here people are becoming increasingly preoccupied with job insecurity and the shifting value of their relations of emotional dependency, then the social pressure towards individualization is liable to increase as they are forced to become more reflexively oriented to the inevitability of change at work . . . [and in] intimate relations."[52]

Observing Gina's attitudes toward friendship, work, and partnership, we might see her as the very archetype of one drawing on independence ideals to cope with this inevitability of change in those realms.

However, the relationship with her children seems to fall into an entirely different category, and rather than taking a similarly dismissive stance with them, she funnels all salience into this one singularly meaningful relationship. With a small baby, caring does not feel dangerous to her. Instead, it is the one relationship where she lets down her guard and allows herself to feel all the love, attachment, and emotional openness she minimizes elsewhere. In this way, the insecurity of her attachment-scape that draws her toward independence in all other realms leaves a vacuum that then draws her toward *connection* with her children to make up for what is lacking.

CONCLUSION

The deep dependency of young children and the unabashed intensity of their love deeply attach them to their caregivers and frequently offer women great personal rewards. Many women see motherhood as enriching them as human beings, stretching them, and filling their lives with beauty as they witness the miracle of human growth. Finding security (or meaning, purpose, intimacy, or joy) in the relationship with one's children—as all mothers in this study do to some degree—does not indicate a woman is using the compensatory-connection security strategy. Compensatory connection only occurs among those particular women who seek security *primarily* through their children as a way to make up for a security deficit elsewhere in their lives. For these women, the mother-child relationship feels like their most guaranteed bond. Unlike work, where layoffs can occur unpredictably, or marriage, where divorce often feels a coin flip away, young children's great dependence on caregivers makes them *dependable*.

As the principal source of lasting connection these women can count on, the mother-child relationship is given far more energy than their other relationships. This includes greater amounts of physical contact, copresence, and thinking about time than other relationships, and also greater identification with one's role as a mother than with the other roles in one's life. Attaching this primacy to the mother-child relationship makes it take up more life space and fills one's attachment-scape with its seemingly most secure element. Although relying so heavily on a single element creates a lopsided attachment-scape, it produces a subjective feeling of security even when the majority of one's life feels insecure.

Reaping security from the mother-child relationship is by no means problematic. However, making up for less secure arenas of one's life by magnifying that relationship does set up dynamics with repercussions, as we have seen with Gina. First, the security one seeks in the relationship with one's child can be at odds with actual or potential forms of security elsewhere in one's life. That is, a woman may not attend to her friendships, partnerships, or work life due to her intense involvement with her child, and these other life realms may become still less secure. Second, the relationship may be highly exclusive, with the compensating mother hoarding the child's attachment and curtailing the child's experiences with caring individuals other than herself. Third, the intensity of the mother's own attachment seeking with the child can sometimes make it hard for her to recognize and respond to the child's cues if they are outside the spectrum of dependency she seeks. This may interfere with the child's needs being met, particularly the needs for separation and individuation. And finally, the mother's reliance on her child's dependency is threatened by the child's growth and the passage of time, so her basis of security in the mother-child relationship is inherently unstable.

While Edin and Kefalas demonstrate how poor women draw their security, identity, honor, and life meaning from bringing children into the world and caring for them,[53] I show that compensatory connection is not unique to poor, single, and unemployed women. It can occur among women of any social class, including married and working mothers. This is because having a job is different from having job security and being married is different from feeling secure in that relationship. Just as significantly, living an upper-middle-class lifestyle is different from feeling economically secure, particularly if one's own income is only a token part of the family economy. In all of these cases, it is a woman's subjective experience of insecurity, rather than her employment status, marital status, or social class, that creates the need for a redemptive mother-child relationship.

The particular insecurities common among women using the compensatory-connection security strategy are insecure work, insecure partnerships, and psychotherapeutic understandings of their current life challenges as stemming from events in their early childhoods. Women using compensatory connection also tend to have a zero-sum view of connection, believing that more attachment with one person must mean less attachment with others. Thus, they vigilantly protect the exclusivity of the mother-child relationship.

On the one hand, we see that the causal arrow seems to fly from one's attachment-scape to one's security strategy. The women whose attachment-scapes are the least secure—whose work, partnerships, and past connections are felt to be inadequate, unimportant, or painfully problematic—are the ones who most aggressively recruit their children into the making-up-for role of compensatory connection.

On the other hand, using compensatory connection with children affects the security of one's attachment-scape. When the mother amplifies the time, meaning, energy, and importance given to the mother-child relationship in order to make up for insecurity elsewhere in her life, she edges out other possible forms of security, often intensifying the very insecurities that drove her to compensatory connection in the first place. When this happens, the causal arrow returns to its bow and the purported solution to her life's insecurities unintentionally exacerbates them. This is not limited to the compensatory connection security strategy. One or another variation of this backfire effect occurs with each of the security strategies, including the independence-oriented ones, and is the cost of heavy-motherload mothering.

In addition to revealing this security backfire, compensatory connection yields theoretical insights. It addresses the seeming contradiction between those theories of society claiming that surrounding instability or threat propels people to seek greater independence and those claiming that it propels them to seek greater connection. The findings presented here lend partial support to the former theories, as women like Gina gravitate toward independence (or at least emotional disengagement) from their more tenuous life realms. Independence becomes a form of safety and immunizes them from the dangers of fluctuating circumstances. But what those theories miss is that this very independence can create a greater need to intensify any connection these women see as more likely to endure. That is, the less security women find elsewhere in their lives, the more attachment they may seek with their children. This second link in the chain lends support to the latter theories claiming that societal insecurity leads to greater connection seeking. Taken together, my data suggest that we should dispense with taking theoretical sides or trying to disentangle these strands with an either-or analysis because independence can beget connection.

Compensatory connection also reveals something about attachment relationships. Though it has long been recognized that children are attached to their mothers, I find that mothers can likewise exhibit attachment behaviors regarding their children. This reliance on children for one's attachment needs is particularly pronounced among those mothers whose work lives and other relationships are weakest or least reliable. This has implications. Specifically, when we pair increasingly widespread experiences of insecurity (economic, marital, and psychotherapeutically framed) with the tendency I have identified to intensify parenting among those with insecure attachment-scapes, we have a new lens with which to understand why motherhood is intensifying. For many women, the single dependable bond they are able to find is with their children.

We already know from other studies that intensive mothers are providing or attempting to provide others—their children in particular—with various benefits.[54] What compensatory connection adds to this is an understanding of a mother's *own* stakes in an intensive relationship and how the undependability of modern society is raising those stakes.

Thousands of attachment studies attest that people gravitate toward attachment figures when they feel threatened. Thus, if there is a continued perception of societal insecurity and risk and a perceived destabilization of other avenues of meeting those security needs, we might expect to see more of this type of heightened attachment to children in the future.

4 Light-Motherload Connection

Don't be overawed by what the experts say . . . The more
people have studied different methods of bringing up
children the more they have come to the conclusion that
what good mothers and fathers instinctively feel like doing
for their babies is usually best after all. Furthermore, all
parents do their best job when they have a natural, easy
confidence in themselves. Better to make a few mistakes
from being natural than to do everything letter-perfect out
of a feeling of worry.

—Dr. Benjamin Spock

Mothering does not have to be so weighty. Even in an insecure society,
there are alternatives to heavy-motherload mothering—and they have
nothing to do with putting the baby down or teaching her to self-soothe.
In fact, they have nothing to do with correct mothering, or mothering
practices at all. They have to do with lightened expectations.

Because this first half of the book is focused on connection, I have looked
thus far at mothers who use connection as their means of bringing about
security. It may therefore be tempting to blame any less-than-desirable outcomes or family dynamics on attachment parenting or on these mothers'
generally hands-on parenting approach. However, mothers who engage in
nearly identical child rearing practices can have radically different relationships with their children and different mothering experiences.

In fact, I will show it is not attachment parenting that leads to the
difficulties we have seen but rather a heavy motherload. I show this by

presenting the cases of mothers who are just as connection oriented as those we have already met, but who do not project life-securing powers onto the mother-child relationship. This comparison brings into focus the determinative influence of intense *expectations* rather than high-intensity mothering *practices* in shaping the unfolding dynamics of the mother-child relationship.

Light-motherload mothering occurs among women with at least one very secure attachment in their lives beyond children and who are either not particularly anxious about various threats in the world or who do not see the mother-child relationship as the principal means by which to address these concerns. They look to multiple forms of support and remediation in their own and their children's lives. And if they do feel responsibility for repairing the ills of society, that responsibility extends to those beyond the confines of their own private families.

These mothers with less intense security concerns or broader security nets, like all mothers, may orient their parenting toward connection or independence. But in contrast to the preceding cases with heavy motherloads, in light-motherload mothering, the connection or independence is not *strategically deployed* to enhance security. This does not mean that connection, for instance, is never used as means to an end, as one may pick up a crying baby in order to comfort her, or sleep with a baby because it allows the parents to get better rest. However, light-motherload connection with a child is not generally intended to assuage uncertainty or threats that a mother perceives in her life or in the world at large. Rather, connection occurs for a host of other reasons: it may simply feel good, the baby may seem more contented with a high level of connection, or baby carrying and co-sleeping may be an assumed part of the mother's ethnic culture.

About a third of the women in this study entered motherhood with light motherloads, and they were fairly evenly divided between connection and independence oriented. This chapter examines light-motherload mothering among connection-oriented mothers. In chapter 7, we will again look at light-motherload mothering, but among independence-oriented mothers. Only by seeing women who do *not* project life-redeeming powers onto the mother-child relationship can we more clearly bring into focus the women who do.

Though some mothers with light motherloads may practice attachment parenting, they may not use or even know that terminology. Nor do they view their parenting style as the correct model that others should follow. Their stories show how mothering in a highly connected way can indeed be a joy, can be shared with partners and others, and can be responsive to the changing needs of the child.

RESPONSIVE ATTACHMENT

The style with which a woman with a light motherload interacts with her child tends to emerge in relation to the child himself rather than according to a preexisting model of correct mothering. In fact, several respondents who did have clear plans about how to mother saw their plans challenged or even reversed by the births of their children. Abandoning their prior models proved to be a positive shift about which they were happy.

For example, Amelia McDaniels, already head of marketing at a well-regarded company at the age of thirty-one, had every intention of raising an independent child and of remaining an independent person herself after the birth of her child. During pregnancy she said:

AM: I'm sure it's bad to say this, but my mom was a stay-at-home mom, and I really saw—my mom was very wimpy and dependent on my dad financially, very much a child in her own right, and I just want to be the complete opposite of that. I'm like, "I'm going to be strong! I'm not going to need"—so I never really put myself in that Mommy thought, even as a kid.

AV: What's the Mommy thought?

AM: Women walking around in Laura Ashley jumpers and their kids are their whole entire lives, they don't do adult things anymore, and you can't have a conversation with them because, you know, it's all about the kids.

Amelia was quite clear about her parenting plans: get the baby into her own room by two months and breast-feed for "six months at the *most* [because] . . . back to my own independence, I don't want to be the milk station forever." Regarding her marketing career, she had a goal of two weeks of maternity leave, though she said she probably wouldn't make it that long since she considered a number of her work responsibilities "just my job, not necessarily something I trust an assistant to do." More realistically, she foresaw herself getting back to certain job duties—from home—within a few days of the birth.

Amelia was also fervent about not losing herself as an individual and being a strong, independent person, as well as being a mom. She ran a ten-mile race in her third trimester of pregnancy and scheduled a trip to the Galapagos Islands to take place shortly after the baby's birth. Amelia appeared to be gearing up for highly independence-oriented mothering.

Then Amelia had her baby. Her daughter, Jazz, had terrible colic—"She cried almost any moment she was not breast-feeding or asleep"—which left Amelia literally staggering, sleepless, "on the verge of a nervous breakdown," and "crumpled and crying on the bathroom floor." Desperate for some solution to her daughter's relentless screaming, she was willing to try anything. "The only thing that worked was breast-feeding, and I fed her so much I got pus in my breasts. [Carrying her in] the sling helped, too, and going outside." Gradually Amelia's independence orientation gave way to a focus on connection and emotional security and she took an open-ended unpaid leave from work to tend to her baby's storm of needs.

After three months, when the colic subsided and Amelia no longer felt forced to co-sleep, breast-feed around the clock, or constantly hold her baby in order to keep the peace, she felt such adoring love for Jazz that she simply wanted to hold her. "When she was a newborn . . . I looked at her as a dreadful duty, and now it's like a *pleasure*. Not that it's not still hard, but it's a whole different thing."

At six months, Amelia is still not back at her workplace but is participating in occasional phone conferences and acting as primary liaison with several key clients, averaging five to ten hours of work a week. I ask whether Jazz is still co-sleeping. "Yeah," Amelia replies, ducking her head in mock shame. "I know, I'm so bad . . . [but it] was just easier to keep her in bed with us. She fits perfect under my arm . . . [and] I love sleeping with her and waking up with her in the morning. I know we've got to get her out, but it's just so *nice* for me to have her there next to me, and she *likes* it so much."

I ask why she is apologetic about it or feels it is necessary to get Jazz out of their bed. She says, "I have friends who make me feel totally awful about sleeping with her. They think it's nutty. 'You *know*, Amelia, you've *got* to transfer her! How are you going to have another baby?' I've been made to feel like I'm supposed to do things a certain way. One friend says I hold her too much, I should have given her solids at three months, I shouldn't co-sleep."

Yet despite the disapproval of her friends, Amelia is asserting her *own* independence, bucking social pressures to "grow her baby up already," and instead surrendering herself to mother-baby connection.

What has changed for Amelia from the idealized version of independent motherhood she shared prior to the birth to her current reality of near-constant physical connection seems to be less about her long-term goals for her daughter (or herself) and more about what simply feels good in the moment for both her and Jazz. Feeling good was not part of Amelia's prior repertoire of parenting values, yet it is a significant factor since her baby's birth. The fact that breast-feeding and sleeping cuddled together were the only ways to calm her baby during the first few months forced her hand at the beginning. But now that things have settled down, she continues these practices because of how much both she and Jazz enjoy them. At six months, she revels in her daughter.

> I bawled my eyes out so many times at the beginning, but now when I cry it's almost always happiness. Like [when] she went over by the Christmas tree and started clapping, or when she cut her first tooth and I felt it, or [when] she crawled over to me with a toy and offered it to me ... I have fallen so in love with this child it is unbelievable. . . . Oh gosh, hearing her laugh is the neatest sound in the whole entire world. And ... she crawls over to me, ach, it's so—When I wake up in the morning, she'll gently paw me in the face to wake me up and I'll look up to this gummy smile and it's just the best thing in the world.

Watching Amelia's eyes crinkle as she twirls her fingers before Jazz's looping gaze, or hearing her delightedly laughing back and forth with the baby as I organize my papers, the joy is palpable.

Another mother, Alma Perez, took an equally surprising turn in the opposite direction. She thought she would practice attachment parenting and ended up engaging in far less touch with her son than anticipated.

To Alma, who had spent part of her life in Mexico and had absorbed the indigenous practice of perpetually carrying babies, holding her infant son, Mateo, most of the time was simply assumed. Before the birth, she purchased a handwoven baby sling in Mexico with the intention of carrying Mateo most of the day. "We were planning to hold him a lot . . . but he had other plans for himself and he seemed to actually prefer to be set down sometimes, to be another separate person in the circle, or to be face-to-face. He also . . . really seemed to prefer the stroller, which totally surprised us, and he'd fuss while carried and then be peaceful in the stroller. Our parenting has become a 'try this, and if it doesn't work, try that' approach."

Mateo also surprised Alma and her husband regarding sleep.

> He became fussy every once in a while, always when he was overtired. . . . We went into this thing thinking that a baby just sleeps when he's tired and we don't have to be quiet or put him off in a room by himself or give him a bed to sleep in. . . . [We assumed] he would just sleep on us while we do things or visit with other people or whatever. That worked great at first, but eventually, he got so interested in all the [goings-on] around him that unless we turned down the stimulation, he wouldn't sleep. And then after a whole day without a nap, he would melt down and just be miserable. So we began to *manage* his sleep for him . . . feeding him down in bed and then leaving him there while I got other things done. Then he wasn't fussy anymore.

In both cases, Alma adjusted how she thought she would mother in order to accommodate her son. She is not dogmatic about her new, custom-built mothering style either, however, and has maintained a self-reflective posture from the beginning: "At about three weeks, my sister came to visit and she pointed out how little I talked with Mateo and how little I stimulated him with playful exchanges. I began to question myself and whether or not I was giving my baby enough of that kind of attention. After about a week of self-doubt, I began to realize that my natural tendency with my baby is to calm him, to avoid him being overstimulated, to keep things gentle rather than entertaining or stimulating."

Again showing a fluid and responsive relationship with Mateo, Alma talks about what happened as he aged: "Once he got more into voices, I began to talk with him more, and once he began to smile, I began to play with him more. . . . I [also] did less of the calming sways that had felt so natural at the beginning. So now I'm not so plagued by self-doubt; I just think that I'm responding differently to him at different stages of his development."

Like many mothers with light motherloads, Alma speaks with great detail about her *child*, not just about their *relationship*. For example, at three months she says:

[H]e is already such a person. I didn't realize that a little baby could be such a well-defined human being. I thought he would just be an incomprehensible lump of warmth that I would cuddle and love, but he's a *person*. He follows conversations between me and my husband as if he were a third person in them, which he is. He's curious about things around him, particularly faces and nature. He likes to study things, and he gets this very serious look on his face when he's trying to figure something out. He also loves to relate to people, and sometimes he and I have conversations with each other and we just go back and forth, back and forth, talking all about things together.

The narratives of light-motherload mothers have a different emotional character than those of mothers who carry heavy motherloads and draw greatly on one of the security strategies. One possible explanation of this difference is that light-motherload connection is less instrumentally driven; connection is not an object to give or keep for the sake of results. With the shielding and antidote strategies, the child-focused connection is a (frequently sacrificial) gift bestowed to the child. With compensatory connection, the more mother-focused connection is a (scarce and vanishing) resource hoarded by the mother from other would-be caregivers and from the passage of time. By contrast, light-motherload connection does not appear to be something one can possess; it has no clear directionality and appears to be more simply an expression. There is little attachment to what the relationship should look like (since the relationship is not relied upon for its insecurity-reducing properties) and great attachment to the individual child.

Furthermore, light-motherload connection differs from its heavy-motherload counterpart insofar as it is not universalized as the right way to mother (particularly since it is so often in response to the individual child), so doing otherwise is not necessarily considered harmful. That is, there is no felt *pressure* to mother this particular way. In fact, like Amelia, whose friends saw her connection-oriented mothering as nutty and who herself had a similar appraisal of connection-oriented mothering prior to her baby's birth, many mothers with light motherloads are parenting as they are *despite* their prior taken-for-granted assumptions about normal or correct mothering or despite what they repeatedly hear from their family and friends.

For example, German-born Lena Wasserman, whose "mother thought I was spoiling my son by responding to him every time he cries and holding him a lot," says, "I have one friend in Germany and she did the cry-it-out method with her boy, and [regarding my baby] she's just like 'Oh god, he's still sleeping in your arms? He's never going to get over that!' And actually I thought about it, and maybe she's right, and maybe I'm just . . . one of those moms who can't let their baby grow up. But then I thought, 'He's a *baby*. He's not going to sleep in my arms forever.'"

Lena has also had to contend with experts telling her how to properly mother.

LW: I have those books and magazines—they just come to me, I didn't order them—and I have read those articles that say babies should learn how to fall asleep by themselves because otherwise they need you to fall asleep. [*pause*] But I think it's perfectly *fine* for him to need me. If he needs me, he needs me. He's not manipulating me and doesn't understand why he has to cry. I don't like the idea of my son going to sleep crying. I want him to feel safe and happy when he's going to sleep. . . .

AV: Do you ever judge other parents who *don't* hold their babies or respond?

LW: Maybe a little bit. It depends. If the baby is happy with that, or if the cry-it-out works quickly, then I don't think there's much damage.

We see from the above quotes that Lena actually considered the possibility that her friend could be right and her co-sleeping might be holding her son back (just as Alma considered her sister's comment that she might be understimulating her newborn). This indicates a degree of continued reflection, refinement, and flexibility in her parenting rather than a single dogmatic approach. She also sees that other parents using the cry-it-out method might be okay—if the baby is happy with that. This openness to others' strikingly different-looking forms of mothering is remarkably absent in heavy-motherload mothering, with its emphasis on right and wrong.

Like other mothers with light motherloads, Lena seems to *know* her child very well and, of all the women in this study, she gives the most detailed answer to the question of what her baby, then six months old, particularly likes doing.

LW: He likes eating solids. He likes being in the water a lot, in the pool or shower or bath. And he likes spending time with his parents. He likes the cats a lot, looking at them and petting them. He likes toys he can take apart and bang. He likes being on the playground. He's just crazy about watching the other kids and sitting in the sand and feeling it on his legs and going on the swing with me. Just coming close to the playground, he gets all excited and his body wiggles. He loves cuddling, loves music, loves dancing. He likes going for walks and just looking around. He loves trees. He's crazy about tearing apart magazines and books and newspaper.

AV: How do you know he likes those things?

LW: He either laughs, or has this intense focused look of wonder. If he doesn't like things, he turns his head away or pushes things away and has angry noises [*imitates the noises*] or he cries.

THE MOTHERING POLICE

In contrast with Lena, among women with heavy motherloads, those with a connection orientation tend to cast judgment on independence-oriented mothers and often view them as self-absorbed or insensitive. Likewise, those with an independence orientation often view connection-oriented mothers as denying their own selfhood, being overly indulgent of children, and not offering children their own legs to stand on.

As egalitarian ideals and the rhetoric of choice permeate our culture, the so-called mommy wars between working and stay-at-home mothers have lost momentum and very few soldiers remain who will heckle a mother regarding her work status. But there is a new—and related—war about correct mothering fought on the contested terrain between independence and connection. This war has abundant soldiers—the mothering police—patrolling its terrain and eagerly telling mothers what they should be doing differently. Here are several examples from various mothers in this study:

> "My mom is critical. [Our baby] was six weeks old and she said, 'Why isn't this kid on a schedule?!'"
>
> "I had a breast-reduction surgery as a teenager and ended up not being able to breast-feed my babies, but with all the messages around about the right way to feed your baby, I had to deal with some real looks when I mixed formula for my two-month-old."
>
> "[Everyone] thinks I need to put her down and leave her. I don't internalize it, but I wonder if they're ever going to give it up."
>
> "The minute you tell someone you're pregnant, you'll be judged for the rest of your life and everyone will tell you how to do things."

Squadrons of mother correctors urge mothers to put the baby down, pick the baby up, not breast-feed in public, or not bottle-feed at all, with the frequent subtext that mothers can control destiny for their children. Like the parenting advice literature, the mothering police tend to either enforce greater independence (Stop being so indulgent!) or greater connection (Be more sensitive to that poor baby!). While women may feel confused or even attacked by these mixed messages, if they carry a heavy motherload, they tend to deal with that confusion by taking their own correct mothering stance and joining the patrol.

To understand even better the differences between light- and heavy-motherload mothering, I present the story of one mother, J. T. Miles, with a light motherload. J. T. makes for a good comparison with Heather Dover and Gina Haley, the prior case studies, because of background similarities. J. T. shares the job insecurity common to many connection-oriented mothers. Furthermore, J. T., like Heather, was living with the baby's father but unmarried when she gave birth to her daughter and currently has little money and insecure housing. All three women report childhoods in which they did not feel their needs were adequately met by their mothers. And perhaps most importantly in the context of this study, J. T. practices attachment parenting to a degree very similar to that of Heather and Gina. However, there are a number of striking differences that will become evident in her story.

J. T. MILES

J. T. Miles is a white twenty-six-year-old living with her boyfriend of three years, Buck, a waiter. J. T.'s prior jobs include waitressing, tutoring immigrant adults in English, and working at an independent bookstore, where she was employed as a stocker and cashier when she became pregnant. While the bookstore provided her an enjoyable job, she did not consider it important work "so [she went] on the hunt for a calling. And [she] got a call. It said, 'Your diaphragm is broken!'"

Though she and Buck had talked about wanting to have children at some point,

> kids were permanently two years down the road. We did know things had gone wrong with two methods of birth control simultaneously and we talked about whether we should go to Planned Parenthood for the morning-after pill. But it almost seemed like fate since these things came together at the same time. I did get a seven-page manifesto from one of my friends saying why I shouldn't keep this baby: I wasn't financially ready and I wasn't mentally or emotionally mature enough. I was kind of pissed off at her, though I didn't take it too personally since she still lives with her parents at thirty.

Despite irritation at this friend's lack of confidence in her as a mother, during pregnancy, J. T. herself questions whether she will do a decent job and be contented as a mother, particularly given how encroached upon the pregnancy makes her feel. In her third trimester, she says:

> I'm physically miserable. Lumbering. I just cry for a half hour each day, eat chocolate, and go on. Sleeping sucks. . . . I don't like pregnancy. I feel totally taken over. I feel like a *pod*. I call myself a pod person. . . . I am worried about hating being a mom, particularly since I hate being pregnant so much. I worry breast-feeding will feel like being a pod person. . . . I can't get into it like other pregnant moms—"oh my sweet baby"—because I don't know if she'll come out and I'll just be horrible.

Her worries about being horrible as a mother stem from fears that she will "turn into [her] mom—nonsnuggly, emotionally shut down—once the baby [is] born." J. T.'s mother was sixteen when she and her teenage boyfriend conceived J. T.

[My coming into the world] was a complete disaster for them. My dad tried to keep going with school; my mom went to work at a grocery store around six months. I was breast-fed for about a day. [My mom] had toxemia [a blood pressure problem] and she couldn't breast-feed and get better. . . . She is really un-maternal, like she holds Daisy away from her body facing out and [Daisy will] spit up all the milk I just fed her. Daisy screams when my mom comes near her. . . . [In my own childhood, my] mom told my [then] six-year-old sister to get out of the car and pump gas, and my sister said she didn't know how and [my mom] said, "*Why not???*" She's completely nonempathetic, can't get into anyone else's head. She tells Daisy, "Don't cry!" My parents divorced when I was four and I saw my mom once or twice a year after that. My sister went with her. My mom just wanted *out* and decided, "This is just going to be too hard with two, so I'll let him have the one who likes him." I called her by her first name.

J. T. is the eldest of eight children (her father remarried and continued to have children with his new wife) and she characterizes her role in her father's family as "the maid."

I did all the work and spent high school just taking care of the family. I resented it, though I didn't know how bad it was until I moved out and they had to get a nanny *and* a maid to replace just me. I couldn't do anything because I was always with the kids, doing dishes for eight. I've already been humiliated by children in public and had childless people look at me and judge me like "What are you doing with that child here?" I realized early on that you can't judge other parents because then *you'll* be the one [being judged].

The birth, like the pregnancy, left much to be desired: "I had to change my birth plan five minutes into inactive labor. [We s]aw meconium [*the same excrement in the amniotic fluid as Heather's babies both had, creating an elevated risk of infection*] and had to make decisions for *her* well-being rather than for my Gaia experience. It was traumatic because I had back labor and was in transition with multipeaks from 10 A.M. until 4 P.M. So it was horrible. I was in so much pain I didn't know what a cow was."

Everything changed when her daughter, Daisy, emerged and looked straight into J. T.'s eyes.

AV: What was Daisy like when she was first born?

JTM: She was great [*J. T. makes a huge glowing smile*]. Her nose was just like Buck's. She didn't cry, just laid there and stared at me and I stared back. I didn't think anything. I was just completely *in* the experience, totally *there*. There was no other thought in my brain except for this feeling for, like, an hour.

AV: How had you anticipated you might respond when the baby was born?

JTM: I got both of us ready with pictures of ugly babies, just in case. I was prepared for squished up, small, etcetera.

AV: How did you actually respond?

JTM: I felt bonding immediately. I can't describe it. Nothing else existed. I would hold her and out of me would come this noise, sighing and sobbing, *mmmm, mmmm*, spilling over the edges, so full. I had blown the pressure in my eyes [during labor] and couldn't see anything but her.

AV: Were your fears of motherhood still there?

JTM: No. After that first moment when I realized I *liked* her so much, I was confident. I knew what to do, I was just afraid about the feelings. I did think it would be difficult and breast-feeding would be tough, but it was great, such an easy adjustment. The pediatrician told us to wait forty days before going to public places—we made it thirty-six days. I don't know that that's helpful immunologically, but it was helpful in terms of bonding. There was no other thing for me to be doing; I was in this liminal space, walking around with her in the front pack.

AV: Did you receive help and support from friends or family when she was born?

JTM: No, it was Buck and I. Buck took a week off. He is a really good partner, completely helpful, recognizes the things most women have to point out to their partner: "You have a full-time job five days a week, and I have one seven days a week." No one was allowed to stay in the house for the first week. It was bliss.

Regarding her emotional responses to having a baby, J. T. has been "*very* emotional, both hormonally and because I've just opened myself up to it. The world is a lot kinder to me [as a mother], so I can become more open than someone in the rat race."

With Daisy now eight months old, J. T. describes herself as a "stay-at-home mom, at least for now," although she is tutoring four immigrant adults in English each week, during which time Daisy is with Buck. J. T. is "just working to maintain contacts" since she says that Buck's waiter job brings in ample income to support the family in their small apartment.

During pregnancy, J. T. had described her approach to her future parenting as "wait and see" rather than according to any plan. Reflecting back, she says the "only plan was to use the sling [to carry the baby]. It really appealed, the closeness . . . etcetera. Then [Daisy] hated the sling for the first four months!" She does hold her baby in her arms, however, to a degree that resembles Heather and Gina.

AV: Under what circumstances did you hold her as a newborn?

JTM: All the time, constantly. I got a heat rash from having her skin to skin all the time. That wasn't the plan, but when she was born, I just didn't want to put her down. People would say, "Put her down!" or, "She's sleeping, so why don't you put her down?" But all I hear from other parents is this passes so quickly, so am I going to push her through *faster* and train her for the *next* phase?

AV: How often do you hold her these days [at eight months]?

JTM: She does her activities and when she's done, then I hold her.

AV: Is it work to hold her or is it generally pleasant for you?

JTM: Yeah, it's pleasant. Never a burden.

Likewise, breast-feeding Daisy is not generally taxing for J. T.

AV: How often does she breast-feed?

JTM: No idea. Whenever she wants to. Maybe five times in the day, three times at night. No idea.

AV: How do you know when she needs to feed at night?

JTM: I have no idea; I don't even wake up for it. I think she wiggles and I have to get her on and if I ignore it, it turns into crying, but as long as I act on it, she doesn't cry.

In the realm of sleep, despite J. T. estimating Daisy's longest sleep stretch at night as being three or four hours (short by US standards for an eight-month-old), J. T. does not echo the US parental focus on getting children to sleep through the night and she does not see sleep as an area of concern.

AV: How is your baby about going to sleep for naps?

JTM: No problem. She naps when she wants and it falls into a schedule generally. She might fall asleep on a walk or in the sling or I'll breast-feed. She sleeps on me [while I'm lying down] about 15 percent of the time, in the sling while [I'm up and around] 45 percent, and the rest lying down—these are short; she much prefers on me.

J. T. reports she is getting enough sleep and says that she has gotten enough sleep since the birth, though part of that is during the day when she naps with Daisy.

While J. T. practices attachment parenting—nearly perpetual togetherness, holding Daisy most of the day, co-sleeping, night feeding—she does not experience this connection as burdensome or involving any sacrifice on her part. This is not to say motherhood is without its moments.

AV: Do you ever have a sense of being overwhelmed by Daisy's needs?

JTM: Yeah, during growth spurts, teething, and when I had the clogged duct [which made it difficult and painful to breast-feed]. I got food poisoning once, too, but it was okay. You just gotta do what you gotta do. It's like running a nuclear plant. You gotta barf? You gotta barf. But you *still* gotta run the nuclear plant. Or like quitting smoking, which I did the minute I got pregnant.

Her unambiguousness regarding meeting her baby's needs is part of her developing philosophy of mothering Daisy.

AV: If you had to describe the tone of your relationship with Daisy, what would that be?

JTM: I can't think of any words. She's engrossing. I do what she seems to need me to and I'm terribly, terribly proud of her all the time. It doesn't take as much out of you when you give yourself to it fully.

J. T.'s theory is that giving herself to motherhood 100 percent removes any give-and-take struggle, which actually makes it easier for her as a mother. "If I ever have trouble with meeting her needs, I usually need to give *more*, not less." For example, when her family comes to visit, she has to "adjust my parenting because they won't slow down so I can fill her needs." Not meeting Daisy's needs then makes things difficult: "My mom came to visit at five weeks and I had to get ready for a wedding, so I put my needs and my mom's needs first and Daisy's needs second, and I felt a bit of guilt and disconnection with [Daisy]. I think guilt negatively affects bonding. I had a 'What do you need *now*?' attitude, a little resentful. So I held [Daisy] and smelled her head and did the things I had been doing, and it felt better."

In a later part of the interview when I ask what has affected her various feelings of love and bonding with Daisy, she again replies, "Smelling her head. I think there's pheromones in there. Or maybe it's what head smelling represents: taking complete time to be with her."

ATTACHMENT-SCAPE SECURITY

J. T. characterizes her father as an abusive rageaholic, and prior to her partnership with Buck, J. T.'s romantic partnerships were with similarly emotionally volatile men. Then four years ago, she met Buck.

> I was married [to someone else] and [Buck] liked me but dropped it since I was married. I didn't even notice him at the time, thought he was boring. I was into guys where there was no hope, who were bad for me. But Buck was a good, decent human being, and he was really intellectually supportive.

First thing I remember him saying was when I was complaining about the trashy editorials and he said, "You should write them," and he thought I'd do a better job since I had interesting things to say. When I became single, I started stalking him. I wanted a nice guy who was boring, with no more chaos, no more father-type guys. We went out once, two weeks later, and I moved in the same day. Spent every night together for the next couple years.

Selecting a nice guy has had an enormous influence on the stability of J. T.'s life. She no longer changes partners every few months and her level of drama has plummeted.

In attachment research, the majority of babies and children are classified as secure in their attachment status, as are the majority of adults. Often the secure baby grows up to be the secure adult. However, there are cases in which someone experiences malevolent parenting during childhood, which might be expected to result in an insecure attachment status, yet the person somehow rises above her early experiences to become secure as an adult.[1] Psychologists use the term *earned secure* to describe this phenomenon.[2]

J. T. has not undergone testing to determine her attachment security status; however, gauging from her description of her mercurial and unstable past, as well as her description of her childhood, one might infer that earlier in her life, she would have fit into one of the insecure statuses. By contrast, she currently appears secure. That is, her current telling of her life story is neither brief and denying of her painful childhood events nor overly dwelling on that pain, with past events intruding on her present discussions of attachment.[3] Her narrative is coherent and, like secure individuals, she appears quite capable of turning to her partner and friends for support when she experiences emotional difficulties. Thus, she may fall into the earned-secure attachment category.

JTM: When I was pregnant, I attended a wedding in Utah, and there's nothing really to do in Salt Lake City except wander around the Mormon temple there. And being pregnant with this baby with someone I was really committed to and walking around and looking at all these totally family oriented depictions on the walls, I really realized: I can see the *value* in this. If you had asked me two years ago to look at this, I would have said this is *cheesy*, this is *crap*! . . . You can't teach someone how good it feels to do something really blah, boring, cliché, until they're actually ready for it. And now we've built a really good amazing life together. . . .

AV: What do you think made it possible for you to stop going for father figures and instead go for nice?

JTM: I heard it on *Loveline* [a call-in syndicated radio show about relationships] when they said, "If you come from the kind of background that J. T. comes from, find a guy that you find *boring*. And right when you're *really bored* and you want to sabotage the relationship—DON'T! Just push through that a little bit and see if anything happens," you know. And I hit that point for sure. I hit that point of, "Who *is* this *good guy*, everything is cool, everything is good?" And I pushed through it. . . . [Then m]aybe a year and a half into our relationship . . . I felt like the wacky, crazy—"I have such a crazy life, look at all these crazy things that happen to me"—that identity of mine died off. And I remember feeling all freaked out about it 'cuz, like, what am I going to be now? Just some *normal* person? What's my identity going to be then if I'm not always the one who's having a catastrophe or, you know, cultivating chaos? So, you know, the little Goth girl in me kind of died off. And I still don't know if there's a name for the boring person that came out after that, but it's been really *pleasant*! And there's been a lot of times I've been, "I can't believe you're being this way about this" with Buck, and he would just be like, "This is how normal people *live*, J. T.," like, he totally knew that he was going to have to teach me like, "This is the way people *treat* each other; this is the way it's *supposed* to be." He must have said, "This is the way it's supposed to be," like, two million times in the first year of our relationship just 'cuz I was—I didn't *know*! I didn't know *how* it was supposed to be. I think he had to teach me to be, you know, a member of a family and a normal human being.

People's experiences of abuse in their childhoods often cycle into the next generation, sometimes despite their best efforts to avoid it. However, a loving relationship with a secure partner sometimes helps remedy this cycle (or possibly the person's ability to *choose* a loving relationship reflects changes within the individual that have already occurred). For example, a study of women who grew up without parents in institutional settings shows that those who formed positive partnerships later in life were able to engage in mothering that did not reflect their early deprivation.[4] Likewise, in psychologists Carolyn and Philip Cowan's landmark longitudinal study of couples transitioning to parenthood, they found that when women with insecure models of relationships from childhood and "unresolved feelings about their growing-up years were married to [secure] men with a coherent view of . . . early family experiences, the women's parenting was as warm, structuring, and engaged as that of the mothers described as securely attached."[5]

This shows the tremendous healing effect even a single secure bond in a woman's attachment-scape can have on her mothering. The mother-child relationship is not drawn on so desperately for either the mother's or the child's security because the mother has already learned to love and be loved before the child enters her life. Some of her insecurity has already been remedied. In this way, Buck's presence in J. T.'s life creates an immense difference between her and, for example, Gina Haley, who does not "let down her guard" emotionally with her partner or with *anyone* except her youngest babies.

J. T.'s relationship with Buck also helps account for how connecting with a baby does not feel particularly sacrificial or burdensome. This is because even while J. T. physically holds and tends to Daisy, she continues with her own self-nurturing activities such as conversing with Buck.

AV: How important is it for you to do things with Buck and what things do you like to do?

JTM: *Everything.* Anything you can talk during.

AV: How important is talking?

JTM: Supremo. Talking is my hobby. We don't like mountain biking; we don't snowboard or anything. We *talk.* Talk about politics, stuff we heard, people that we saw, books we read. It's kind of—I don't want to sound geeky or elitist—but it's generally intellectual, asking about our opinions and thoughts. We read all of each

other's books so we'll have the same context from which to discuss
the world.

J. T. attributes her ease of mothering to this hobby of talking. When
asked how hard it is to mother Daisy, she says, "Not very. Even compared
to not working at all. It's the best, easiest job I've ever had—fun, really
fun. But [Buck and I] have conducive lifestyles. We think, 'God, why do
people get all bent out of shape about having a kid?' but maybe that's because we just like to *talk*, and we can do that with a baby!" Elaborating
on this theme, she says that maintaining adult-centered activities after
having a baby is *very* important to her. "That's why [Daisy] fits so well
into our lives, because taking care of her needs and doing what I'm doing
[for myself] go together."

MOTHERING WITHOUT A SET
MOTHERING MODEL

AV: What is your image of a good mom?

JTM: I don't know. I guess fairly, yeah, very empathizing, able to see
what the kid wants, and just kind of tireless.

AV: What do you imagine the consequences might be if a parent *isn't*
that way?

JTM: Hard to say. Having a philosophy about child raising, it's still—
it's—um—most of our philosophies are: "NOT what our parents
did!" but *we're* the results and we're not reprobates. Cry-it-out
babies can grow up great. . . .

There are two key aspects of her answers to notice. First is that her
initial answer to the good mom question is: "I don't know." The answer is
not right there for her, not a fixed construct already fully conjured in her
mind, ripe and ready to be plucked.[6] Second, and relatedly, we see from
J. T.'s response that she believes children can grow up great under a *variety* of parental practices. She does not cast judgment that her way is su-
perior to someone else's way.

Likewise, in responding to what level of closeness she would like to experience with her child, she says, "That is so hard [to know]. I think some of the best parents I know are able to be both the adult and a friend at the same time. And others are able to keep themselves a little separated, and they're not so swayed by what their kid wants them to do, still able to say what we do and don't do. I like a lot of single parents because they've worked it out . . . [They] have to have a certain amount of give and take and their kids are a lot more compassionate. Mom counts *and* baby counts."

Again, it is not that she lacks answers, but her images of correct mothering are not predefined in one single fashion. She finally lands on both mother and baby counting; however, that ideal is so hard for her to know since she has friends with various levels of closeness and separation with their children that all seem to have worked it out.

Furthermore, when I ask J. T. whether she had done a lot of Internet research either regarding what to buy—such as a car seat—or on various other parenting issues, she replies, "I'm not so *agro* [over-the-top intense]. Since she was born, I've focused on what her development is, and less about baby products and safety. . . . I feel like she's like me and Buck, [strong] like horses, so she'll be fine."

THE SOURCE OF VALIDATION

J. T. is not a part of any attachment parenting groups and, given her and Buck's wait-and-see approach to parenting, it had been unclear during pregnancy that this was the way they would parent. In her social circle, the loudest advocates of a specific parenting approach are discordant with her own practices.

AV: Have you ever felt judged by family members, friends, or strangers about your parenting?

JTM: My mom's family. Her cousin believes in putting babies in their own room and using babysitters at three weeks. My mom left me for her honeymoon at two and a half weeks, and she wanted us to leave Daisy [at the same age].

Rather than her parenting conforming to the practices advocated by her correct mothering advisors, it is at odds with them. Likewise, regarding whether books have influenced her parenting choices, she says, "All my books—mostly that others gave me—were just causing inner conflict because they were advocating baby training. *What to Expect the First Year* I just didn't agree with so I threw it out."

With Daisy eight months old, J. T. has not read any of the books that might actually validate her parenting choices. She does later read *The Baby Book* (that Heather Dover refers to as the attachment parenting bible) and finds it helpful, but more emotionally proscriptive than what she seeks. She does not want a book to tell her what to do or how to feel and prefers more analytical texts with cold, hard facts about human evolution or developmental stages. She says, "You can't get the touchy-feely out of the book. People try, they say, 'I'm going to parent like it says here,' and they end up contorting themselves into what it's supposed to look like, and it just feels like it's forcing something."

While the books and sleep-training advocates that overwhelmingly surround her during Daisy's infancy do not reinforce her mothering style, someone else does.

AV: Has anyone made you feel particularly *validated* as a parent?

JTM: Daisy has. Every step along the way. When I start freaking out and think I should start to do what everyone else says I should do, then I see she's just sprouted a tooth and *that's* why she's fussy.

J. T.'s childrearing practices are not heavily motivated by correct mothering proponents, either within her immediate social circle or from books, or by a quest to measure up to a particular model in her head. Rather, she is validated by her *baby*.

AV: What experiences have influenced your parenting choices?

JTM: I started out just really willing to do whatever works best. *She's* the main influence.

In summary, among connection-oriented women, the differences we see between a heavy and light motherload are as follows:

Table 2   Differences between heavy- and light-motherload mothering

Heavy Motherload	Light Motherload
Mother-child *relationship* focused	*Person* focused
Singularity of mother-child relationship for security	Major alternative source(s) of security
One good mothering model	*Multiple* models considered acceptable
Preplanned mothering, rigid adherence	Wait-and-see mothering, flexible
Validation from experts or social group proponents of correct mothering	Validation from child and one's own sensibility
Guiding principle: correct-mothering models	Guiding principle: when it feels good and works for the whole family
Children fragile, easily wounded	Children generally strong like horses

In addition to these differences, J. T. appears ready to welcome independence when it inevitably occurs, with the same wait-and-see approach to her future parenting that she had during pregnancy.

AV: When are you planning to wean?

JTM: No plans. Whenever she wants to. If she continues to be like me, I'm going to be trying to get her to be *less* independent rather than more, since I toilet-trained on my own at eighteen months— "Get me out of here and into my own apartment!"

AV: Do you think you'll continue to hold her a lot?

JTM: If I want to hold her or she wants me to hold her, I [will]. I try to be completely into each moment so I can say it's going too fast, but I can't say I spent it doing other things.

LIGHT-MOTHERLOAD CONNECTION
WITH OLDER CHILDREN

The baby days are behind them. Daisy has just had her fifth birthday party at the local children's museum and J. T. and Buck, now married, have had a second child, Trish, currently two and a half. The family has moved to a new state where they can afford to live on Buck's part-time waiter and J. T.'s part-time English tutor incomes.

Aside from preschool three mornings a week for Daisy, J. T. and Buck are the girls' sole caregivers, taking turns working for pay mostly in the evenings and spending most days together as a family. "We've been able to look at what our values are and say, 'Okay, here's the jobs that allow us to be with our kids pretty much all the time.' And we've managed to create this really wonderful life together." They collectively earn thirty-five thousand dollars a year and live frugally in an excellent public school district. Initially, Buck worked more hours than J. T. when each of the girls was born to accommodate frequent breast-feeding, but J. T. is gearing up to be the primary earner this summer teaching ESL classes and tutoring immigrant adults in English.

Their new home is in a family oriented apartment complex on the edge of an urban area. J. T. says, "Up here, all the kids hang out at my house—I'm that mom. And all my friends from [before I had kids], they're like, 'No way! You're that Betty Crocker mom where everyone comes over to your house and has cookies?' The kids just run in and out of my house now—I *am* the block mom."

While she finds the parent culture in her new suburban life a little superficial and somewhat pines for her former city populated with "intellectuals and colorful neurotics," she says steadfastly, "We're not sacrificing ourselves for our kids." She quotes a Muriel Rukeyser poem that says, "[T]here is no sacrifice. There is a choice, and the rest falls away."[7] She sees her life "as a stream of the best choices we could make" and, even if there are certain elements in her life that could have been better with an alternative choice, "90 percent of what I want in life is here. Why bemoan what's missing when any other choice and I'd only have 60 percent of what I'd like? This is no sacrifice!"

She also attempts to avoid sacrifice in her daily interactions with her children. For example, unlike Heather Dover, who believes a mother should follow the child's lead—which may mean playing Barbie with her child for much of the day—J. T. does not take on the playmate role as a major aspect of her maternal identity: "That was one of our motivations for having a second child. I thought, 'If I have to play Candy Land one more time, someone please just shoot me in the head! We've got to *make* someone who wants to play Candy Land more than I do. There's only so much Candy Land I can *take*, honey!'"

It is not always easy for J. T. (or Buck) to be primary caregivers to two rambunctious little girls.

[F]or at least the first six months [after Trish was born], we wondered if we had made a *huge* miscalculation. [*laughs*] We knew we wanted this, but we were still just "*HOLY MOSES*, what did we *do*?" ... [Daisy] was two and a half, just moving into the stage when you have to put the rope around the baby elephant so when it becomes a big elephant it doesn't push those boundaries, and figuring out how to get that authority is hard. Then you have a baby, so you basically have *no hands*. So I started using my voice. Maybe if I'm *louder* she won't notice that I'm completely incapacitated. Maybe I can control her through sheer *volume*. So it was hard. And there were a lot of times when we were, "Okay, the kids are in bed, so let's use the two hours before Trish gets up again to do some serious strategizing." And I feel like that [made a huge difference] ... those moments of sitting our- selves down ... and saying, *this* is what I can't live with anymore—what do I do? Do I throw out all the shoes that don't have Velcro? Do I reshape her behavior in some ways? What am I going to have to cut?

Parenting can be difficult, but she and Buck are active agents trying to resolve those difficulties and they are constantly refining their parent- ing—as a couple—in order to make their family life as workable and pleasant as possible.

Recall that part of what made early mothering work for J. T. was that her needs (to engage in frequent conversations with Buck and her other friends) and her baby's needs (to be held, changed, fed, etc.) were compat- ible. This becomes harder as Daisy and Trish become more verbal.

AV: Do your needs—particularly for adult conversation—and theirs collide more often than when Daisy was young?

JTM: Oh, yeah, definitely ... [though] now I can talk *with* them ... But we've definitely hit the point now where the minute you're doing anything else is the minute they go haywire. What kind of reward chart do you make for leaving me the heck alone so I can have some personal time? It's like the minute your butt hits the computer chair, it's like, "Hello, hello, *hello!*"—they're like those bacon strips on that commercial, jumping all around.

At the same time, she says the joys of motherhood are "just the kids themselves. *They* are joyful, watching them grow, and go through stages, hearing the things they say."

Rather than grieve the loss of their littleness, she announces with pride that Daisy is voracious for growth, on a quest for independence, and always wanting the next achievement. She says, "At this point, Daisy is a *person*. There's no more little baby in there, she's a whole person, and . . . I'm totally stoked. . . ."

AV: How do you feel about your daughters' growing independence?

JTM: I feel good about it. My kids are definitely, they're the kids who walk in and are "Bye, Mom!" and I feel proud of that. Maybe just because that's the way *my* family has always been. I was a bye-mom kid, too. But they're not afraid of anything; they're very gregarious. They just go out and get stuff.

I do not present J. T. as a perfect, unerringly happy mother for whom mothering is always easy. She yells, gets annoyed by too much direct play with her daughters, and is acutely aware when things are not working and is driven to make changes to make them better. But despite the difficulties, she deeply enjoys mothering and she both values her deep connection with her children and is proud of her daughters' growing independence.

Here I summarize how the mothering experience differs between women with heavy motherloads (using the antidote security strategy as an example of such mothering) and those with light motherloads.

Table 3 Mothering experiences with differing motherloads

Heavy Motherload (Antidote Strategy)	Light Motherload
Motherhood sacrificial and hard	Motherhood nonsacrificial and sometimes hard but mostly enjoyable
Child first, mother second	Child's and mother's needs count
Mother's own pent-up needs→sorrow, resentment, and rage	Mother meets her own needs through at least one source beyond the child
Needs to be needed	Proud of child's independence
Not joyful?→*GUILT* (bad mother)	Not joyful?→*REFINE* (no judgment)
Keep doing the same thing but try harder.	*Make changes in how one parents.*

CONCLUSION

J. T. Miles's mothering is markedly different from heavy-motherload parenting. For example, unlike mothers using compensatory connection, J. T. entered motherhood with one very secure attachment already established in her life through her relationship with Buck. This meant she did not need to compensate for an insecure attachment-scape through intensifying the mother-child relationship. She is also nonexclusive in her maternal role, sharing this role with her partner and being secondary to him at times as they trade off work and family. Also, J. T. does not *need* to be needed by her children and is equally enthralled with her daughters' overtures of independence as with their willingness to connect.

J. T. also differs from women using shielding and antidote mothering. Most significantly, she is not fearful about Daisy's well-being and sees her as emotionally resilient, physically healthy, and generally fine. As she does not assume vulnerability, her parenting need not provide a cure-all for the world's ills or offer protection from foreseen threats.

An additional difference is that J. T.'s love is not given in a sacrificial way. Rather, she and Buck engage in late-night strategy sessions and are continuously trying to find ways (with varying degrees of success) to meet their own needs alongside those of their children.

Unlike mothers with heavy motherloads, J. T. has a wait-and-see approach and her major philosophy upon entering motherhood was to simply do what works. She has a flexible, work-in-progress view of mothering. Furthermore, she is not trying to do right by the experts, an attachment gestapo, or other social groups telling her she *has* to be connection oriented and judging her degree of compliance. Quite to the contrary, during Daisy's babyhood, J. T.'s own parenting police told her to sleep separately, to put the baby down, and to let Daisy cry it out. Thus, rather than trying to accommodate an externally imposed correct mothering model, she is rebelling against the primary model advocated by those around her and by the collection of books she was given as she entered motherhood. J. T. is loving in the way she wants to, not because of but in *spite* of the way others tell her she should. This creates a very different dynamic.

Finally, J. T. is candid about her limits. She quite blatantly decries another round of the game Candy Land and she does not enter motherhood with a larger-than-life expectation of how great a mother she will be. In fact, she is initially somewhat braced for the possibility that she may be horrible as a mother and may not feel a great emotional attachment to her child. While this may be a protective mechanism stemming from her own childhood injuries, her acknowledgment of this possibility may also have contributed to her sense of permission to feel *anything* she might feel and may have helped remove the compulsion to have a particular emotional experience as a mother. All of this lightens J. T.'s motherload.

On a more philosophical level, J. T. does not objectify connection or *deploy* it in the service of saving either her children or herself from an insecure world. With connection as more a verb than a noun, more an emergent expression of what already is than a holy grail of hoped-for redemption, there is no need for her to guard her mother-child connection from others who might take it away, no resentment for its loss when her children display independence, and no need to freeze time to maintain it—for connection is not a thing.

Thus, with minimal compulsion, minimal fear, and no one in need of saving, J. T. is simply parenting in the way that feels right to her and that works for her family.

PART II Independence

5 Inoculation Strategy

PUNCHING BACK AT FEAR

The beauty of life is its unpredictability. So danger is part
of it.

—Julia, thirty-three-year-old mother

Security is mostly a superstition. It does not exist in
nature, nor do the children of men as a whole experience
it. Avoiding danger is no safer in the long run than outright
exposure.

—Helen Keller

Sarah Gordon, a white thirty-five-year-old mother of one- and three-
year-old sons, is a journalist who lived in Kazakhstan for several years
before she had children. There she would get e-mails from the US em-
bassy saying, "We have intelligence that suggests Americans should avoid
gathering at ex-pat bars and hangouts this week," or "There is increased
chatter from the bin Laden cohort. Please alter your usual routes." After
that, she moved to New York and began working at a theoretically safe
office job downtown. "And that's where I was on September 11, watching
the fireballs and the papers and people flying through the air, running
with the crowd when that first building started crashing down. Turns out
going to Central Asia wasn't what put me close to a terrorist act. But it
did give me a deeper, nuanced understanding of what's now affecting my
own 'safe' country. And it taught me: you just never know."

Since then she married, became a mother, and is living in a West Coast
city with her husband and two young sons. Sarah follows police statistics

and refuses to close her eyes to the murders and rampant violence across town in the city where they live. Her belief that "you just never know" persists and she fully acknowledges that random violence could at some point involve her or her children. However, in her refusal to gear her life around avoiding randomness, she brings her children with her into high-crime areas of the city when she finds something worthwhile for them to experience there. She is also committed to "not altering travel plans based on terrorist threats." She says, "I have worked so hard in my life to shed anxiety as a ball and chain—through sheer willpower and putting myself in difficult but rewarding situations" and is therefore "determined *not* to pass fear on to my kids."

Deb Feldman, a white thirty-five-year-old former business manager who gives her two children a great amount of physical affection, deliberately did not gate the stairs when her children began to crawl because she wanted them to learn how to negotiate stairs safely. She and her husband also bypassed the crib phase when they moved their daughter from the family bed because their then eleven-month-old baby "did not want to have the railings there." So the couple put their baby directly into a bed of her own with no guardrail. Deb recalls that she let her daughter go down the slide by herself starting at six months, sometimes headfirst, and while "people at the playground would look at me like I was being neglectful, [my daughter is now] more physically coordinated than any two-year-old I've ever seen, and she's only sixteen months."

Deb believes "human babies are much more capable of keeping themselves safe than we give them credit for" and that much of today's over-childproofing and cautionary parenting conveys to children the message that they are *not* capable of making safe decisions. She believes that children "pick up on that message" of ineptness, to which they then readily comply as a way to conform to social expectations. "Children don't do what we *ask* them to; they do what we *expect* them to."

Sarah taking her children into high-crime areas and Deb not gating the stairs are both examples of the *inoculation* security strategy. This strategy describes independence-oriented mothering practices intended to prepare one's children for encounters with a diversity of forces, including challenging or menacing ones, by giving children measured doses of danger or hardship to navigate early on. It is parallel to a medical vaccine that exposes the patient to an attenuated dose of germs in a controlled setting for the purpose of making her body stronger and more capable of dealing with germs on a larger scale later on. It is intentional *exposure* to risk.

Inoculation (using independence to enhance the child's security) and compensatory connection (using connection to enhance the mother's security) are the two most common security strategies in this study, with each occurring in about one-fourth of the mothers. However, the types of insecurity associated with these two strategies are quite different. Whereas compensatory connection stems more from an insecure attachment-scape—that is, an insecure job and partnership and an emphasis on deficiencies in how one was mothered—that is not necessarily the case with inoculation. In fact, most women who use this strategy have histories of stable full-time work that they characterize as careers, describe being acceptably loved and cared for as children, and are married or cohabitating in self-described mutually supportive partnerships. However, women who inoculate are not immune to fear and they are often preoccupied with security threats in the world at large, such as terrorism, environmental catastrophes, epidemic illnesses, and crime.

INOCULATION IN FAMILIES OF COLOR

Despite the prevalence of inoculation, scholars generally bypass this strategy completely, at least regarding white middle-class women, focusing instead on "overprotective parenting," "helicopter parenting," or the ethic of "total motherhood."[1] The way intensive mothering is typically assumed to manifest is through shielding the child from risk and from information about "bad things" in the world. Protection by exposure is routinely overlooked. The popular press likewise vigilantly attends to "hyperparenting" or "mothering madness," but pays little notice to this wholly different form of strategic parenting.[2]

The exception to this is the body of work on families of color. "[P]arents recognize the enduring nature of racial troubles and issues their offspring are likely to face" and teach them "a repertoire of responses" with which "to cope and contend with racial mistreatment."[3] Some parents of color use direct engagement with hardship or conflict as teaching tools to equip their children to survive in a racist world, exemplifying the inoculation strategy. As feminist rap artist Lauryn Hill, says, "That strong mother doesn't tell her cub, 'Son, stay weak so the wolves can get you.' She says, 'Toughen up, this is reality we are living in.'" Education scholar Suzanne Carothers gives the example of mothers in all-black communities who intentionally expose their daughters to conflict or crisis situations with whites. This is partially to convey the reality of racism and partially to model how mature people of color will not bow down to it. Carothers writes, "By introducing their daughters and granddaughters to such potentially explosive situations and showing the growing girls how older women could handle the problems spurred by racism, mothers and grandmothers taught the lessons needed for survival, culturally defined as coping with the wider world."[4]

Sociologist Allison Pugh describes the practices of affluent African American parents in the opposite position of living in all-white neighborhoods. Sending their children to schools where their skin color marks them as other is already exposing them to difficulty with purpose (teaching them to navigate the white world that holds the reins of power in American society). These parents then put their children in further uncomfortable situations by enrolling them in sports teams dominated by street-smart African American children from low-income families. Here the children are again other, this time not by race but by class. They experience culture shock as they are thrown into a street culture with different rules of survival. The parents seek out this alternative cultural knowledge, however, because they believe black street smarts are necessary for their children's survival.[5] This consistent prioritization of their children's learning over their social comfort, like some poorer black parents' exposure of their children to potentially explosive interactions with whites, is a racialized variant of what I call inoculation.

Interestingly, in my research, I do not find the inoculation strategy particularly prevalent among African American or Latina mothers. In part, this is testament of the great variation within families of color. For example, some "black parents, like white parents, try to protect their children from pain and particularly from the pain that they have experienced themselves" and therefore protect their children from exposure to racial prejudice.[6] This, along with color-blind parenting, downplays racial categories entirely, and is a variant of the shielding security strategy.[7] Anglocizing children by helping them to pass in the white world, or its alternative—instilling individual and racial pride—are likewise possible either with or without information about or exposure to racism.[8] So although racial socialization research is where we have seen glimpses of inoculation in the past, it is only one of the many parenting strategies families of color use to deal with the challenges of racism.

One reason the mothers of color in my research may not gravitate toward inoculation is that their children are still so young. Risk exposure may emerge later when their children are out in the world more frequently and therefore more likely to encounter racism.

Another reason these mothers may not converge in inoculation is that other factors besides race may contribute to their parenting. In fact, much as Lareau found social class had a greater influence than race on her informants' parenting approaches,[9] among the women in this study, I find that one's personal income, job status, and marital status have a greater influence than race on one's parenting strategy. For example, I find that single unemployed mothers, regardless of their racial identification, most often use the compensatory-connection strategy, drawing their own security from their relationships with their children. We might have expected working-class parents' premium on toughness to instead predispose these women to inoculation. Nelson finds that working-class parents, "who often live with more present, concrete dangers in their daily environments . . . believe it is necessary for their children to toughen up and deal with the world around them."[10] However, age may again be a factor, as Nelson studies parents of older adolescents who are more likely to be navigating those concrete dangers.

So who *is* toughening up their young children? I find inoculation is actually in greatest abundance among those in whom we might expect it the least: economically privileged white women. I also find this strategy among economically privileged Chinese American women (who describe the inoculation practiced by their own Chinese-born mothers as well).

A strategy of risk exposure, formerly found in racially oppressed or financially struggling families, could be occurring among today's privileged mothers for different reasons. It may be due to acute economic anxiety and an increasing fear of loss among seemingly secure people. Alternately, in-oculation may be a backlash against helicopter parenting, which the media, bloggers, scholars, and other parents keep telling us has gone over the top among the privileged. Whatever the explanation, previous research has yet to explore inoculation as a white middle-class phenomenon or even to acknowledge it as a possible variant of intensive mothering.

Mothers themselves seem well aware that inoculation exists in white middle-class communities. Patricia Tate, a white twenty-four-year-old mother of a toddler, sees many of her white friends trying to unduly "toughen their children up." Rather than viewing this toughening as a strategy of protection, however, she interprets it as negligence or insensi-tivity to children and sees it as overly harsh. She believes these mothers are "setting [their] kids up to be emotionally traumatized. [They]'re mak-ing them feel like . . . they've got to do it all on their own, and there's not always someone there for them. . . . I just think it's going to cause self-esteem issues and confidence issues down the road."

To illustrate the wide range within the inoculation strategy, I will de-scribe two cases: Daphne Petrolis and Julia Freitag. Both women experi-ence risk-society fears—of crime, terrorism, global catastrophe, and so on—and both believe in helping a child to survive by giving her practice in surviving. However, Julia experiences these broader fears from a perch of marital and career security, whereas Daphne experiences them from within an insecure attachment-scape. So while they both see their mothering actions as crucial to the *child's* survival (by training the child to cope effectively with threats), Daphne additionally sees the mother-child relationship as key to saving *herself.* Thus, her motherload is heavier still, creating very different dynamics.

DAPHNE PETROLIS

Daphne Petrolis is a thirty-one-year-old Greek immigrant with tightly wound black curls dressed in a tailored blouse and professional skirt.[11] She talks quickly and nervously and her body frequently jolts in response to noises. She characterizes herself as "right wing" because of her concern with national and international security issues and her belief that the right deals most aggressively with military threats. Her concern with safety is also evident on the road. Driving on the highway in her large, black SUV on a sunny afternoon, she audibly gasps several times in response to seeing other cars beside her, as if their presence on the road were unexpected. She once whispers, "Crazy drivers," and is so preoccupied with avoiding other cars hitting her that she repeatedly swerves and makes sudden lane changes, causing several honks in response.

To help her infant son, Adrian, navigate the scary world she believes awaits him, she wishes to instill three basic forms of independence: "I want him to learn to be strong and not easily offended by people. I don't want him to come home crying because this kid said this to him and that kid said that. Almost to the point where I want if someone hits him for him to hit back. I really want him to be strong."

Daphne's first meaning of independence, then, is the ability to be tough under duress, to not falter or cry when people say unkind things to him or are violent with him but rather to respond with emotional indifference or possibly a return of force. Second, she wants her son to be emotionally okay being alone: "You can't live your life always with other people—that's the way it is—so I want Adrian to know how to be on his own and enjoy that." Third, she wants him not to have to rely on others for practical help: "Independence and self-reliance is most important [to instill in a child] because it helps to get along in life as an adult, to do stuff, not to need other people to do things . . . because if I won't help myself, probably no one will."

Daphne's meanings of independence all imply either a capacity for aloneness or stoicism and tolerance for pain. If the people around Adrian do not come to his aid or if they act unkindly toward him, she wants him to be okay with that.

In order to create this pain tolerance and to prepare Adrian for life's potential hurts, she toughens him with small amounts of discomfort. One example of this is bottle warming. She believes that babies prefer their bottles warm, but life cannot be perfectly controlled and she knows a circumstance might arise when that is impossible. So rather than risk his discomfort in those circumstances, she decided never to warm his bottles at all so he would not get accustomed to that comfort and suffer from its loss. Her sister told her, "Poor guy! Because once in a lifetime you won't be able to give it to him warm, three hundred times he gets it cold." But this is perfectly in keeping with her chosen form of protectiveness, and giving her baby cold milk has the caring intention behind it of sparing him from a rude awakening later on.

JULIA FREITAG

Julia Freitag, a thirty-three-year-old German-born photographer and mother of one- and two-year-old boys and a seven-year-old girl, is on the opposite end of the personality spectrum from Daphne. She speaks in mellow tones, her posture is loose, and her hair is rubber banded up in a messy bun.[12]

Julia's personal world appears relatively secure, as she has "never worried about not finding work" and her family of origin "was a secure and safe place" with happily married parents. Furthermore, her "husband is the closest relationship I have," a statement I never heard from connection-oriented women. The overlap with Daphne is her keen awareness of fearful occurrences in the world and her use of an inoculating parenting strategy. In Julia's version of inoculation, however, confidence, education, and honesty, rather than tolerance of pain, are the means by which to expose her children to the harsher aspects of life.

Julia's parenting is self-consciously set apart from overprotection. She believes a confident, relaxed mother will make children feel safe, whereas a nervous, hovering mother will upset children. Speaking to a friend who is anxious about managing her two very young children on a long upcoming flight, she says, "My piece of advice for you is: *Relax!* It'll be all right and it'll be over in a few hours. Whenever we board a plane, I can point out the families at the gate who are going to have trouble with their kids during the flight. It's always the families with the nervous and worried parents. The more relaxed you are, the calmer your children will be."

To illustrate her relaxed attitude, she recounts an incident of losing track of one of her children at a large airport food court: "I remember him taking off [as a two-year-old] in the airport, trying to find a table for us while I was still paying for our lunch. Everyone just freaked out, and I just took my tray and started looking around the tables until I spotted him, proudly sitting at a vacant table." Likewise, she shares with pride how her youngest child "cannot walk yet, but still will climb to the top of the biggest climbing structure in the park, coming down the big spiral slide without any assistance."

Furthermore, Julia, who lives on a busy street in a large metropolitan area, allows her seven-year-old daughter, Megan, to walk alone to the park to play, often for much of the day on weekends, "pop[ping] in only occasionally for food or stuff she needs." Julia is not doing so because she views cars and strangers as safe, nor is she a hands-off, permissive mother— though she acknowledges that the stress of her two much younger children may have *something* to do with it. Rather, she believes that giving her daughter an education in how to cope with fast, careless drivers and would-be abductors will give her the strength and confidence necessary for her daughter to navigate the world. She says, "We have set firm rules and explained them to her. Besides the obvious such as 'Look when you cross the street,' or 'Don't walk up to a car,' some of our family rules are: 'If there are no other children in the park, you need to come home.' Single children are easier targets. I also believe in teaching her strategies of how to defend herself." As an example of these self-defense strategies, if someone tries to abduct Megan, rather than kick and scream, Julia has instructed Megan to yell, "I don't know you!" so witnesses will not simply dismiss her as a child having a tantrum and will more likely come to her aid.

Describing children as "targets," thinking through the ineffectiveness of an abducted child simply screaming, "No!" and creating an alternate tactic and teaching it to her daughter all convey how seriously Julia takes the threat of abduction by a stranger. It is not always easy for her to let her daughter be vulnerable to such threats. Julia was "worried the first few times Megan walked a couple of blocks by herself," but overcame this worry for her daughter's sake because, she says, "I refuse to deprive my child of her freedom."

This high value placed on children's freedom is reflected by Lenore Skenazy of the *New York Sun*, whose 2008 editorial entitled "Why I Let My 9-Year-Old Ride the Subway Alone" proclaimed the author's own inoculating approach to mothering. Skenazy left her nine-year-old son in a New York City department store, at his adamant request, so he could have a solo adventure and then find his own way home. She writes:

> I didn't trail him, like a mommy private eye. I trusted him to figure out that he should take the Lexington Avenue subway down, and the 34th

Street crosstown bus home. If he couldn't do that, I trusted him to ask a stranger. And then I even trusted that stranger not to think, "Gee, I was about to catch my train home, but now I think I'll abduct this adorable child instead." Long story short: My son got home, ecstatic with independence. Long story longer . . . [h]alf the people I've told this episode to now want to turn me in for child abuse. As if keeping kids under lock and key and helmet and cell phone and nanny and surveillance is the right way to rear kids. It's not. It's debilitating—for us and for them.[13]

Skenazy's editorial hit a public hot button and she quickly found herself on the *Today Show*, *Talk of the Nation*, Fox News, and MSNBC, among others, sometimes with the title "World's Worst Mother?" beneath her. While Skenazy received a flurry of letters in response to her editorial and subsequent media appearances, many accusing her of reckless endangerment, the majority of the letters were supportive, written by other inoculating parents who thanked her for breaking the silence on this formerly taboo type of child rearing.

Like Skenazy, Julia believes confining children to safe environments is debilitating. "If I want to raise strong children, I will have to let them practice their skills of survival." Julia herself experienced great freedom as a child. She grew up in a small town in Germany where, at her daughter's age, she likewise roamed the streets until a church bell rang in the evening at six o'clock and summoned her back home for dinner. "This was common practice and my parents were not more or any less protective than the other parents." She walked alone to elementary school and to her music lessons and went unsupervised with friends to the swimming pool beginning in third grade when she learned to swim.

Julia does not fully replicate her parents' practices, however. "Although they did a great job raising independent children," a value that Julia shares, "they also did stuff I'd never do with my kids, like leaving us home alone in the evening when they went out." The reason Julia does not leave her children alone is "partially because it is illegal," but "also the fact that we live in earthquake country and even the most responsible firstborn would be certainly overwhelmed dealing with a catastrophe in a leading role." Notice that, in keeping with the social amplification of risk framework, it is not primarily worry about more common hazards such as choking on a grape that keeps her from leaving her children alone. Nor does she voice a fear of her one- and two-year-old children having needs or an emotional meltdown in her absence that her seven-year-old would not be able to handle. Rather, she is concerned that her eldest child would not be able to lead the family during a large-scale catastrophe.

Julia did, however, upset some of her friends when she left her baby unattended in the car, parked just behind her at an ATM. She says:

> One of my—former—friends accused me of not watching my baby, for turning my back to her at the ATM when we got the parking spot right in front of it! And everyone in my moms' group agreed with her that they would never leave their children unattended in the car because somebody might steal the car while they turned their backs. I replied that I did not leave my child unattended since I could see her the entire time by just turning around, and that the car was about fifteen feet away from me. That was the first time I noticed the hysteria [of] some parents . . . because they see bad stuff happening on the news all the time.

While Julia believes today's hysteria about risk is at least partly a social construction amplified by the media, her own act of teaching her daughter what to yell if an abductor drags her off reflects a perception of *real* hazards in the world as well. She responds to this by positioning her daughter to navigate among those hazards in as safe a manner as she can.

Like Daphne, she believes independence is critical to such a navigation. Much as connection-oriented mothers with heavy motherloads view connection as essential to correct mothering, Julia views independence as essential and sees alternative mothering models as suboptimal. For example, in her goal of "rais[ing] strong and independent children like [her] parents did," she sees overprotection as stunting. "I know so many families who will watch their kids like hawks, drive them everywhere, pick them up, control their teens by putting them in so many after-school activities that they don't get any crazy ideas. But do they get *any* ideas that way? What will happen to these children if they leave to go to college? If they never had to look out for themselves, they are much more likely to get in trouble at that point without the adult supervision."

Julia has two alternative parenting models in her mind: (1) inoculating children by teaching them to deal with a difficult world from the beginning and (2) shielding and sequestering children, which provides a level of immediate comfort and safety but which she believes ultimately puts children at *greater* risk. Most parents posting at freerangekids.com, a website created in 2008 in which inoculating parents can connect with one another, agree with Julia's calculus of risk. For example, one such parent writes: "I think that *not* teaching children . . . how to be self-reliant and think for themselves is a lot more dangerous than exposing them gradually to certain calculated levels of risk-taking" and another writes: "[I]f you don't give them room to make small mistakes, I fear they will make *big mistakes.*"[14]

Beyond the ultimately greater risk Julia sees in letting children loose in society without the survival skills gained from practice, she believes protecting children from frightening information is also a disservice to them and leaves them ignorant. This parallels the research on racial socialization, mentioned earlier, that shows how some families of color not only expose their children to difficult situations but also equip them with knowledge about racism, which is viewed as critical to children's survival. Sharon Van Epps writes, "As parents, we live in constant tension: How thoroughly should we prepare our kids for the ugliness that exists in the world? For my son's safety, I can't afford to be vague when it comes to racism."[15] Likewise, Carothers writes that the collective work necessary for communities of color to survive requires "a free flow of information, which in turn supports the teaching and learning process. It is important for mothers to teach daughters how to cope with the world; therefore, they do not hide the world from their children. Rather, information about what it takes to deal with their reality is readily available to Black daughters . . ."[16]

Although Julia is a white woman, she expresses similar sentiments. She says, "I don't create a safe haven for my daughter by withholding bad news from her. She . . . knows about 9/11 and the resulting wars. . . . When her favorite preschool teacher was diagnosed with terminal cancer, I did not give her the common 'yes, honey, she's really sick, but she'll be better soon' version many of her classmates got. I'm not lying to my child. I tell her about the bad stuff."

Julia does not see herself as exposing her daughter to hard truths any more than beautiful truths; she is simply trying to give her child an accurate representation of the world in all its complexity. She says her daughter "knows that I'm sad, angry, and upset about many things on this planet. But she also knows what wonderful things there are, and what we can do to protect these. I believe in empowering children, because they have to deal with our world when we're gone."

Thus, we see two distinct variants of inoculation mothering practiced by Daphne and Julia. While either of them may be mistaken for negligence upon cursory glance, they both represent highly deliberate parenting actions taken to prepare children for a potentially hazardous world. For Daphne, who gives her baby cold milk, inoculation means tough medicine and subjecting her infant son to mini-harm in order to make him resilient to the potentially greater harms out there. Her underlying message is as follows: "The world is a harsh and scary place, and I will help you to gradually get used to it so you won't be emotionally destroyed when it hits you for real." For Julia, who lets her daughter walk alone across busy streets to play in the park unsupervised, inoculation means giving her children the necessary information and guidance to freely roam. Her underlying message is: "Freedom is a human right, but in order for me to let you free in a sometimes scary world, we will need to make it *less* scary through your education and empowerment." Despite these differences, the common thread weaving these women's stories together is a belief that exposure to, rather than isolation from, potentially fearful elements of society is the best way to raise a child capable of dealing with those elements when they inevitably present themselves in the child's life.

DIFFERENCES IN INOCULATION

While Daphne and Julia both aim to help their children survive in the world by giving them practice in surviving, Daphne's motherload is heavier, both by virtue of how she assesses risk and what she seeks in the mother-child relationship for herself. I discuss here a number of interrelated differences between Daphne and Julia's mothering, which do not reflect merely idiosyncratic differences between the two women but rather an underlying logic of the motherload.

The first difference is in the *type* of insecurity that is most salient in each of their lives. Daphne expresses two types of insecurity: impersonal

fears—such as of accidents, crime, and terrorism—and fears of an interpersonal nature, that is, an insecure attachment-scape. Regarding the
latter, Daphne is skeptical about partnership. As a child, her parents never
got along, and after years of what Daphne describes as their giving "no
indication that they cared about each other," they finally divorced when
Daphne began college. She also saw many of her friends' parents divorce,
and for most of her life she was a self-described marriage cynic who fully
intended to remain single in order to not depend on a man. She reports
feeling lonely, but she threw herself into her work as an administrative assistant to a high-level manager of a Greek newspaper to fill her hours.
Only when a friend sat her down and confronted her with what she saw as
the meaninglessness of Daphne's life did Daphne make the life-changing
decision to find a man to marry. She met a man with the right characteristics the following week and six months later they were married.

Yet even now, she does not lean on or fully trust the institution of marriage. Referring to her daughter, born two years after Adrian, Daphne
says, "I want her to have a job and be independent and make money so if
things go wrong and she gets a divorce, she'll be okay." She strongly believes in a backup plan. Regarding her own marriage, while it appears to
be stable, she does not appear to put her heart into it. She says her husband, Jeff, is more emotionally invested in the marriage than she is, and
though *she* has considered divorce, she describes Jeff as "intensely loyal."
Likewise, she says, he "[tells] everyone he loves me—I don't do that." In
fact, she hardly speaks of Jeff in interviews unless directly questioned
about him, and when she does, it is perfunctory. She explains how she
and Jeff get along for the most part and are compatible in their spiritual
and political values and in their enjoyment of similar sports and activities, but she shares no evidence of emotional connection or comfort-
seeking attachment with him. Thus, the apparent *stability* of the marriage does not translate into it being a place where she actively seeks out
emotional *security*. Recall that this was also the case in the marriages
(and work lives) of women who engage in compensatory connection. While
some elements of their attachment-scapes seemed fairly stable, these relationships were not where the women put their own emotional stock. In
Gina Haley's case, her aloofness was due to her view of caring as dangerous and her finding safety only when the other person cares more. Daphne's dynamic seems similar.

Likewise, Daphne finds little refuge in work. She left her job as an administrative assistant when she moved from Greece to the United States to be with Jeff. Prior to Adrian's birth, she did clerical work at home for Jeff's property management business, but that did not feel like a "real job" to her. Being a full-time mother does not feel like a real job to her either, and although staying home with her son allays some of her work anxiety and functions as a way for her not to deal with issues of finding work, she sees mothering as more "an excuse not to find a job" than a bona fide work activity in itself. She expresses anxiety over seeing her life as on hold.

Julia's story is different. She left a lucrative position as a commercial photographer to freelance after having her second child and expresses no anxiety about her work or her prospects for full employment once that decision is made. She says, "I love my work. I have been working two to four days a week since my youngest was six months old. I will probably keep this up until he is in preschool, at which point I'll slowly up those hours, and then up them again when he enters school. [My current freelance work gives me] real flexibility in setting my schedule. I could work more, but . . . I basically only work to cover child care costs and keep my name in the field so I can go back full-time later."

She likewise describes her childhood as objectively safe. She grew up in a small town where there was little fear of crime. Furthermore, she views her marriage as her closest relationship and says she and her partner take good care of each other physically and emotionally, though, she adds, "I do have additional support. My ties to my family [of origin] are very close. I talk to my mom on the phone about five times a week, and also often to my siblings. I have friends . . . [that I've known] for twenty to thirty years. . . . I think the consistency of these relationships gives me the confidence to give my children all the independence they crave rather than tying them to me."

Engaging in her own sociological analysis here, she believes the security and strength of her various attachments allow her to give her children wings rather than binding them to her in compensatory connection.

In sum, the first difference between these women is the *object* of fear. Julia is a personally secure woman who has an underlying sense of danger in the world at large, whereas Daphne's fears stem both from a sense of danger in the world and from an insecure attachment-scape.

The second difference is in these mothers' appraisal of the *nature* of risk, which parallels the discourse in social scientific theories. The first paradigm is *realism*, set forth by such theorists as Ulrich Beck, in which the current explosion of new technologies with global reach endangers the very continuation of life on Earth.[17] Beck sees the current era as the first time in the history of our planet that there has been a real possibility of self-annihilation and discusses the social consequences of this and other new forms of uncertainty. Mary Douglas, by contrast, an early proponent of the *social construction* of risk, asserts that risk, like cultural categories in general, is a "cognitive container." She views risk as a concept used to maintain the social order, uphold boundaries, and strengthen an "us-versus-them" mentality by ascribing blame to socially maligned groups.[18]

Within this theoretical divide, we find Daphne is a realist. She gives no hints of viewing today's fears as overblown, and says, for example, "Realistically, times have changed. There is more crime now."[19] By contrast, Julia has at least some social constructionist leanings. Despite fearing such perils as child abductors and reckless drivers and framing her parenting partly as a response to such hazards, she also believes there is a media-amplified hysteria over risk. Furthermore, she sees this hysteria as harmful, causing parents to unnecessarily restrict their children's freedom and inadvertently creating greater vulnerability in children who have never been prepared to cope with the world as it actually is.

The third difference between these women vis-à-vis risk is in their perception of whether the risks that do exist are alterable. Julia sees the world as potentially threatening but believes there are ways to bypass some of that through education and empowerment. Her parenting goal is to teach and model for her child safer ways to deal with the world that will lower the probability of harm. By contrast, Daphne views external harm as inevitable; therefore, the solution is not to help the child deflect harm but rather to be emotionally unfazed when harm invariably occurs. In her worldview, personal control is less over what happens and more over one's capacity to bear it.

Given that some of Daphne's own insecurities lie in personal realms such as work and marriage (realms in which individuals might be in a good position to influence outcomes), it is interesting and paradoxical that she views risk as unalterable. Conversely, Julia's insecurities lie primarily in impersonal realms, related to strangers, natural disasters, and world risk (all of which one would suppose is less subject to individual control). Yet she seizes whatever degree of control is available and is aware of her own and her children's power to create different, less harmful types of interactions and outcomes.

According to the literature on anxiety, Julia's view of personal control is the healthiest response to threat. "[M]ore than any other factor, 'self-efficacy' or 'perceived control over life circumstances' has been identified as the most valuable coping resource and the foundation for mental health."[20]

To summarize, despite Daphne and Julia sharing a fear of the world at large and an inoculating approach to mothering, we see that (1) Daphne has an insecure attachment-scape, whereas Julia does not; (2) Daphne views threats as looming and real, whereas Julia believes that only some threats are real and others are amplified to the detriment of parents and children; and finally, (3) Daphne sees threats as unalterable, so she tries to convey to her children control only over how they react to harm, whereas Julia is teaching her children ways of dealing with the world that she hopes will lessen the harm that befalls them in the first place.

THE SECURITY BIND

The fourth difference among these women is in the level of conflict in their mothering and whether they experience a *security bind*: a contradiction between the type of mother-child relationship they view as producing security for the child and the type of relationship they would like in order to feel secure themselves.

Whereas many women with insecure attachment-scapes resist their children's growing independence, this is decidedly not the case for Julia, who has plentiful sources of attachment security. Nor, it bears adding, is she threatened by her children's overtures of neediness; she responds quickly to cries and gives her children abundant physical contact. Thus, she embraces both child dependency and independence; the tension between these drives does not present much conflict in her parenting.

This is in marked contrast to Daphne. She strives to instill toughness and independence in Adrian, but at the same time she desires unconditional devotion from him, as I will show. This desire, which might ordinarily propel her toward a consuming, connection-oriented relationship, is at odds with her desire to protect Adrian through independence. That is, she uses the inoculation security strategy for the sake of her *child*, but inwardly feels the tug of compensatory connection. These dueling urges create a security bind that makes mothering a painful experience for her.

This finding unpacks and builds on Nelson's finding that elite parents' own greatest satisfactions are in "their open and close relationships with their children," yet they have concerns of being "*too* involved in their children's lives, of having difficulty in drawing appropriate limits."[21] So their own satisfactions from the relationship (connection) bump up against the boundaries they think might be best for the children (independence).

Daphne's own satisfaction and what she thinks is best for Adrian are greatly at odds, possibly because she does not satisfactorily meet her security needs with anyone but him. Whereas her testimony is replete with evidence of emotional longing and comfort-seeking attachment with Adrian, there is no such evidence regarding her husband. For example, she says that Jeff is "always saying I'm not showing enough affection [to him], and I think it's because I'm so consumed with showing affection to [the kids]. I'm just driven to smooch and hug them, but when they go to sleep, I just don't want it any more. I mean, I love Jeff a lot, but I don't feel like hugging." By contrast, Daphne's feelings for Adrian, her firstborn, are intense. She says, "[Adrian] will always be my most beloved man. He's my man, my love. I will never be able to love a man more than I love him." Furthermore, in response to the question of to whom she would turn for comfort if her purse were stolen or she received a scary medical test result, and what type of comfort she would seek, she ducks her head and says, "Adrian." She pauses and adds in baby talk, "Huggy would be the best." Her delivery implies that she understands it to be more socially correct to seek solace from one's partner or another adult, yet the content reveals a yearning for the special comforts reaped from the connection with her son.

If either Daphne's connection seeking with Adrian or her desire to make him independent were the whole story, she would not be in a security bind. But the combination of these intense drives creates conflict.

Daphne believes she knows how to teach Adrian independence—"by having him sleep in a crib on his own, by letting him play by himself, and by not holding him all the time"—yet she lacks a blueprint for how to teach connection. "I want him to be able to say he's close to me, but I don't really know how you do that. I want him to be able to talk with me, but it's hard to know what to do."

The greatest difficulties she experiences in connecting with him are, in fact, the repercussions of her own efforts to instill independence. One difficult step in her independence training occurred when he was twelve weeks old and she decided to let him cry it out so he would not continue to wake up in the middle of the night. He was waking up twice a night and she would often feel forced to bring him back to bed with her from his crib—for her own sake, so she could get more sleep. This is because the only place he slept well was snuggled next to her in bed. However, she was frightened of rolling over onto him or of him suffocating in her bedding. Thus, when he reached twelve weeks of age, she made the decision against Jeff's protests to leave Adrian in his crib in his room and not to respond to his cries. She says, "In my Lamaze group, it seems like all the other women had done sleep training and I didn't want to be behind. So we trained for three weeks, and he's been sleeping through the night ever since."

During those three weeks, she reports her son screamed and cried for about two hours each time he woke up. She closed his door and hers, but she could still hear it, and occasionally rather than trying to escape the noise, she sat awake in the living room just outside his door, listening and agonizing. "It was very hard for me to do it, hard to train him. I was depressed, like postpartum, for three weeks; it was really hard for me. Plus I had a lot of fights with Jeff because he didn't want to do it."

Prior to that experience, she had thought it was cruel to let babies cry it out. "I still think that and it's hard to leave him to cry. I still have mixed feelings about it. I'm glad I did it and it's good for me, and I'm also happy that he can fall asleep on his own . . . but I feel guilty and wonder if I did it at too early an age."

On the face of it, she accomplished what she set out to: her baby is more independent and now sleeps through the night in a separate room. Daphne has also attained success in her quest for Adrian to be independent in other realms, as he frequently plays alone and is not distressed when she walks away. However, she sometimes wishes for a little *less* success. She says:

DP: I [have friends who] sleep with their babies, and [one of them] says her baby is clingy. So maybe the fact Adrian is not very attached to me or doesn't want to be held . . . [means] I've damaged the bonding [and] he doesn't love me anymore. He never whines when I'm not around, and I should say *thank you*, but it's hard for me because maybe whining is a sign of love. Why is he so independent? I *want* him to be independent—it's healthy—but it's also hard for me. . . .

AV: What if he was clingy?

DP: I think it would drive me nuts if I'm honest with myself! It would be annoying and I need my space and want to do things around the house, speak to friends. But I do need it for my ego, that my kid loves me, even though it doesn't fit my character. Since he can't speak and say, "Mommy, I love you," clinginess is the only way to reassure me. [*turns to the baby and speaks to him*] A little clinginess would be nice!

With Adrian still in diapers, she is already experiencing the pain of him leaving her and she interprets his growing independence (at her insistence) as a lack of love.

Daphne characterizes Adrian as very independent and she repeatedly brings up the clingy babies of her friends and how perhaps those children love their mothers more than Adrian loves her. "For the past two months, I've been telling Jeff that Adrian doesn't love me." She wonders if she "screwed up" and damaged the bond by sleeping separately, by leaving him to cry alone during sleep training, by not holding him or being with him during his first two hours of his life, or by leaving him at day care.

The beginning of day care, at ten months of age, is a key moment when her desire to foster independence collides with her own need for reassurance through connection. We had an interview scheduled for the day after he began attending a home-based day care and she called me that morning in tears, asking if we could meet somewhere besides her house since it was too painful for her to be at home alone without Adrian. The first day of day care had been very upsetting for her. "I felt as if I was hit by a car. I couldn't be at home without him. I felt like a woman who was dumped by the love of her life. My heart was so broken." As with all the various forms of independence that she initiates between herself and Adrian, despite her being the architect of the separation, she experiences it as *him* rejecting *her*. She feels dumped.

Despite how difficult this and other forms of separation are for her, she sees it as good for him: "Adrian sees other kids and starts giggling. It's *healthy* for him to be around other kids. I'm trying to be reasonable and tell myself I'm doing the right thing. But he's already so independent— what if I'm pushing him away more? Maybe I'm missing the train."

She fears that these early experiences with her son may be laying the bedrock for a troubled relationship in the future. She says, "[W]hat if this is already the beginning of him hating me as a teenager, the first mistake? . . . It's against the odds to be a perfect parent. In my moms' group, what are the odds that all those babies will love their moms in the future? They won't! And it's sad, because I want to be a perfect mom."

The stakes are high for Daphne. Her statements about missing the train and the first mistake each indicate she sees her current independence-seeking choices as laying a track toward Adrian hating her. The start of day care brings into full relief the tension between her desire to foster independence for his sake and her own need for connection, a heightened moment of the common push-pull between the modern day ideology of independence and many mothers' emotional longings to connect.

Figure 1 on the following page depicts this tension.

This is by no means simply an empty nest syndrome that occurs only when children leave home. It is a continuous occurrence, beginning in babyhood, as children are taught to fare without their parents. Another independence-oriented mother, Amira Blankenship, like Daphne feels a little sad that her son is so independent—yet she shares this when her son is five months old and not yet able to feed himself, crawl, or even sit up. Being saddened by premobile babies' independence is not uncommon among my research participants, especially those with elements of compensatory connection in their parenting.

In sum, Daphne is using not one but two of the security strategies I highlight. On the one hand, to make her child secure, she is independence oriented and training him to survive on his own in the face of perils (inoculation). On the other hand, to make *herself* feel secure she is connection oriented and turning to her child as an attachment figure

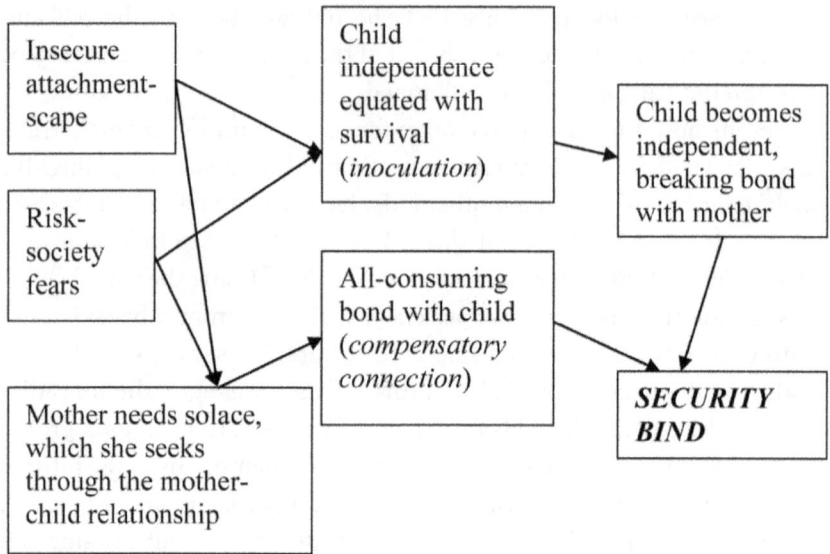

Figure 1. Dynamics of the security bind.

(compensatory connection). Seeking comfort in the mother-child relationship, paired with the sting of getting what one wants regarding child independence, creates a security bind, personified in Daphne's story.

A HOLDING ENVIRONMENT

The final difference among mothers who inoculate is how they utilize the mother-child relationship in the inoculation process. As we saw in chapter 2, mothers using the antidote strategy use *themselves* as their child's antidote for the world's ills. The world is scary, but this mother-child womb of love is not, so there is always at least one place the child can go for sanctuary. We might suspect that mothers who use inoculation would therefore also use themselves, but to the opposite end. That is, in teaching their children to navigate the dangerous and unreliable elements of the world, these mothers might use themselves as a gentle version of that danger and unreliability on which their children can safely practice. After all, these women describe their children as benefiting from contained experiences of hardship, be that in the form of cold milk, taking falls and getting back up, or dealing with frightening truths about the world.

However, Daphne and Julia use themselves very differently toward these ends: Daphne inoculates her son by being a tough *mother* and Julia inoculates her children by exposing them to a tough *world*. Recall that the way Daphne believes she can teach her son to be independent is "by having him sleep in a crib on his own, by letting him play by himself, and by not holding him all the time." For her, his independence lessons come from his learning to cope without her affection and attention. She is his training ground. He learns to sleep independently because she does not go to him. He learns to be okay without physical contact because she does not hold him all the time. She is the supplier of cold milk. In her attempt to impart pain tolerance and strength and to have him "learn to be strong and not easily offended by people," she withholds her own comforts. Thus, she is using herself as the inoculating substance, the taste of challenges and separations to come, which she hopes will prepare him to fare successfully in a harsh world.

But this is not the only way mothers use themselves to inoculate their children. Julia lets her children explore in a potentially hazardous world, and she does use herself as the most frequent bearer of bad news, such as when she directly told her daughter that her favorite preschool teacher was going to die. Unlike many connection-oriented mothers who protect their children from such experiences and information, she does not offer her mothering as a shield. However, like these connection-oriented mothers, she creates a space for the child to safely dwell, and that is *with her*. For example, she creates a safe space when she discusses difficult information. "I try to make time for the bad news, cuddling up on the couch together or in her bed, usually starting with 'I have something very sad to tell you. . . .' I don't talk around it then, but bring out the news first, then giving more details, letting her ask questions."

That is, Julia inoculates within a connected context, attempting to create an emotionally safe environment for hard truths rather than letting her daughter be exposed to them unexpectedly in a random context without a safety figure present.

This parallels Winnicott's concept of a *holding environment*.[22] The holding environment refers to the caregiver's ability to "create the world in such a way [that] the baby . . . feels held, safe, and protected from dangers without and protected as well from the danger of emotions within."[23] This environment is one in which the parent is paying close enough attention to the child as a person that she can empathize with the child and recognize his emotional needs. If the parent is able to contain potentially unsettling experiences for the child, then from this safe place, the child can theoretically learn to cope with a frightening world. This is precisely what Julia is attempting to do. While she deliberately exposes her child to challenging, confusing, and even frightening experiences in the broader world, she offers herself as comfort against those experiences. Thus, the training and practice in surviving that she values for her children regards the harshness "out there" processed from within an emotionally safe environment "in here." When her children are upset, she says, "I just pick them up and hug them, cover them with kisses, lie down on the floor with them." Far from pulling back from her children so they can learn to cope with separation from her, she positions herself as the hugger, the kisser, and the person down on the floor with them at their level. There is no great connection cost to her inoculation because the mother-child relationship is not the site of her children's independence lessons and Julia herself is not the inoculant. The *world* is the source of hardship and challenge and Julia can therefore both have her independent children *and* a warm, intimate bond with them as well.

She is also judicious in her independence orientation to begin with.

> I don't think of myself as pushing independence on my kids willy-nilly. For instance, we needed to do some sleep training with our youngest because he was getting used to nursing all night, but I waited until six months when I was going back to work and I just had to start sleeping. And we used a very gradual approach that involved a lot of walking around [with him in our arms] at two, three, and four [in the morning] trying to stall his feedings. So I'm definitely not a hard-core, independence, cry-it-out person who wanted my babies to just sit in bouncy chairs or strollers or take bottles if I was able to nurse.

Julia, like Daphne, did sleep training. However, unlike Daphne's closed-door training, which left Daphne herself traumatized, Julia's training was not intended to make her son be okay without *her*; it was intended to have him be okay without *milk*. Therefore, she and her husband held their son and walked around with him in the middle of the night, physically connecting and comforting the child even as they were refusing him that for which he was clamoring.

Because Julia remains intimately connected with her children even as she encourages high levels of independence, we do not find the conflict in her between independence and connection or between what she wants for herself and what she wants for her children that is so apparent in Daphne's case.

CONCLUSION

While it might be tempting to claim that independence-oriented women have lighter motherloads than connection-oriented mothers on the basis of their less intensive-seeming practices, the weight of one's motherload is not related to one's mothering practices. Rather, it relates to how much security one expects to be produced in the mother-child relationship. Mothers who use the inoculation security strategy have heavy motherloads. Their fears of crime, terrorism, accidents, and environmental catastrophes result in a deep wish to create security for their children. To do so, they have a well-developed correct-mothering model: exposing children to risk or mini-harms will equip them to independently navigate greater threats in the world.

Despite the above commonalities, we have seen in this chapter's case studies how the inoculation security strategy can vary greatly. In Daphne's case, her risk-society fears are paired with weak personal attachments and insecurity about her job. Lacking a secure base elsewhere in her life, she finds comfort leaning on her child as an attachment object. This adds further weight to her motherload and is greatly at odds with the independence she seeks for the child.

Julia, too, carries a motherload, as her mothering likewise serves as the primary tool by which to impart survival skills to her children in a threatening-seeming world. Furthermore, her judgment of overprotective mothers for *not* imparting such skills suggests a strong view of correct (and thereby of incorrect) mothering, further evidence of the purported security-producing power of a just-right mother-child relationship. However, because Julia relies on her husband, family of origin, friends, and job to meet her own security needs—that is, because she has a secure

Table 4 Differences in mothers who inoculate

	Inoculation with Heavier Motherload (Daphne)	Inoculation with Lighter Motherload (Julia)
VIEW OF WORLD	Dangerous and scary	Dangerous and scary, but not to the degree that everyone thinks
ATTACHMENT-SCAPE	Insecure	Secure
SEES CHILDREN AS:	Breakable, need toughening	Resilient, need education and empowerment
VIEW OF RISK	Risk inescapable "Get used to it."	Risk malleable "Learn to interact safely."
VIEW OF PERSONAL AGENCY	Control only of emotional response to harm	Control of process that brings about or deflects harm
ANXIETY LEVEL	High	Low
MOTHER USES HERSELF AS:	The actual inoculant, a taste of the challenges and separations to come	Emotionally safe perch for child to experience the world's challenges
SECURITY BIND?	Yes	No

attachment-scape—and also because she sees many threats to children as at least partly socially constructed, her motherload is lighter than Daphne's and her experience of mothering is less anxious.

The table above summarizes the differences we have seen in this chapter.

These differences convey an inner logic of the motherload that goes beyond the personal idiosyncrasies of the highlighted cases. For example, the more the mother views risk-society threats as real rather than constructed, the more she may feel she needs to combat those threats on behalf of her child through her acts of mothering, producing a heavy motherload. Likewise, if she has a worldview wherein risk is fixed, then danger cannot be minimized and she can only hope to reduce how much it hurts. In this case, it is quite logical to teach stoicism and emotional disengagement and to inure the child to life's pain by intentionally inflicting small bits of it in advance. In this more emotion-based survival, independence training may require the mother to use herself as the inoculating substance and to use the mother-child relationship as the basis for the child's independence lessons (that is, the mother teaches the child to emotionally disengage and to tolerate separation from herself as the child's primary other). Given the mother's insecure attachment-scape, however, the child's emotional disengagement creates a conflict with the mother's own security needs in her relationship with the child, creating a security bind wherein the mother's own needs and what she perceives as the child's needs conflict.

By contrast, a secure attachment-scape pairs with risk-society fears in a different way. These mothers have a more self-efficacious view of harm; they believe children can do something to deflect threats given a proper education (with the mother as the teacher) and practice navigating threats (with the mother as the source of comfort when this is frightening). In either case, the mother remains central and available as the child processes the harsher elements of life that function as the inoculant. The distinction between the safe mother and the threatening world allows the mother's desires for connection to *align* with rather than conflict with the independence she seeks for her child.

This alignment between connection and independence among those with secure attachment-scapes holds true beyond inoculating mothers, and in general, the lighter the woman's motherload, the less her drives toward independence and connection appear to conflict.[24]

Most recent research regarding motherhood discusses the rise of the helicopter mother phenomenon, and often assumes risk avoidance (the strategy I call shielding) is the obvious and therefore dominant mothering strategy in the face of fear. What is missing is a discussion of alternative forms of maternal involvement with children that might even be thought of as the backlash to helicopter mothering.

The inoculation strategy reveals how risk avoidance is not the only mothering response to fear. Protection by *exposure* to risks is an alternative and—in this research, even more prevalent—protective strategy. While many classically protective parents may wince at these mothers' inoculating practices and the potential harm to which they expose their children, it is clear that these practices are not acts of neglect but are rather conscious, intentional attempts to produce security and prepare children to thrive in an unpredictable world.

6 Friendship Strategy

PUNCHING BACK AT RESPONSIBILITY

Security is when everything is settled. When nothing can
happen to you. Security is the denial of life.

—Germaine Greer

[M]any of us can't even commit to a hair color, let alone
a full-fledged, long-term relationship.

—Elina Furman[1]

Katie Garber, nine months pregnant and experiencing intermittent labor
contractions, has read *What to Expect When You're Expecting*, but she
still does not know what to expect. When her friends ask how she is, she
says scared. She elaborates that she is scared of labor—scared she might
not be able to do it—and also scared about the baby being born physically
or mentally challenged. Above all, however, she is scared of mothering.
What will her life look like tomorrow when she has a child? How will she
both keep her job and care for a baby as a single mom? With all her flaws,
will her son grow up well-adjusted? Will she know what to do, how to
care for such a fragile creature? Can she keep him safe? One of her friends
needs to leave and says with a smile, "Next time I see you, you will probably be a mom." Katie gives a little shudder of fear and says, "Oh, God."

We have seen example after example of women's Herculean efforts to
provide security through or reap security from what they see as the singularly powerful mother-child relationship. However, as motherhood becomes a taller and taller order in our society, there is another way a woman
might respond to it: she might flee from it. In fact, the expectation that

she should provide another human being with ultimate security—enough to keep him physically, emotionally, and economically safe in the face of surrounding hazards—may terrify her. As Daphne, highlighted earlier, says, "I was extremely afraid of [having a baby] and not into it . . . I was afraid I would be a bad mom, that I wouldn't love him enough. I was afraid of the responsibility . . . and afraid of the vulnerability, because what if something happens to him? Plus it's a lot of *work*. You lose your freedom and always have to be around. And you can't change your mind after seven years if you decide you don't like this job. You're his mom forever, and that long-term commitment kind of scared me because I like my freedom."

This quote highlights the security *costs* women bear when they become mothers. The costs to mothers' careers and earnings have been well examined.[2] Additional costs, such as to one's other relationships, to one's time, and to one's *freedom* were all recurrent themes in my interviews as well. During their pregnancies, I repeatedly heard women discuss their determination to have a life after their children were born, with the underlying assumption that having that life was in jeopardy.

We have already seen how women with heavy motherloads harbor fears about the insecure state of the world or of their lives. Now we turn to the fear of motherhood itself and the recoiling against expectations that one is somehow personally responsible for making it all better.

The rate of women remaining childless has dramatically increased in recent years, doubling since the 1970s, with nearly one in five women not bearing a child today.[3] Women are also postponing childbearing longer. Part of this may relate to middle-class women's attempts to get their careers in order and establish themselves economically prior to taking on the financial and career hits that often accompany motherhood.[4] However, a fear of motherhood and intimidation by the perceived enormity of the task may also play a role in this delay or in the decisions not to bear children.

With women now increasingly economically independent of men, some women also have the opportunity for less encumbered lifestyles that in the past would have been mainly identified with bachelors. They have the option of fully committing to jobs: working nights and weekends toward scientific discovery, earning their way up the corporate ladder, or giving their all to social causes. They also have the option of couch surfing,

living abroad, performing in bands, or having multiple romantic partners. Some may describe women living without the encumbrances of a partner or child as liberated; others may describe such women as commitment-
phobic. Yet an increased attempt to avoid personal entanglements is
consistent both with many women's ideals of financial independence
from men[5] and with social theories that claim that insecurity and rapid
social changes lead to increasing levels of independence.[6]

Furthermore, in a culture of warning labels and media exposure to
worst-case scenarios, and with parenting advice books drawing attention
to all that could go wrong and to what mothers should do to avoid it, a
woman may also fear becoming attached to and ultimately responsible for
something so precious that could be lost in a moment. What if she woke up
in the morning and found her baby had died of SIDS? It is little wonder
some women take a good look at the motherload and decide to pass.

Even so, most women do have children. Conceiving a child, however,
does not mean one has overcome these intimidations. Women may continue to be overwhelmed by the high expectations, by the intensity of the
responsibilities they associate with motherhood, or by what they believe
is required in today's world to keep a child safe. They may have a strong
urge to flee or to offload their motherloads—but once a mother has a child,
how can she do that?

The *friendship security strategy* is one way independence-oriented
women with heavy motherloads and an aversion to being tied down to
commitments can deal with motherhood. One in eight women in this
study uses this strategy and—ironically—manages her doubts about long-
term commitment *by having a child*.

Myra Rossi, a forty-one-year-old with three graduate degrees (in Ital-
ian, social work, and business) is a short, feisty, and very talkative woman.
She has a self-described type-A personality: "My friends call me 'Miss
Exact Change'—I'm always on top of it" and "my brother calls me 'the hall
monitor of life.'" Myra likes to be in control and to have things just so.
Until fairly recently, just so did not include being settled with a partner
and child. She says, "My life: 'Why can't you do things like normal people?'
Because I'd probably blow my brains out! I've always done things differently. Regular life among my old Denver friends doing nanny searches and
going to Target is just so boring to me."

Two years ago, however, Myra made a deliberate decision to change her nomadic ways and to find a partner with whom to have children. "I spent so long on my own. I'd been living in Africa and came home partly to settle down and here was this single dad driving a Volvo living in a cul-de-sac. Watch out what you ask for!" She and Mark met through a speed-dating service. They were engaged six months later and began immediate wedding preparations. Myra says, "We were planning this elaborate wedding which was getting out of control. Neither of us was working, it was all we were doing, and he was drinking a lot. . . . I saw his complacency and wondered if he would be a good provider. So we had a big fight and split up." They called the wedding off several weeks before it was to have taken place, returned the gifts, and Myra moved back into her parents' house (she was forty at the time). In the aftermath of the breakup, she had mixed feelings about partnership, but her longing for a child remained. "I was so clear that I wanted to have a child. When [Mark and I] were split up, I went to a sperm bank because I was thinking an anonymous dad might be the best in case Mark and I didn't get back together." First, however, she needed a final fling with international travel, so she "ran away" to Java. She was there during an earthquake that devastated the country "and Mark was the only person to call." His being there for her when she was literally and figuratively shaken up made an emotional impact, and, five months after she returned to her parents' house in Denver, she recommitted to Mark in an exclusive but long-distance relationship (he now lived on the West Coast). Still unclear whether this relationship would last but aware of her advancing age and declining fertility, she made a proposition.

> We wanted a normal period to see if it worked, etcetera. But as an expensive insurance policy, I asked my dad if he wanted to spend all the money of the expensive wedding that didn't happen on freezing grandchildren. So we did one cycle of IVF [in vitro fertilization] and froze four embryos for the future. I got pregnant naturally the next cycle and assumed I'd miscarry. I had had a positive pregnancy test the month before we froze—I was faintly pregnant for, like, one second, got a period, then we froze the next month— and got pregnant a second time the month after that. That was Giovanna.

At the same time as Myra was pregnant with Giovanna, another mother-to-be, thirty-six-year-old Ellie Ryder, was pregnant with her own first

child. Like Myra, Ellie had been a world traveler, with parenting philosophies inspired by the Quicha women of the Amazon as well as by chim-
panzee mothers, since she "worked with chimps in Kenya and . . . saw
how they mothered." Despite her indigenous-inspired beliefs in attachment parenting, her own background and needs for independence are
similar to Myra's.[7] Ellie says, "I thrive on instability, refuse to commit
to anything . . . so marriage was a huge step for me. Before [I started
living with my husband, Frank], in fifteen years I probably lived in thirty
residences." She explains this as follows: "My fear of commitment is
about the accountability that goes along with commitment. If I commit,
I *have* to do this, and it's choice limiting. Frank smothered me in the beginning of our relationship, he was overwatering me, and I told him he
needed to back off!"

While we might assume stability is a good that people seek, particularly to counterbalance the economic insecurity, culture of divorce, and
risk-society threats discussed in the earlier chapters, these women challenge that assumption. They thrive on movement and a revolving cast of
characters in their lives and seem to *eschew* stability. In fact, it takes an
act of will and the overcoming of much internal resistance for them to
settle down.

The threat a baby poses to such a woman's independence may cause
her to remain childless. As I only interviewed women who were pregnant
and then kept their babies, I cannot say anything about those women.
But I can speak of those who are threatened by motherhood even as they
seek it. The *friendship strategy* is one way women, as least economically
privileged women, cope with that fear and restore, to some degree, the
security of their prior independence. A mother using this strategy seeks
a low-dependency, yet highly personal friendship with her child, with
whom she can enact independence as a twosome and explore the greater
world through joint adventures, travel, and outings to places she enjoys.

Unlike the inoculation strategy, which is independence seeking for the
sake of the child, the friendship strategy is independence seeking for the
sake of the mother. Her parenting actions are geared toward maintaining
her former independence and lifestyle as much as possible. It is a strategy
in which a baby is seen as almost impossibly needy and fragile and a caregiver's job in keeping her safe as almost impossibly difficult—so the

woman carries a very heavy motherload. However, the first element of this strategy is that she does not see the baby as needing *her* in particular, which means it is emotionally unproblematic for her to outsource care to others. (Perhaps it would be more correct to say she has a heavy *otherload* during babyhood.)

Being *identified* as a mother, however, is socially important to women using the friendship security strategy, and they foster strong social connections with other mothers, mainly through mothers' groups. Their social universes are geared around girlfriends, not partners, and they either consider their children additional friends with whom to engage in enjoyable adult-oriented activities or attempt to minimize their parenting.

In this chapter, we will examine the life histories and independence drives of the women who draw on friendship as their primary security strategy. We will then investigate the expectations these women have of mothering, the changing nature of the mother-child relationship as their children age, and how they manage the practical responsibilities and emotional commitments of work, partnership, and child rearing.

HISTORIES OF DEPENDENCY

The women in this study who use the friendship security strategy have certain aspects of their backgrounds in common. They come from middle-class homes and have mothers who stayed home with them as children and who were highly involved in their lives. Indeed, their mothers "lived and died" for their children. Myra says:

MR: My mom was a full-time mom and still is *so* dedicated to her family, so she was always there for me, always the first to pick me up from a party—I was never forgotten. . . . She is the most selfless, supportive, do-anything-for-anyone-you-love kind of person. . . . She doesn't really have a self. She defines herself by others. . . . She never worked. If I push: "What interests you, why don't you take a class, go on a trip?" . . . my dad says, "That's what *you* [Myra] want, *your* agenda, but that's not her." I wish she did more for herself.

AV: Growing up, did you ever feel your parents were *too* involved?

MR: No. It felt wonderful. I don't think I fully realized the extent of
their love and dedication until I realized other people don't have it.
And my father had an active interest in our lives. If I was getting a
degree, he knew the difference between an MSW, MA, or MBA, he
knew my friends . . . I mean, maybe at times when you're an
adolescent and you see other kids whose parents don't give a shit
and who can do anything, and when your parents always do the
right thing, you wish for more freedom. . . . Maybe it felt a little
intrusive sometimes. . . . But they let me have blow-out parties,
didn't lock the liquor cabinets, they'd feed all my friends—they
were quite permissive. But their active involvement sometimes
felt—but we talked at the dinner table. In other families, the
parents are not around. . . . My parents were *always there*, so stable
and comforting, and if [they] hadn't been there I would miss [their
presence]. I did want to be home alone sometimes, for them to *not*
know what I was doing. You know, when you drive and you have to
call when you get there. . . .

Myra gives minor glimpses, repeatedly interrupted midsentence, of a
longing for greater freedom or to occasionally not be accountable to her
parents. Perhaps these are a precursor to her intense independence orientation as an adult. However, these longings appear to be subsumed by
a much greater sense of gratitude, solidness, and joy in response to her
parents' high levels of investment and involvement in her life.

Paradoxically, women using the friendship strategy—more fiercely
committed to an ideology of independence than any other women in this
study—are the most dependent on their families of origin, continuing as
adults to be supported by their own parents in various ways. Beyond the
emotional support of frequent phone calls and visits, their parents provide far more care for the grandchildren than parents of the other women
I studied. If local, the children may routinely nap or spend mornings or
afternoons at the grandparents' home while the mother shops, works out
at the gym, or visits with friends. If living further away, then during visits, which are frequent and typically last for weeks rather than for days,
the grandparents assume the role of primary caregivers to the children

for the duration and the mother mostly does as she pleases. These mothers also typically continue to financially depend upon their parents. Examples of this include their parents paying for the grandchildren's schooling or buying the women homes as gifts (sometimes in the same neighborhood as the parents).

Myra—who currently lives in a large and luxurious home her parents bought for her, complete with expensive beds and an industrial-sized washer and dryer set they paid for as well—says of her early years while her father was financially struggling: "My parents didn't have the money or the wherewithal to take us to the opera or enroll us in classes. . . . Now Giovanna is in private school and my dad is footing the bill. He's compensating."

Additionally, these women may live with their parents on and off as adults. "Boomerang children"—adult children living with their parents—are becoming increasingly commonplace in US families, even as the ideological value placed on independence continues to increase.[8]

Regarding work, Myra's career history is colorful, but her aversion to long-term relationships with romantic partners seems to apply equally to her job situation. She has been an Italian teacher, a book translator, a hospital social worker, a publicist, a fund-raiser for a public television station, and the coordinator of a conference center and retreat house. These are all well-respected positions and she was successful at every one of them, but she held them all for three years or less, at which point she voluntarily moved on. She also has graduate degrees in three unrelated fields, including one PhD. Looking at this alongside her geographic mobility—having traveled to all seven continents and having lived in four—gives a sense of her passion for doing it all. However, "doing it all" means doing nothing for too long and that runs counter to the long-term commitment often associated with having a child. This creates the need for a highly creative strategy to continue as an independent go-getter while still experiencing the love and connection of motherhood.

Among women using the friendship strategy, it is unclear whether there is a link between their attraction to novelty and movement, on the one hand, and the high stability of their own parents' safety net, involvement, and financial support, on the other. It is certainly plausible that they seek the *challenge* of unfamiliar faces, places, and job responsibilities either due to the lack of similar challenges in childhood or simply because they have such a secure home base that there are fewer risks associated with launching into unknown territory.

There are also, however, certain elements of insecurity in each of these women's backgrounds as well. For example, Myra's mother was not an income earner and her father's job situation was tenuous for most of her childhood. "He was a grocery stocker, then a line chef, and he was out of work when my younger brother was due." He did eventually find another chef job and began to have his own ideas about the restaurant business, but he was "scared to go off on his own" and pursue his ideas through starting a restaurant. "He made the break when I was ten or eleven from steady paycheck [to starting his own restaurant] with a friend from third grade as his partner." The restaurant was initially slow to take off, but eventually its unique décor and foods caught on and it grew to become one of the ten most successful restaurant chains in the county, which made him a very wealthy man. "It took five years to be sure he made the right choice. My mom wanted him to keep the stable job, you know, two kids, new house. She thought he should not take the risk. But he did."

Women who use the friendship strategy may also have experienced high levels of geographic mobility as children. Ellie says, "I changed schools every two years and never lived in one house more than four years." Likewise, Myra lived in "seven houses in my first seven years. I didn't know that wasn't what people did. But it shows that if you have the foundation of the family, the rest doesn't really matter. . . . It didn't make me feel insecure." The difference between their childhood mobility and the mobility these women gravitate toward as adults is that, as adults, they do not take loved ones with them but prefer to travel solo and meet new people as they go. In fact, as evidenced by their self-stated fears of commitment, aside from their enduring connections with their families of origin, they are generally not comfortable with ongoing relationships.

Myra says her partner, Mark, sees a connection between her relationship with her parents and her lack of effort in their partnership. "He says I have such an emotional and financial safety net [with them], so maybe I'm not trying [with him]."

INSECURE PREGNANCIES

All of these mothers experienced some form of insecurity during their pregnancies. On the social level, given their ambivalence regarding long-term relationships, there was a context of tenuousness between them and their children's fathers. For example, Myra, whose pregnancy was welcomed but accidental and who was unmarried and uncertain about whether she would stay with Mark, says: "If we hadn't gotten pregnant and had waited until the time was right [between me and Mark], I'm not sure it would have happened. . . . [But] if I end up being a single mom, it's nice that he's there and that Giovanna will know her dad."

Beyond the insecure relational context surrounding the pregnancy, the pregnancy itself was typically regarded as insecure and prone to miscarry. This may be partly due to subjective fears and projections and partly due to their postponement of childbearing, making them significantly older mothers than most—typically in their mid-thirties or forties during pregnancy.

> I was almost sure I would lose the baby; I was almost resigned. I didn't tell people about it until really late. . . . I was worried about an ectopic pregnancy [where the embryo implants in a fallopian tube rather than the uterus]. I was worried about every problem du jour. . . . I didn't feel her a lot, so I rented a fetal heart monitor [an expensive piece of obstetric medical equipment to determine if the fetus is still alive], and we'd do that fairly frequently at home to hear her.

Myra did not experience her pregnancy as merely physically insecure, however. It was also emotionally stressful, which led her to further concerns about the baby's health. "It was hard. I was a lot more sensitive, and worried about the responsibility. I wasn't in the space and relationship—so many conditions were not as I'd hoped. At the same time, I loved reading about it, looking at the development. I was on the Internet and in pregnancy groups. . . . [But] I thought about what stresses I had during pregnancy: moved twice, relationship issues, totaled my car—and I worried about *worrying*, worried my stress would lead to an underweight baby."

Myra's "worry about worrying" is not unique to her or even to the friendship strategy. William Sears warns that "if your pregnancy is cluttered with emotional stress (especially the last three months), you have a higher risk of having a child who is anxious," which in turn increases the child's risk of other negative outcomes.[9] So being worried is itself a cause for concern and women are advised to calm down, especially those last three months. However, it can be hard not to be stressed while absorbing the onslaught of purported threats to healthy pregnancies, including alcohol, sugar, jostling, airborne toxins, and stress itself.

Many pregnant women experience some uncertainty about a baby being born "normal," and fear over this uncertainty is more evident among women using the friendship strategy than among other women in this study. For example, Ellie says:

> I had horrible thoughts in my head about her being born deformed or ugly. I was concerned that I might not accept her. I even worried about it before I got pregnant. I think it's [due to my own] insecurity. Nothing is more an extension of yourself than your own baby, and it's out there in the world for them to judge. It's shallow because it's basing my perception of her on the rest of the world. It's my own fear of rejection externalized onto the baby. I do this with boyfriends. Frank was not the best dresser in the world when I met him, and that really bothered me. It's about my own need not to be rejected.

This focus on appearances continues after the birth, and women using the friendship strategy are the most critical of how their babies look. Myra says:

> [W]hen she was born, she looked like she'd come through a war. . . . [S]he didn't look like I'd thought. She was so scrawny and fragile. She couldn't even cry; she went *ee ee* like a mouse. I was scared of the fragility. . . . [W]ho did I give birth to? She doesn't look like me, so scrawny, wasn't what I thought. I didn't identify with her as my daughter, more a person I'm responsible for. I was so sore, still bleeding—it was very jarring. . . . We were making so many jokes about how ugly and scrawny she was—"We should have gotten her for half price!" or looking at other babies and saying, "Now *that's* a baby!" We called her runt and when other people said, "Oh she's so beautiful, what an angel," we'd say, "You must have seen a lot of *ugly babies* if you think this one's an angel!" In my family, we call it like it is.

Ellie likewise does not see her newborn baby as physically attractive.

She has been scowling at me for a month, and always has a mad look on her face, possibly because of how her forehead got squished in the birth process. It's hard to bond with someone who is scowling all the time. . . . Frank got upset with me when I said I think she's kind of ugly. . . . [T]hat didn't fit his archetype of what a mother is supposed to say about her baby. . . . [But] I didn't really like the way she smelled, I didn't like the way she looked. . . . I didn't find her very endearing, frankly.

Part of what accounts for this may be that these mothers are simply less excited by babies than they are by older children, teens, or adults. My interviews include a question asking if the woman feels particularly drawn to babies or children of a specific age. In contrast to women who use the compensatory-connection strategy, who are most drawn to babies and very young children for their intense level of dependence on the mother and the physical intimacy, women who use the friendship strategy are drawn to older children, typically because an older child more closely approaches the mother's abilities and interests and can therefore be a better friend. At four months, Ellie says of her infant daughter, "How close can you get to her? . . . I mean there's only so close you can be with a baby." Similarly, at one year, she says, "She doesn't have language now, so how intimate can you be without knowing someone's thoughts and feelings? There's no comparison with a one-year-old versus a sixteen-year-old."

I should point out that these women's underwhelming initial bond with their infants does not make them exceptional among mothers. Many other mothers in this study who do not use the friendship strategy likewise experienced disappointment in the initial months of their babies' lives and then harbored their lack of bonded feelings as a dirty secret. What is unique in this group is not their ambivalent feelings about their babies but rather how forthcoming they are with it, how little shame is associated with it, and how casually and unapologetically they say things that others might fear would mark them as bad mothers.

THE MATERNAL IDENTITY

As these women do not describe themselves as baby people, their initial drive to have children is often framed less around having a baby than it is around the identity of being a mother. This includes viewing motherhood as an act of personal accomplishment or badge of honor.

AV: How old were you when you first experienced a desire to have a child?

MR: Teenager. It just got stronger over time. Life wouldn't be whole without it. I have this thing about doing it all.

AV: Do you know why you wanted to have a child?

MR: So many reasons and no reason. I think I feel like it makes you a better person, makes you more of everything: more sensitive, more aware, more conscious. Oh, and there's that narcissistic "leave a legacy," impart my views, so there's something left of me after I'm gone. Then the less selfish thing: I've always learned from my students, and this is learning from someone I *create*.

For these mothers, having a child also creates a sense of belonging among other mothers. Myra says, "I had this one chance to be a mom. It was a club I wanted to belong to. If I were to die tomorrow, I'd regret not being a mom much more than I'd regret not being a wife. . . . Now I've joined that club." Ellie, too, uses the club metaphor: "[I]t's *such* a part of my identity, belonging to the motherhood club, and I can't imagine *not* being one." Notice that while my question is about why each wanted to have a child (that is, about a relationship), both of them switch this to a discussion of being a mother (that is, about an identity). Myra says, "I'd regret not being a mom" rather than saying she would regret not having a child, suggesting the importance to her of the maternal identity as well as the affiliation with a group to which she wishes to belong. Absent from these reasons to mother are the more typical responses such as "I want somebody to love and who loves me" or "I think it will be so rewarding to see a little person developing."

Membership in the motherhood club is more than a subjective sense of belonging. It is quite literal. With breadwinning partners tied up in long hours of professional work and babies who have yet to verbally develop, women using the friendship strategy find togetherness and intimacy by cultivating a network of adult girlfriends. They belong to an average of three mothers' social groups and their calendars are filled with these women: wine-tastings, lunches, parties, working out at the gym together, or group marathon training. This allows them to depend less on their partners for their social needs. For example, at four months, Ellie explains how she and her daughter spend their days: "We have our outing days and we have—God, it's so different every day. We spend a lot of time with other moms, at art museums, out walking and hiking. She's already been to the Smithsonian, seen the San Francisco symphony, been to Yosemite and Carmel. We go clothes shopping, we do yoga. Each weekday has an activity that we do once a week that day."

Before the babies are old enough to be girlfriends in their own right, taking them on outings with other mothers and babies meets the mothers' needs for adventure.

The road trip is another element of the friendship strategy. At eight months, Myra says, "We had more of a bond once she made her first smile and we had our first road trip together. That was more my vision of the girlfriends-on-the-road thing." Being on the road was an important aspect of these women's lives prior to motherhood, when they generally traveled alone rather than with romantic partners or even with girlfriends. Myra says, "The greatest adventures I've had are putting myself out in the globe, by myself. I've been to Cambodia, Mongolia, and the Congo, not speaking the language, not knowing anyone. There's such a sense of confidence and empowerment that comes from that."

The empowerment that stems from putting oneself out there without knowing anyone continues to some degree, but after the birth of babies, trips become solo-with-baby. Ellie, for example, flew across the country with her then nine-week-old baby (and without her husband) to attend the opening of a new museum. Another mother, Deb Feldman, explains how travel with children and without one's partner can be a test of one's independence mettle: "I'm very independent—though I am close to my friends and my family. But I don't feel dependent on anyone, not even my husband. And I have to prove that to myself sometimes when I'm feeling down. Like, I took my two kids [both under twenty-four months] for a week to New York [across the country] to prove I could do it without my husband, like a rite of passage. People thought I was crazy, taking both kids on such a trip alone, but I needed to know I could."

As these empowering partner-free travels reveal, the girlfriends dynamic and the need to assert independence from one's partner are interrelated.

BABYHOOD AND CONSTRAINT

Given that these women's expressed rationale for mothering includes more about the maternal identity and less about the child than other women's narratives do, we might wonder how they respond to the day-in and day-out experience of an actual baby in their lives. Myra says of her four-day-old baby, "When I rode in the backseat with her [on the way home from the hospital], I thought, 'I'll never be in the front with Mark again.' You worry that you'll never have your life again. The negative is the feeling of constraint: you can't go off to see the film with the filmmaker talking afterwards. No more exotic travel to Vietnam for a long time." The backseat is a hard place for a hall monitor of life to sit. And a newborn is unlikely to satisfy the wanderlust of a woman hungry for constant newness.

AV: How was it during the newborn phase?

MR: Hard. It felt like the movie *Groundhog Day*. Didn't I *just* change the diaper? Didn't I *just* feed her? I was pumping, then feeding her, then supplementing, and over again. And "sleep when the baby sleeps" doesn't work because there's things you *need* to do. It's an exhausting cycle.

For Myra and other women who intensely guard their independence, motherhood's diminishment of their freedom, status, and control within the broader world is particularly problematic. The friendship strategy at least partially resolves some of these problems through the outsourcing of care.

Being a stay-at-home mother often means taking care of one's children full-time, and not all stay-at-home mothers feel comfortable paying for someone else to do that. For example, Belinda Landers, a white stay-at-home mother of three young children, is feeling burned out and is considering putting her younger two children in a preschool twice a week for three hours (her eldest is in kindergarten). She tells her mothering group:

Having my boys go there would give me some alone time to relax, shop, go to appointments, work out, pay bills, or whatever. It would also, I believe, leave me feeling more available on the weekend [to care for all three kids so my husband can also get some downtime] since I got a break during the week. It's not super cheap, but we can afford it. But just thinking about doing it makes me feel like a serious cop-out. I'm already feeling guilty about it and I haven't even signed up yet. I know I need more consistent kid-free time, but it feels slightly wrong for a stay-home mom to drop her kids off just to get a break.

Nina Meyers, a white stay-at-home mother of two young children, says she was talking with her husband about this very thing the night before. She offers a remarkably sociological response to Belinda: "People used to stay close to their families and then when they had kids they would have babysitting help. . . . But now so many of us don't live near our parents or siblings . . . [so we] have to get a break by purchasing it. That's just the new order. It's not a cop-out to use a day care or preschool—you are just having to formalize something that [in the past] would have happened without really thinking about it."

Unlike Belinda—who has three children and who, even after five years of full-time caring for them, feels guilty for even considering paying for two mornings of care each week—neither Myra nor Ellie experience a contradiction between stay-at-home motherhood and the use of paid help. Ellie says, "We have three babysitters off of craigslist. We use these sitters when I'm at home so I can get things done around the house, or occasionally I'll go out to lunch or read a book or do some writing. It's about fifteen to twenty hours a week of help."

Myra likewise found her babysitters on craigslist. After her postpartum doula was no longer coming to help out daily, Myra hired regular babysitters. "[T]hings weren't really in place, and I wasn't really comfortable with [the babysitters] I was leaving Giovanna with, but I needed a break." Initially, the babysitters watched Giovanna one to two days a week, but this quickly became what Myra describes as three part-days a week. When pressed for a specific schedule, she says these part-days are from 9 a.m. to 4 p.m., from 10 a.m. to 3 p.m., and from 10 a.m. to 6 p.m., plus one evening a week. Myra estimates her paid care at fifteen to twenty hours a week, the same as the estimate Ellie gave, but according to the more specific schedule she shared with me, she utilizes twenty-four hours of paid help per week. "During that time, I go to therapy, Weight Watchers, errands, get stuff done, lunch with a friend, a manicure this Friday, etcetera." In addition to that paid care, Mark's mother babysits Giovanna two evenings a week, once so Myra and Mark can go to couples counseling and once so they can have a date. This is a total of thirty hours a week of nonparental child care, excluding time at the share-care around the corner from Myra's house, where she occasionally drops Giovanna off "just to get a break." Giovanna, at eight months old and with a stay-at-home mother, therefore receives more nonparental child care than the twenty-eight-hour weekly average of preschool age children whose mothers work in the paid labor force.[10]

Some mothers' devotion to family is evident in their intense research and scrupulous choices of caregivers to whom they entrust their children.[11] Working mothers in this study describe their children's caregivers with great animation, sharing details of what makes those caregivers so superb and how they enrich the children's lives. By contrast, Myra never describes Giovanna's babysitters (beyond their not being particularly good), what they spend their days doing with Giovanna, or how Myra's choice of these caregivers reflects well on her and is good for Giovanna in some way. Likewise, Ellie never describes any of her daughter's paid caregivers except to say that they are college students from craigslist.

It is paradoxical that Myra, who is highly anxious about her daughter's physical health and development, is willing to defer responsibility to less-than-ideal caregivers.

> I'm a germ-phobe. I pour hot water over toys when they fall down; I put a paper towel on the counter when I set things on it. But sometimes now I'm too tired to care, sometimes even letting random people hold her if they ask to. It's this conflict between wanting to keep control and wanting to let go. On the letting go side, Giovanna has had *so* many babysitters, has stayed in hotels, and once I needed to pee when I was checking out of a store so I left her with the clerk [a stranger] while I went to the bathroom.

Clearly the qualifications and quality of the people she leaves Giovanna with is not how Myra maintains her sense of maternal concern during her thirty-some hours of weekly absence.

When asked how much separation from her baby feels like too much, she says that when Giovanna is with a sitter or at the share-care "and I'm gone all day, [then] when I come back, I just want to hold and squeeze her all night. . . . [If] I'm out that evening, that feels like too much. I really want a piece of each day. I *do* it [go out the entire day and also that same night] if it's important, but I try not to do it two days in a row."

In addition to paid caregivers and Mark's mother twice a week, Giovanna receives regular care from Myra's own parents. Myra says, "Probably I've stayed at my parents for a couple months total [since Giovanna was born eight months ago], and when I pass her off to them at seven in the morning knowing I can go back to sleep, what helps is knowing I can check out, that I don't have to be the one to deal with it all the time. Like, 'Tomorrow, I have a babysitter. This too shall pass!'"

On a subjective level, despite the support she receives caring for her baby, her own child-care responsibilities still feel intense to Myra. When asked how much time she focuses solely on Giovanna each day, she answers, "A *lot*. Much of the day is either feeding her or walking her—usually while catching up with people on the cell phone—then twenty minute periods of leaving her—thank God for *Baby Einstein*—to check my e-mail, groom myself . . ."

Myra's impression of spending a lot of her time focused on Giovanna seems incongruous not only with thirty-some hours of nonparental child care per week but also with how she and Giovanna spend their time when they are together.

> I leave her alone a lot so she doesn't get overindulged with too much attention. I leave her in the Pack 'n Play [playpen] to just be, or in the saucer or swing while I put on music. Or in her crib, I put her down awake. And I give her a fuzzy baby sock as a lovie and a bunch of pacifiers, and she'll talk and then go to sleep. When I leave the room, she's just beginning to whimper. I used to rush to her side when she'd fuss, but the research I've read says it's just as problematic to rush to them immediately as to not respond at all. So now I've learned the importance of sometimes letting her cry so she can learn self-soothing. . . . I've left her alone in a room from the beginning. She was never this clingy, needing-to-be-held baby. . . . [S]he's just always been happy in a swing and I do my own thing.

They are also in separate rooms at night. Myra explains their sleep arrangement and how they moved Giovanna to a separate floor of the house: "At six weeks, we moved her into the downstairs bedroom to sleep and we turned the monitor [listening device to know when the baby is off crying]. I was scared, but if it's SIDS, you won't hear it anyway, and if she's upset and cries loud enough, we'll hear it [from upstairs]."

We see a two-pronged approach taking place. The first is a tactic of needs reduction and the fostering of early independence through the use of baby swings, toys, and videos, during the times when the mother and child are together.[12] The second is the utilization of paid caregivers to buy one's continued freedom. The women using the friendship mothering strategy in this study—all stay-at-home mothers—utilize an average of twenty-three hours of nonparental care per week for their babies. This may be through mother's helpers such as those Ellie uses, through regular help from grandparents, or through daily trips to the gym with friends so the mother and her girlfriends can take fitness classes while the babies are cared for in the gym's babysitting program. These mothers generally arrange their schedules such that their own period of responsibility for the child coincides with the child's naps.

The outsourcing of care continues as the child ages. At three years of age, Giovanna's schedule is:

> [p]reschool three mornings and Spanish one morning a week. The babysitter picks her up on preschool days and stays with her until 6:00 or 6:30 [at night, and we have] an older woman who babysits some evenings. . . . My time: the house stuff takes a lot of time. Bugs, maintaining the tile grout, gotta seal it, get an estimate. Stuff breaks, wrong light bulb, laundry, changing sheets, dishes—a lot of time maintaining the household. I get anxious with bad feng shui, and Mark is a slob. Lots of errands and shopping. For "me things" I do friend time, meals with friends, do my nails . . . film festivals, or going to hear a speaker in the city . . . [and] I spend a lot of time in Denver at my parents' [house].

The hours of nonparental child care have expanded since the baby days, yet due to Mark's frequent absence for business trips, she still feels like she is shouldering a lot. Longing for some of the advantages of divorce, she says, "[M]y divorced friends have these days off when the kid is with the ex. And I'm doing it alone anyway! But he takes her to day care."

With Mark taking Giovanna to school, the babysitter picking her up from school and taking care of her until evening, and a sitter caring for her a couple evenings a week so she and Mark can go out, it still subjectively feels to Myra like she is doing it alone and that her single mother friends have certain freedoms from child-care responsibilities that she lacks.

Ellie, too, now with two children, uses paid caregivers far more than the other stay-at-home mothers in this study. For example, when she flies to visit friends, she often brings her nanny with her. On such trips, her children and the nanny accompany her on outings with friends, but the nanny is in charge of attending to the children's needs so Ellie is free to focus more on her friends.

PARTNERSHIP AND WORK

Jealousy

During the baby phase, when the primary approaches are outsourcing care and needs minimizing, these women's narratives highlight how much their babies cost them in sleep, time, and freedom. An additional cost is the diminishment of their partners' attention. At eight months, Myra says (and notice that she refers to her daughter as *the baby* rather than by her name in this particular description), "Mark will make dinner, bring flowers, dress the baby, take care of the baby—but he doesn't say things so much anymore about how much he feels for me."

Ellie shares a similar dynamic (also referring to her daughter as *the baby*):

> [T]here might have been competition between me and the baby for Frank's attention. So I didn't actually want to bond with the baby because she was taking attention away that I thought I should be getting from my husband. . . . You hear a lot about the male jealousy, but I've never heard of Mommy jealousy towards Daddy, but I think there might have been some of it. Why is he taking such good care of her and not [of] me? So I sort of rejected the baby in some way—I mean, I never *rejected* her, but I think there was some jealousy. I just think if Frank had been really nurturing, taking care of me, it would have been a much, much easier process.

These women have not only lost their prior front-seat statuses through having children but they have also lost some of their centrality in their partners' lives, a loss which they more keenly feel (or at least express) than the other women in this study.

Feminism, Independence, and Work

Recall that these globe-trotting, hypermobile, historically short-term partnering women define themselves by independence. The discrepancy between their independence and their high levels of practical, financial, and emotional dependency on their families of origin does not strike them as problematic. They make no attempt to resolve this apparent contradiction or to frame their relationships with their own mothers or fathers as independent in any way. They have a home base of support into which they dip as needed and that appears not to cause an identity crisis.

However, in addition to relying on their parents, they financially depend on their partners. Ellie says, "I've never fully, responsibly supported myself and I'm thirty-six years old. I'm a financial disaster. Thank God I'm married to Frank because I'm a disaster in that area." This type of relying on others is much more at odds with their self-images as strong, autonomous women. For example, a year after Giovanna's birth, Myra says of her financial dependency on Mark: "I am forty-two, and right now, I'm dependent. . . . It's horrible. It makes me feel childlike."

Myra is not alone in eschewing financial dependency. Such dependency smacks up against both the American ideology of independence and an egalitarian worldview—which leaves many stay-at-home mothers, like Myra, feeling uneasy. Women's desires for independence became resoundingly clear during the second-wave feminist movement of the 1960s and 1970s when a concomitant spike in the divorce rate made women's financial independence all the more crucial. Many women at that time— and to this day—saw earning their own incomes not only as establishing themselves as people and giving them ownership of their own lifework but as allowing them to choose partnerships based on criteria other than financial need, freeing them from financial bondage to abusive or otherwise unacceptable husbands and lowering their risk of impoverishment at a man's prerogative.[13] Thus, working for a wage is not merely a form of personal empowerment for women or the claiming of a public identity; it is also a form of security.

Feminist women's valuing of independence and viewing work as a path to selfhood was initially given voice by middle-class white women. African American and working-class women had worked for others throughout

US history and neither glorified paid work nor viewed it as self-defining.[14] They had also historically survived through pooling resources with their communities and were therefore not prone to seeing independence from others as essential to their personhoods.[15] Nonetheless, African American mothers were even less likely than white mothers to financially depend on men, and they carved out distinct ideals of "community-based independence" that embraced community ties while resisting both legal marriage and exclusive mothering.[16] Thus, while emerging from entirely different circumstances and manifesting in distinctive ways, by the turn of the twenty-first century, independence became a widespread value among US women from a variety of backgrounds, 92 percent of whom consider independence important in defining themselves as people.[17]

Dubiousness about heterosexual marriage may have a lot to do with this, and in my interviews, I often found that when women said "independence," they often meant "financial independence from men." This is generally the case, and a Roper poll investigating the relative importance of women's financial goals found that women rank being financially independent of others as their single most important goal, even above such other (more family inclusive) goals as "hav[ing] enough for me and my family to live as well as we can."[18] Putting this differently, when women compare the relative importance of (1) their own piece of the family pie being enough to live on without a partner and (2) the whole pie giving their families the best possible standard of living, the former ability to live without their partners is more important. The backup plan—or the financial security to go it alone—takes precedence over the goodness of one's current circumstances for most US women.

Under these cultural conditions, and with so many marriages ending in divorce, many mothers seek paid work not simply because economic realities today dictate that most two-parent families need two incomes to get by but also—and crucially on the level of felt security—as a way to avoid financial dependence on men.[19] However, if a woman lacks the security of an income of her own or has been unable to establish this financial independence from her partner, she may be forced to strive for independence in different ways.

Myra had not intended to be a stay-at-home mother ("What a term!" she says. "I prefer to call myself a run-around mom."). In fact, during pregnancy—before her father bought her a house—she said Mark did not earn enough to support them on just his salary. So initially, being a full-time mother was neither desirable nor financially feasible. Despite her intention to work, however, eight months after Giovanna's birth she was still unemployed: "I'm still not back at work, while other women just whip right back into the saddle. But I'm trying to cut myself some slack. Maybe there's a reason that there's not something I'm so excited about in the world, like a job opportunity, etcetera. Maybe it's because I'm supposed to be home with Giovanna now and I should just lose the guilt. Something is getting in the way, but I think I'll be ready soon."

Recall her earlier statement about how she does not do things like normal people who spend their days going to Target, and how "regular life . . . is just so boring to me. . . . I'd probably blow my brains out." Checking in with her three years after Giovanna's birth, we find her precisely at Target and pining for more. "I thought I'd go back to work at six months; it was clearer that I'd be a working mom . . . [but life today] still goes on [without me finding an appropriate career]. Like what did I do today? I went to Target and Costco. I used to be on page at the ER and I knew not everyone can do what I'm doing—it's gratifying. Anyone can go to Target. I was used to living a bigger life, contributing more, being out there in the world."

Although Myra finds her own regular life unappealing, she is not willing to compromise her values to live a bigger life by taking the job opportunities that present themselves, as they tend not to offer the flexibility she seeks. Much as she is unwilling to make a lifelong commitment to an imperfect partner, she is unwilling to commit to imperfect or overly demanding work. At this point, the only work she has found that somewhat utilizes her special talents without overly impinging upon her freedom is promoting a line of children's educational books through having occasional parties similar to Tupperware parties. She says the pay is abysmal so it is not her ultimate ideal, but at least it is a beginning.

> I'm not going to jump on just any job . . . I want it all on my terms. If I can't be at a staff meeting because I'm going to Denver [to stay with my parents] for a week, that has to be okay. So that's hard, but that's what I finally found. So now I can say I'm working; I don't have the gap. I still wish I knew something bigger was around the corner . . . [but] I do believe if I

schmooze enough and connect to people high enough up, someone will have my résumé in hand and know about a job and I'll be ready to make a difference in the world.

Meanwhile, she says she is grateful that so far in life she has been blessed "because I've never felt like I *need* to be with a man, or I *need* to take this job, so I never compromise my integrity or feelings or values in order to be with someone or do something." Being blessed to not need a job, however, means she does need someone else to financially support her, which creates a conflict with the part about not needing to be with a man. She says, "I don't like being dependent, or asking permission. My desire is to be self-sufficient, but I also don't want to account to somebody. It just doesn't feel right."

Between her desires to be self-sufficient (free from a man financially) and to not have to account to somebody (free from a boss, regarding her time), something has to give. In the moral calculus of not compromising her values by needing either a man or a job, she has chosen to stick with her values on the job front and to not take jobs that restrict her freedom. However, this choice means she cannot earn a living, which leaves her needing financial resources, particularly with a child to support. She therefore financially depends on Mark, which according to her, feels childlike and horrible.

Solutions to Dependency

Myra has various ways of emotionally resolving her dependence on Mark: "I *hope* Mark and I are together for the long haul, but I wouldn't be surprised if we were not. I have no *intention* of splitting up, but I look around and see so many couples breaking up. Our parents stayed together because that's what you *did*. But now, maybe you're together for a huge life chapter—raising children—and then maybe I go into the Peace Corp when I'm sixty."

This first solution to her dependency, therefore, is to segment her life into three parts. In two of those parts, before and after raising a child, she is a free agent. Only during child rearing itself is she tied to a man. "[I]t's just a life chapter. My skills aren't going anywhere. *Carpe decade!!!*"

With their daughter now three years old, she and Mark are still unmarried. "As Giovanna gets older, we get more questions. But it's hard to get that piece of paper when I'm not totally sure." The transition to a more stable life has not been easy for Myra. "I'm always the one with the escape fantasies. [Mark is] the domestic one, the suburban dad, the home guy. His expectations are lower, more realistic. I thought if I'd been to every continent, I could settle down, but it's hard. I get this panicky feeling like: 'I don't want this!' When I was jet setting, I wanted a home and a kid [*notice she does not mention wanting a partner*], and now I have it so I'm, 'Okay, shut up already!'"

Despite her desire to overcome the flight impulse, she is preparing the way to flee just in case. The house (a recent gift from her father) is in her name only. She is working not so she can make money but so she can keep her résumé current for her future employability. She is also maintaining and strengthening ties with her own family of origin as a form of alternative support.

> I nurture [Giovanna's] relationship with my parents. If [Mark and I] ever split up, I'd want her to have all these people. . . . It helps to acknowledge that it's hard. Most of the time, we have our fights and our differences, but we make up quickly. But I'm the escapist: Wouldn't it be better elsewhere? But also the guilt: this beautiful house, this wonderful child, right under my nose, and I can't just be okay with it. Intellectually, I know my work is to let it go and do my life, my work, be with Giovanna—but "let it go" is so *not me*. I either do it a hundred percent or don't do it. So it's hard.

In summary, Myra has three ways of reconciling her fear of long-term commitment with Mark with her financial dependence on him. First, she has an understanding that even *long term* may just indicate a life-stage-specific relationship, tied exclusively to child rearing, so the relationship is fine for now, but she can still envision a future without it. Second, she maintains a level of emotional independence by remaining ambivalent about the relationship. This includes not getting married, but also escape fantasies and a continuously stated uncertainty over whether the relationship will last. And third, she makes just-in-case strategic plans so if the relationship does dissolve, it will have the least negative impact on her and Giovanna's lives.

The fourth way she maintains her independence from her partner is through her friendship with Giovanna. While the initial babyhood strategy of outsourcing care has continued, as Giovanna moves from being a baby to being a toddler and then a preschooler, the character of the interaction when she and Giovanna are alone together qualitatively changes. At this stage, Myra's strategy is no longer one of needs reduction—letting the baby cry or putting her into a mechanical swing or in front of a *Baby Einstein* video in a separate room. Rather, Giovanna is now old enough that they can go to Starbucks together, head out on a road trip, or do lunch at a chic patio restaurant in the city.

GIRLFRIENDS

Giovanna is a gorgeous, stylishly dressed three-year-old with long black eyelashes who talks precociously about planets and horses. She likes jazz and sushi. She has become *fun*. While her hours of nonparental care have grown, the degree of connection between Myra and Giovanna has also grown. They have become girlfriends.

This is exactly what Myra had hoped for during pregnancy. Beyond her drive to do it all by joining the motherhood club, she also desired a daughter-girlfriend. In her pregnancy interview, Myra foreshadowed the present relationship:

MR: After the amnio [testing of a fetus for genetic disorders that also reveals the baby's sex] . . . we found out it was a girl, which I secretly wanted. . . . I selfishly want a girlfriend. . . .

AV: What is your image of what your life will be like after the baby is born?

MR: Fantasies of her being a girlfriend, enjoying the same things I enjoy, traveling the world together. I'm naming her "Giovanna" since I hope she will have a love of languages.

For Myra, the fact that Giovanna is a girl appears to particularly qualify her for friendship. Myra says, "When I was pregnant, my mom said you *have* to have a girl because every woman should have a daughter. Me and my mom have traveled together, did a little shopping together, and we just *hung out* together. There's just a different quality to a girl relationship. Sons leave you. Guys tend to join the girl's family. There's a closer emotional connection with girls. . . ."

For my purposes, it is quite unfortunate that the women in this study who use the friendship strategy all have daughters. It would have been highly interesting to see how they would relate to a boy, but even those who had second children happened to have girls again. As an aside, the first-born daughter is the only child to assume the girlfriend role. The second daughter's babyhood is not nearly as difficult for the mothers, her attractive or unattractive appearance is not as highlighted, and she rarely goes on solo excursions with her mother, whereas the elder daughter continues to go on frequent dates while the younger is watched by someone else.

Among parents of adolescents, Nelson finds that seeking friendship with one's children is a class-based phenomenon. "Over and over, professional middle-class parents told me, with pride in their voices . . . that an adolescent child was their 'best friend'" whereas less privileged parents "knew well the difference between being a parent and being a friend."[20] All of the women using the friendship strategy in my study are likewise economically privileged.

With Giovanna now three, I ask Myra to tell me about her daughter, and, like the women who use the compensatory-connection and antidote strategies, she begins instead by focusing on the mother-child *relationship*: "She's the best thing that ever happened to me. It's so much fun. She's my girlfriend. We got our nails done together the other day. People say she'd be a perfect talk-show host. She's joyful, inquisitive, social, bilingual—which I'm happy about—she'll say 'sure' to almost anything you propose."

Their time together is filled with interaction. "In the car, we play word games and engage in incessant conversation. We go exploring sometimes and I let her decide which way to turn the car. It's fun!"

There are three ways motherhood makes the partner relationship less imperative for women using the friendship strategy. First, it connects them to a network of other mothers, giving them an instant social network of girlfriends. Second, these women have, in their children, more available playmates, companions, and dates than they have with their partners who are generally working long hours. Third, they use travel with their children and without their partners as a form of empowerment to assert their independence from men. They prove to themselves that, despite their financial dependence, they (and their little girlfriends) do not *need* the child's father.

CONCLUSION

Not every woman with a heavy motherload is willing to carry the load herself. In fact, a heavy motherload can cause some women to *retreat* from the responsibility and accountability they believe mothering entails. Unlike women with light motherloads who are less intimidated by mothering and who embrace coresponsibility for child care with their partners, extended family members, and paid caregivers, a woman whose motherload has grown too heavy to bear may be overwhelmed by those responsibilities.

The gravity of Myra's health-related fears and the constant monitoring it required (paired, no doubt, with the total-giving model of her own stay-at-home mother) may have added such weight to her motherload that it ultimately catapulted her in the other direction. After a stint of hypervigilance when Giovanna was first born, Myra had simply had enough. Recall that she was so concerned about fetal death that she rented a medical Doppler machine to monitor the fetus at home and receive constant reassurance there was still a heartbeat. This high level of worry was extreme among study participants. By contrast, several weeks after the birth, with her newborn sleeping on a different floor of the house, she showed an unusually low level of worry by turning off the baby monitor, considered essential by many parents to hear crying or other problems from across the house, since, she said, "you won't hear [SIDS] anyway."[21] Likewise, the fear of germs that initially led her to sanitize any toy that touched the floor and to place the baby's things on paper towels rather than directly on the counter may have also contributed to her feeling overwhelmed and retreating from responsibility. The sheer impossibility of keeping her baby safe, given such an assessment of the threat, may explain how this germ-phobic mother could hand her baby to a random checkout clerk at Bed Bath & Beyond in order to go to the bathroom in peace. Safety—as Myra originally defined it—was simply impossible, so at some point, why try?

A too-heavy motherload and the unattainability of unrealistically high demands is one way to explain the retreat from responsibility of the friendship security strategy. These women, typically raised by highly attentive stay-at-home mothers, could see the responsibility that was coming if they settled down, so they often delayed or did without marriage and delayed childbearing almost to the end points of their fertility.

Once such a woman does become a mother, she is overwhelmed by babyhood and may outsource a significant portion of the baby's care to other caregivers. During the hours when it is the mother's turn to care for the baby, her strategy is to minimize the baby's needs using videos, swings, and playpens to help promote early independence. The mother also socializes with other mothers (the woman's girlfriends) and centers her social universe there.

As the child ages, the outsourcing of care continues. However, during the mother's periods of responsibility, she replaces the needs-minimizing strategy with a girlfriend strategy. She and her child strike out into the world on their own as a duo (each other's girlfriends), travel to places near and far, and participate in cultural and recreational activities that the mother enjoys. This pairing of outsourced care and shared adventures creates a low-dependency but highly interactive and spirited relationship.

The woman who uses the friendship strategy is attempting to forge meaningful ties while still maintaining her freedom, yet each new freedom extracts a cost. Regarding work, she resists accountability to a job, boss, and work schedule. Stay-at-home motherhood frees her from labor market responsibilities and socially justifies her lack of employment. In a sense, then, *having a child liberates her from entanglements.* However, there are two major caveats. First, her freedom from paid work requires dependence on a financial provider. Second, having a child itself requires accountability. Thus, freedom from one entanglement comes at the cost of others.

Addressing the partnership entanglement, just as the child liberates the mother from paid work, the child eases the burden of partnership by lessening the mother's emotional dependence on the father. Mothers' groups create an instant network of intimacy and fun for her, giving her a world away from him. And, over time, the child-companion becomes available for chats, snuggles, dates, and road trips, effectively replacing the partner as the mother's significant other. Going on solo excursions with the child also creates a sense of empowerment that the two can manage on their own without the child's father. All of this helps the woman feel independent from the man on whom she financially depends.

The child, then, is her ticket to freedom in the realms of both work and partnership. However, before a child companion emerges, there is a period in which the mother finds herself with a preverbal, premobile, pre-*girlfriend* infant who initially offers little and has enormous around-the-clock needs. This is its own entanglement. She finds her freedom from this primarily through the paid-care labor market. However, paying for care requires money, so the mother must either reenter the labor market, which requires accountability, or rely on a working partner, which requires financial dependence—and the cycle continues again.

The friendship security strategy is, at its core, a way to maintain freedom among mothers whose security comes from *not* being tied down. These women want to experience the intimacy and grand adventure of motherhood, yet they value their independence in multiple realms. To each problematic commitment, they find a solution that, interestingly enough, comes from having a child.

These women turn the motherload on its head. For most women, having a child requires the greatest commitment of their lives. For these women, having a child is a way to maintain their freedom.

7 Light-Motherload Independence

MOTHERING WITHOUT THE ORDEAL

Society has rightly rejected the myth of domestic bliss of
the 1950s, but in so doing it has swung in the opposite
direction. The myth of the naturally competent parent
who finds fulfillment in family life has given way to a myth
of parenting as an ordeal.

—Frank Furedi

BARB WINTERS

It is Barb Winters's due date with her second child and she is struggling
unsuccessfully to get comfortable on her green corduroy sofa. Two cats
are sprawled over her, one on her legs, one over her shoulder. Her sixteen-
month-old son, Ryan, is at a family day care down the block.

From the day Ryan was born and Barb and her husband, David,
brought him home from the hospital, he has slept separately in a crib in
his own room.

> Sleep is just so important for [me]. . . . [When a baby is in the room with
> you], you literally wake up with every little burp or wiggle or hiccup. It's
> cheating yourself of good sleep . . . [a]nd if you co-sleep, you *still* have to get
> up to change their diaper every time they feed, so it doesn't even save a get-
> up. You know, we have friends who co-sleep, with a seven- and a four-year-
> old, and the couple hasn't slept with each other for four years. The father is in
> the room with the older one, and the mom is with the younger one. But with
> [my husband] David, I'm like, I want you here—*you're* my sleeping buddy!

Maintaining her partnership is important to Barb, as is generally the
case among partnered women with light motherloads.

Barb is a fund-raiser who works mostly with nonprofit and government agencies on a contract basis. She is well-known and very successful at her work, so she is continuously employed full-time and turns down more projects than she accepts. Two months after Ryan was born, she began to take him with her to networking lunches to meet with former colleagues and stay connected up, and at four months, she plunged back into her career full-time. She intends to do the same after her daughter is born.

> Four months is when they come out of that "loaf of bread" phase and start to realize that there's a world out there, and that's an okay time for me to say, "You're ready now for interaction with other children and to be exposed to the world." And it's enough time for *me*, because I kind of go batty not working. . . . When [my daughter is born], I'll be consumed with that. But at four months, you start to get your brain back, your command of the English language comes back, like *you* start being human again, and you think, wow, I could do more. . . . [With Ryan,] I was ready to go back. I needed the stimulation of adult contact.

Like other independence-oriented women with light motherloads, Barb's career is a secure, gainful realm into which she enjoys putting her energy.

Independence and self-reliance are among her top parenting values. "[I]ndependence is *huge* for me . . . [because it was] one of those things that was taught to me really young and it has served me well in getting jobs, going to college, and just everything. Like, my parents never said, 'You're going to go to college.' I just *did*. That's just what I wanted to do." We see that her definition of independence relates, in part, to a child taking charge of her own decisions. Barb attributes her valuing of independence to the fact that her parents raised her and her two sisters with a lot of freedom.

> I want to give [my children] the freedom that they need to explore their world, because I had a lot of that as a child and I really *loved* it. My dad worked in the home [making furniture] and my mom worked outside of the home, so my dad was around. But I think dads watch kids differently than moms. They're not directing your play. So [my sisters and I] would say, "We're going to build a fort in the backyard," and my dad would hand us scrap wood and hammer and nails and say, "Okay, kids, have at it!" I'm sure he kept an eye on us . . . but I really felt like we could run amok and do what we wanted. And when we stubbed our toes or skinned our knees or whatever, we'd come

running to him and he'd clean it and put Bactine on it and bandage us up and send us back out. So he was *there*, but he was not a hoverer. He wasn't like, "Okay, *now* we're going to finger paint" and "*Now* we're going to read books" and "Now it's naptime." There was none of that going on. . . . [N]obody thought *for* us. We had to be like, "What do you want to do?" "Well, what do *you* want to do?" . . . So we had the whole negotiation of play. . . . I mean, we did bad things, too: we killed bugs. But we learned about our world. My sisters also really valued that freedom of play. And we do the same thing with Ryan. Within this safe environment, we let him run amok.

In addition to letting Ryan run amok, another way she conveys independence is by not coddling him. For example, while she claims she and David never had to endure their son crying it out, Ryan does cry himself to sleep each night.

There's different baby cries, and it's so true that you learn to recognize them. There's the "hurt myself" cry where I stop whatever I'm doing and comfort him. He's very quick to recover, which I love. And there was the crying he did as a newborn when he had gas bubbles, and all we could do was hold him while he tried to work it out. . . . But sometimes, when he's tired and playing, he'll, like, drop a ball and start to cry, and I look at him and think, *Okay, that's not a tragedy.* He's just tired and can't deal with play not going the way he wants it to go. That's just a signal to me to ask if he wants a bottle. . . . [There's also] a cry that Ryan does at the end of the day [in his crib] and it's a tired cry, almost a letting go cry, and I can tell he's doing that cry because he takes his blankie and kind of muffles his own cries, and he's letting go of his day. There are times *I'm* so tired *I* cry, and I kind of liken it to that. And literally we'll look at the clock and say, "Five minutes," and he's never made it past two or three. He's unwound, had his little cry, and then he's *down* for like twelve to fourteen hours at this point. So *that* cry, I don't answer.

Like women who use the inoculation strategy, Barb does not always choose the path of minimal risk for her child. For example, she allows Ryan to eat grapes, nuts, popcorn, and other foods that were once common childhood staples but which she knows pediatricians today consider choking hazards for children less than four years old. Also, starting from the age that he could hold his own bottle, she let him feed himself his final bottle of the day in his crib, despite pediatric warnings that a bottle in bed could cause milk to pool in a baby's mouth and cause tooth decay.

"[A] lot of people tell you not to hand them a bottle, but . . . he usually drinks his bottle, throws it out of the crib, rolls over and falls asleep." Likewise, she was happy to have scores of friends and family hold him as a newborn, with extremely little concern for germs. However, these actions are not intended to toughen the child up or inure him to the hardships to come, as with the inoculation security strategy. Rather, she gives him nuts because he *likes* them and she considers them a healthy snack. She gives him his final bottle in his crib because then he goes to sleep so easily. She allowed her family and friends to hold him as a newborn because even if he catches a virus, she does not see that as a catastrophe, and she believes these people deserve to hold her son and he deserves to be held by them. Some would consider her actions irresponsible and needlessly exposing the child to risks; others would applaud her for not giving in to our zero-risk-tolerance culture regarding children and would appreciate her for taking *appropriate* minor risks when they are outweighed by the benefits. Barb says, "I simply believe that, ultimately, what is best for my son is a relaxed mom."

Having a child was not part of Barb's initial life plan due to what she saw as babies' intense needs and her desire to maintain a decent life for herself. She says, "When I was fourteen or fifteen, I babysat for a couple hours each day for a twenty-one-year-old single mom. I took her two-year-old to the park so she could have a break. But occasionally she'd leave me with the newborn, too, and that was just so freaky! [*laughs*] . . . So that totally freaked me out about baby-babies and I decided I was probably not going to have kids because of that experience." Only in college, when she discovered parenthood could be a joint venture between two adults rather than a mother-child cocoon, did it begin to appeal.

> I had a boyfriend who was totally into kids, and we were at the beach and there was this little red-headed boy pulling a giant trail of seaweed along, and my boyfriend went up to him really excitedly and explained what seaweed is and the boy just was blown away. And I thought, "Okay, so if I ever have kids, *that's* the way to do it." You get with someone who is equally enthralled with the process, and then they're *involved*, and that takes the pressure off you to be *everything* for kids. . . . Many years later, I met David, and . . . I knew he would be a really involved dad. . . . When Ryan was born, I never changed a meconium diaper because David was so on it. Since

I was nursing, I got all that together time, so changing the diapers was a way for David to get involved and have that contact.

We see how Barb nearly opted out of motherhood due to the pressure for women to be *everything* for their kids. The motherload was too great. Only when she realized that this load could be shared did she realize "*that's* the way to do it" and embark on this journey. The load is shared between her, David, and their beloved paid caregiver, along with both her own and David's parents. Once a week Ryan has a date at her parents' house, and David's parents pick Ryan up from day care twice a week to spend time with him.

Researchers have long known that poor black families have strong kin and community networks of exchange and support[1] and more recent research has shown that economic necessity, rather than culturally specific values, is the driving force of this.[2] Because economically privileged families "have a stable hold on a decent income, there is little forcing them together into [this] sort of private safety net."[3] In my own research, however, we see multiple families with decent incomes relying on kin, though it is less for goods and more for services, especially the *time* the grandparents free up by watching their grandchildren.[4]

Among the women I studied, independence-oriented women like Barb depend on extended family support more than connection-oriented women. This dependence among independence-oriented women may seem like a contradiction. However, much as we saw earlier that connection seeking with a child does not correspond to connection seeking with a partner, here we see that independence seeking with a child does not mean a woman seeks independence from her own parents (or partner, friends, or paid caregivers). In fact, part of the way she hopes to maintain a degree of independence in the mother-child relationship is that she fully expects others in the child's life to play a sizable part in child rearing. That is, she allows herself to depend on others so that the child will not have to depend exclusively on her.

This is particularly evident regarding her partner. David, like the other husbands of independence-oriented women, plays a much larger role in parenting than husbands of connection-oriented women. One piece of the explanation for this may be differences in maternal gatekeeping.[5] As we saw in chapter 3, connection seekers sometimes guard mothering as their private terrain and "hesitate to relinquish their responsibility for family work because they . . . may lose valued outcomes from doing family work."[6] Nowhere are these valued outcomes from doing family work more evident than in compensatory connection, in which the mother's caregiving is motivated by her own security needs. By contrast, women like Barb hesitate to relinquish their responsibility for *paid* work. For them, the way they maintain responsibility to (and the valued outcomes of) work in the world at large is by ensuring that motherhood is not their responsibility alone.

I do not mean to imply that maternal gatekeeping is all that separates eager fathers from their children's dirty diapers. But Barb's very conscious choice of a partner who wanted to take on fathering responsibilities, paired with her lack of proprietorship around mothering, did make a difference for her. This is not always the case for independence-oriented women, even those who solicit their partners' help. For example, Wanda Ferrina, an independence-oriented white real estate agent, says her husband just "doesn't know what the baby wants. [He] 'helps out,' but otherwise it's me." Likewise, Vivian Yee, an independence-oriented Chinese American scientist, is "not looking forward to football season, since I lose my husband."

An independence orientation is no guarantee of full partnership in parenting. To increase the likelihood of shared parenting, some women today test out prospective partners, exactly as Barb did, and only accept those who seem egalitarian. However, sociologist Kathleen Gerson finds that even those men who initially pass the egalitarian test often fall back on neotraditional arrangements once a child comes along and they are pushed to the wall by colliding work and family demands.[7] Gatekeeping is thus only one piece of the story, possibly a very minor piece, as many full-time working women want a true parenting partner and allow space for the other parent to develop his or her own ways of doing things and *still* find themselves doing the lion's share of the work. Barb, however, got lucky.

Barb and David maintain a degree of independence from each other as well. For example, they do not talk to each other by phone during the workday ("We're not *on* each other."), though she says they love to connect. "We are both extraverted, highly communicative people. We always talk." They talk together about their families and friends. They "do a lot of supportive talk—we both have friends who are dying: 'It's okay to be sad, it's okay to cry your eyes out right now.'" They also "crack each other up a lot." And since having Ryan, they talk a lot about him.

> We cannot believe how beautiful and wonderful and amazing our baby is, and we talk about him all the time. Also we're self-congratulatory 'cuz I think we've both handled parenting very well. There was this one night at three o'clock when we had to rush Ryan to the emergency room and he needed an IV, and the ER doctors said, "You guys are *so calm*." Mostly Ryan slept through it, but we were very solid, very grounded, and whatever this was, we knew we needed to take care of it. As soon as they pumped him full of liquids, that was what he needed to get him stable, and he was fine. . . . And we're like: "You really handled that well!" . . . [W]e've got all these friends becoming parents, and it's kind of natural that there's this anxiety thing that happens because you've got this new person, you've got the stress of taking care of it, but it's just so funny. [David and I] look at each other and say, "Why didn't *we* have that kind of anxiety? Why weren't we having problems and yelling at each other and having fights?" . . . We just really appreciate that, for whatever reason, it was easy for us.

In addition to verbally connecting with one another, Barb and David have a visible physical connection. I see them hug and kiss each time they greet or say good-bye. Though it took almost a year to conceive Ryan, Barb says, "Sex stayed fun." She says some couples "get into this 'chop-chop! Let's get it on and get back to our movie' thing," but she and David "always had a good time." At nine months pregnant with their second child, Barb says:

> This is the heyday of the pregnancy since the more sex you have the more cervical ripening you have getting you ready for labor. He kind of jokes around, "I'm on C.R. duty!" So we have a lot of fun with that because sex when you're this—*big*, is kind of funny and we laugh a lot about that. We're very lovey and touchy. We hold hands when we walk somewhere. . . . When we walk by each other, I pat his butt. I didn't see my own parents hugging or kissing much, but when I *did* sneak a peek, like, of them smooching in the kitchen, I'd always go, "awww." It was nice and I want my kids to know their mom and dad are into each other.

Barb's highly participatory husband, her loving and stable relationship with him, her strong and secure connection to her work and the money she earns from it (which allows them to pay for quality caregivers for their children) are all factors influencing how she parents. Furthermore, her going back to full-time work at four months and having her children sleep in a separate room from the beginning helps her preserve these valuable elements of her life while being a mother. It is a self-reinforcing cycle: her secure attachments allow her to parent in a relaxed way, and parenting that way allows her to maintain those secure attachments.

The independence she seeks for her children is decidedly not geared at helping them to survive in a malevolent or risky-seeming world; instead, she frames it as a freedom to explore, play, and express their creativity and selfhood. Furthermore, while she eagerly shares the work of parenting, her independence orientation does not appear to stem from being overwhelmed by her children's dependency.

AV: How do you feel about meeting the needs of a baby?

BW: I have never doubted my ability to be a good mom. Even though I've had *clueless* moments, like leaving the doors open to the car, I've never feared for the health or safety or needs or whatever of my baby. We're still trying to figure it all out—I think it's a discovery process—but in terms of, like, my confidence level in recognizing his needs and my comfort level in meeting those needs, all that is fine. . . . There's a certain amount of *work* and if you're going to make it a big deal, then it's a big deal. But I've never made it a big deal.

Barb also does not appear to be minimizing her children's needs. Despite the high value she places on her own and her children's independence, when asked what a baby's greatest needs are, she almost sounds like an attachment mother:

The main newborn need beyond what it needs to survive—warmth, sleep, food—is just touch. We [used to do] massage treatments to Ryan every day before he went to bed. It took about a half hour, and then we would float him in this big plastic tub: we'd put it on our kitchen island and we'd hold his neck up and float him around. I would do the massage part, and David would do the floating, and Ryan would just kind of uncurl, let his muscles take a break from holding himself together. It was so beautiful to see him just relax.... I think that level of touch helped him feel good. Gave him that until he was old enough to scoot away. He became so curious about the world and his focus just became more out rather than in. It was so intriguing to him, and he didn't look back—"Okay, see you later!" We baby proofed the house enough that he can run around and we don't have to worry about him and he can just explore his world. It's still important to him that we're around, and he comes to check in, but mostly he's just off exploring.

Although Barb feels she had a good childhood, *some* of her parenting is in response to the aspects of her childhood that she wishes had been a bit different, similar to antidote mothering (but without the sacrifice of self in order to save the child). For example, she says she is the "classic middle child with a high-profile older sister and a high-profile younger sister" with only a year between each. She says she was "the peacemaker, the diplomat, and just kind of *maintained*—the average girl, just kinda doing my thing." But at the same time, she had "all those other middle-child issues of 'Well is anybody watching *me*? Is anybody paying *attention*?'"

This history may, in part, color her goals for the little girl to whom she is about to give birth.

My whole parenting philosophy is, um, and it's really challenging ... but I really want to be able to watch and see what *she's* into.... Like, I want to know if she's a girly-girl or a tomboy, and not push her, just because *I* want ... to be the mommy that braids her hair every morning and makes her look super-cute. But if she wants to wear purple shoes and green tights and a red jumper, and I think that looks like hell, oh well. Because in the grand scheme, how important is that? ... I was taking this two-part class where the first class was preparing for the birth and the second was preparing for parenting, and the teacher asked us to think of the first time we felt really *seen* for who we are, like someone really got us. And as we went around the room and shared, everyone except me and David had their first experience of this later in life, and it was never anyone's parents who had seen them, it was like a girlfriend or a boyfriend—and some of them were still waiting. And I was just *amazed*. So my goal is that she'll be *seen* and heard, that she'll feel like she's understood....

Two weeks later, Barb is back on the same green corduroy sofa holding newborn Abby, a rosy-cheeked baby with a full head of fire-red hair. David was changing Abby's diaper when I arrived, then put the baby on Barb's lap and brought us water.

A few days earlier, I had observed the three of them out at a gathering of pregnant women (they explained that their son, Ryan, was on a date that evening with David's parents). Barb exuded an almost giddy joyfulness, her voice fast and exuberant as she told her birth story with great comic flair. For example, she explained how she was contracted to nine centimeters (almost ready to push) and had to give a urine sample, and as she squatted over the toilet, she had the urge to push and burst out, "I do *not* want to birth my baby into the toilet!!!"

Her baby, Abby, was nine days old at the time of the gathering, which is much earlier than most mothers I spoke with took their children out to social events, mostly due to a fear of germs and of the baby's underdeveloped immune system. Without asking people to wash their hands or giving any instructions, she and David passed Abby around the party so everyone who wanted to could get a chance to meet and hold her. They had packed but forgotten to bring their diaper bag, but were unflustered, and someone else loaned them a diaper when Abby needed changing. Furthermore, Barb adds, "This is *civilization*. Diapers and wipes are never more than a few blocks away."

Back at their home, with Abby twelve days old, Barb holds her for the entirety of the interview, except during diaper changes, and she breastfeeds her twice. "I like to hold her. If she's awake, I like to interact with her. I like the over-the-lap talking and patting her bum."

Barb informs me that both children sleep in the second bedroom of Barb and David's two-bedroom home and the arrangement is going well so far. When Abby wakes up in the night for feedings, Barb enters the children's room, "scoop[s] Abby up and bring[s] her out here to the chair [in the living room where she breast-feeds]. Ryan is a really good sleeper."

As Barb and I discuss the birth and how life is with a newborn, she shifts Abby's position frequently in response to little wiggles. The two times Abby fusses, Barb responds (once by putting Abby over her shoulder and walking around the living room a bit, once by breast-feeding) and the issue is quickly resolved even as Barb continues with the interview. Ryan is again at day care to maintain his routine and David, who is going back to work tomorrow, is in the kitchen making meatballs for dinner tonight. The greatest subjective impressions I have watching Barb holding and adjusting little Abby is tenderness and ease. Barb jokes that "the nurse came to our house for the well-baby and said, 'Are you guys *always* this calm?' and I said, 'Are we supposed to be *stressed out*?'"

Barb believes having a newborn has actually made their lives easier. She says, "Life is easier now that Abby's been born since the pregnancy was really restricting my movement and I couldn't wrestle and play with Ryan so much. Now I can give him more attention. We put Abby in the bouncy seat while we feed him dinner or play with him before bed."

Barb and David appear to be simply *unafraid*. Like connection-oriented women with light motherloads, they assume children are resilient and generally healthy, safe, and okay. Likewise, they do not recoil from the *work* of child raising or fear that their lives will be overwhelmed by their children. A child's testing, fussing, and even severe illness do not create a panic. They feel they can handle these things. Thus, they are not anxious about the world or about the high stakes of parenting and they have other stable, loving, and meaningful connections in their lives besides their children. That is, Barb and David carry light motherloads.

Fast-forward four months: Back on her green corduroy sofa, Barb is more playful in her interactions with Abby. She kisses and caresses, but at the same time, she does not protect Abby with her hands or carry her with tender care to ensure the position is just right. Her touch seems a little more rough and tumble, playfully jostling Abby back and forth in an upright position, a bit more like a stereotypical wrestling father with his "chip off the ol' block" baby boy dressed in a tiny baseball cap. I sense a message in her rough handling: "You are not fragile. You are strong. You are okay."

Barb is going back to work next week and is excited to "get back into the swing of things." Her daughter will go to the same family day care that Ryan attends, where the caregiver (whom Barb refers to as the teacher) is someone Barb "would trust with my life." Barb says this teacher has seen it all with children and describes her as unflappable. When Barb first went to interview her for Ryan's care, one of the day-care children had a tantrum regarding some LEGOs. The teacher helped the child back into the circle around the LEGOs and pushed some blocks closer to the child, then smiled at Barb and David and said, "You know, he's *two*. He's still finding himself." Barb was instantly in love. "That total ease and nonjudgmentalness—I thought, '*That* is the vibe I want around my son.'"

She is pleased with her son's growing independence and classifies him as "a low-needs child. We see the other kids at day care and they go to check in with their parents all the time. Ryan doesn't do that."

Fast-forward again: Abby is a two-year-old playing race cars with Ryan on the floor in the dining room. Barb yells, "Bath time!" and Abby comes running, tearing her sparkly unicorn shirt off as she runs. Ryan, age three, does not look up from his play. "Ryan, do *you* want to pick the bath color?" Ryan keeps playing with his car. "Okay, Buddy, here we go," and she picks him up. "You can bring your car." She puts both children into the bath and washes their bodies and hair within two minutes while Ryan continues to whine and does not assist her in the washing. "You want out?" she asks when she has finished rinsing him and he says yes, so she pulls him out and playfully throws a towel over his head. He plays ghost for a minute, then dries himself and goes into his room to get into his pajamas. Barb stays with Abby, singing songs and clapping hands. After fifteen minutes, she dries and dresses Abby. Then she and Abby join David, who is reading to Ryan on the green sofa. After the book, David gets up to make popcorn and then he does dishes while Barb snuggles with the children on the sofa. They all eat popcorn and watch a ten-minute video about two sibling bunnies. When the popcorn is finished, Ryan lays his head on Barb's lap and she strokes his hair for the duration of the video. Abby still has some energy and is swinging her legs up and down while watching the video. When the video ends, Barb kisses Ryan's cheek and says, "Goodnight, Sweetie," and he goes off to brush his teeth and go to bed. Barb carries Abby into the kitchen, pours her a sippy cup of milk to take to bed, puts her into her crib next to Ryan's bed, and flips off the light.

The house is then quiet. I am a little perplexed, in a sort of Twilight Zone, being a mother of a toddler myself with whom things are just a *little* different at bedtime. Barb pours us a couple glasses of Merlot and we begin our interview.

MARIA CASTILLO

Since women with light motherloads do not draw on independence or connection as tools for security production and since they do not adhere to rigid, well-defined models of correct mothering, they sometimes defy classification as independence oriented or connection oriented. Much as Barb's frequent holding of her children and use of baby massage evoke a connection orientation alongside her strong verbalized commitment to independence, Maria Castillo's parenting is likewise complex and difficult to classify.

Maria emigrated from Guatemala twenty years ago, as an adolescent, along with her entire family. She was the fifth of six children and "came from a poor family, but it was always happy." Her mother was "a very clever woman, very smart, and she had her own business. A merchant, she would buy things and resell them. She always worked from home so she could keep an eye on [the children]." Maria's parents split up shortly after she was born (and then her mother had another child from a different man with whom she did not partner) and her mother raised the six children as a single working woman. "Since I didn't have a father figure . . . I just don't know the difference if I had one. So I can't say, 'Oh, it was awful,' because childhood for me was really, really happy . . . with a lot of people, a lot of friends. We didn't have an extended family—my mom was never close to them—but we always had neighbors and friends who replaced them, even someone I called Grandma—tons of friends from there that I consider my family though we weren't related."

Maria regards her mother with the highest esteem and feels that she was very well loved as a child.

> I was breast-fed for longer than a year, and I slept with my mom. All of us kids roomed in when we were little, not even in a cradle next to the bed; we were always with her in bed. She said that was the best because she never had to get out of bed, and she was never sleep-deprived since we could just eat when we were hungry, and she was happily asleep. I imagine I was held a lot. One of my first memories I can remember is that every evening to put me to sleep, my mom would walk me around the park, you know, carried me, and by the time we were walking back home, I was already asleep. Sometimes she would just walk half a block and I was out and she would come back home from that. And also, my older sister is ten years older than me, and she's very nurturing. She always did my hair.

During Maria's childhood, Guatemala was engaged in a civil war and one of her brothers fought in the resistance movement. When he became blacklisted and targeted for capture and possible execution, he was granted asylum in the United States. Maria says, "Then one Christmas he said, 'I'm coming back [to Guatemala]; I can't spend another Christmas alone!' So [the whole family] made a trip to visit him on Christmas, and we never went back. Once we came here, my mom never worked outside the house. My brothers and sisters supported her."

Maria worked her way through college in the United States and became an assistant at a hospice where she eventually became the manager. She oversees hospice operations and also trains family members of critically diagnosed people to care for them at home. She loves her very demanding work, helping families through an immensely difficult time in their lives, and gives her all to this full-time job where, in addition to her regular work hours, she is on call sixteen hours a day, four days a week.

AV: Is your salary necessary for your family?

MC: We definitely could get by without it and have the same rhythm of lifestyle. Work just gives me meaning and helps me stay current.

AV: Have you considered being a full-time mom?

MC: No. I think I probably would get bored. Maybe with another child not so much—but probably still I would get bored with the routine. . . . I would miss the interaction with adults [that I get at work]—maybe I would do volunteer work. And I really like what I do, the hours are flexible, I get time off whenever I want to, and it's so independent, the work that I do.

With her due date imminent, she stopped working last Thursday and plans to go back full-time when the baby is around three or four months old. Her sister will be the child's caregiver when Maria returns to work, revealing again the welcomed interdependence with kin of women who orient their parenting around independence.

She lives in an upscale four-thousand-square-foot home with a built-in stone-lined pool in a wealthy gated community. She has been married for two years to Steven, an attorney who has made partner.

With the world, [Steven is] shy, but with me, he's like a different person. We're best friends, so he tells me things he wouldn't dare tell anybody else, or . . . how he acts with me, he wouldn't dare be that way with anybody else . . . and for me, that's very special. We have a lot of values in common: family, as well as independence. We see each other as an individual who has needs, and therefore we're going to do certain things the way we want to, but at the same time we're—we can be together and we can be apart.

Her discussion about the specialness of her relationship with Steven and her recognition of his needs is typical of independence-oriented mothers who generally place greater priority on the romantic couple relationship than connection-oriented mothers do.

Maria has enjoyed pregnancy immensely. "At the eleventh week, I felt her move, and it was so real and like, 'Oh my God, this is amazing!' It felt like she was running inside me, and I could feel it. It made me so excited and made the pregnancy really real." She relates to the baby a lot, even *in utero*, and Maria characterizes herself as "a very physical person. I do a lot of touching, so I'm constantly rubbing her inside my belly." She also "talk[s] to the belly about everything, especially when I'm by myself. I let her know what I'm doing, how I'm feeling. When I'm [driving] back from work, I talk with her, walk her through the day. Since I'm pregnant, I'm never alone."

In contrast with the vast majority of other women in this study, Maria has not read expert books about birth or parenting. Given copious nieces and nephews, she says, "I know what to do with a child so I don't feel I need instructions." She did pick up one pregnancy magazine in the waiting room of her obstetrician and began to read an article.

> [It was] about care of a newborn, and to me, it sounds so basic, but I guess it's for people who have never been exposed to babies, and for them, it could be *frightening*. I didn't realize that until I read it. All my sisters just had children and that's it. There's no anxiety about knowing what to do. It's just like people *know* what to do, so [the idea that parenting could be frightening] never crossed my mind. [In the article] there's just . . . this "perfect." But things are the way they are and sometimes they just come and they're perfectly fine and you don't have to do anything about it; it just happens.

Thus, the one expert article she read showed her that parenting could be *frightening* for people—an idea that had never crossed her mind before. Furedi finds that parents are frightened by the expert culture that maintains that "children cannot cope with adverse experiences" and that unpleasant encounters will "scar children for life."[8] Because of that, "parents are directed to adopt a state of high alert" in attempts to ward off such adversity.[9] But Maria does not seek this adversity-free perfection. Instead she sees it as perfectly fine to take things the way they are.

When Maria does seek counsel, it is from her family rather than from books. She talks, she says, "with my sisters, just wanting to know their experiences. And I talk with my mom a lot . . . [but] she hasn't come to me giving advice: 'You should do this.' When I inquire, you know, looking for information, she says: 'You know what to do!'"

The message of her primary social network, her family, is not that of a narrowly defined correct mothering guided by experts. Rather, it is a wide acceptance that she is a competent mother who will be adequately guided by the baby's needs and her own common sense.

Maria is realistic about how a baby will change her life, but not particularly concerned about it. "I know that it's a lot of work, and I know you have to make adjustments in your life. I'm not scared of those changes; I know they're going to happen, just part of the process. It's just one big excitement—there's going to be a lot of happiness."

Unlike many mothers, there is no sense of fear in her anticipation of motherhood, no concerns about the fragility or at-risk-ness of babies, or about being overwhelmed by her responsibilities in dealing with those. What she most looks forward to is simply "having someone like, like a little miracle that happens out of nothing, you know, out of love that just grew and developed and then you have this little thing, you have a *person* that came like, wow, out of nowhere."

Her primary concern is for Steven.

> I worry about him more than myself about the adjustment [to parenthood]. I spoil him completely and he just adores that, and there's going to be a point where I'm going to need help or where he's going to come second because I'm taking care of the baby. Right now he's the baby. I take care of him and everything, which I don't mind; I love it. Once I go back to work, we're going to have help, so hopefully that will balance that, kind of shifting one thing for another. I won't do laundry, but I'll be with the baby.

Regarding the birth, Maria acknowledges the impossibility of perfect control. She says, "I would like things to happen as naturally as possible, but I don't disregard the possibility that things could go out of my control and that I would need some interventions that I would prefer not to have done. But I'm okay with that, you know, because I feel that as long as the baby comes safely, if things need to happen to protect me and the baby, then things happen." Things did indeed go out of her control a week later when their daughter, Rosa, was born. Rosa would not descend in the birth canal and her heart rate was irregular. Maria says, "It was very hard for Steven, because every time I had a contraction, her heart rate on the monitor went down. He was like, 'Oh my gosh, *this cannot happen!*' . . . It was so terrible for him." In the end, Maria had an emergency C-section, and it turned out the umbilical cord was wrapped twice around Rosa's neck. Without some kind of intervention, there was simply not enough length for the baby to emerge without strangling herself.

Maria remembers the birth with mixed emotions, but mostly joy. "When she was born, she was so, so healthy. I was so happy when I heard her strong cry from the other side of the [C-section] curtain. That is what I was waiting for."

What Maria describes as "so, so healthy" is what others might describe as horrifically frightening. The doctors also discovered that Rosa had a blood problem since Maria's blood had crossed the placenta, as well as jaundice, and her temperature fell dangerously low. She was admitted to the neonatal intensive care unit and put under lights and heating lamps.

AV: Did that whole hospital experience make you extra cautious with her, or make you wonder if she was going to be okay?

MC: Not really, not myself, because—well, when we got home, our heater upstairs was broken, and it was during that time with that really bad storm and it was *so cold*. So we brought the mattress into the library and had a fire going in there and we had a heater right next to us—it was really nice. Then I didn't have to go up the stairs. So she slept with me, you know; I had her next to me in the bed so she could stay warm, and to tell the truth, I think I liked that better. [*Note: The sleeping plan had originally been to put Rosa in a cradle next to the bed for the first few weeks, then in a crib in a separate nursery. They adjusted this due to Rosa's difficulty in regulating her temperature. Once she could maintain her own*

*temperature better, after three nights of co-sleeping, they did move
her to the cradle.*] It was fun and easy [to co-sleep] and my sister
slept right next to me. Actually, everybody took turns: my mom,
my sister, and Steven. And the first night, she would not take the
breast, but I didn't want to take her back to the doctors because I
knew she just needed her fluids. My sister said it would be easier
for her to drink through a bigger hole, and I thought that made
sense, so I sent my husband out for a breast pump. I pumped and
then we fed her two and a half ounces over an hour. The next
time, she took the breast fine so we didn't have to do that again. I
did set an alarm, though, to go off every three hours so I could
feed her since she really needs her fluids [necessary to overcome
jaundice]. I didn't plan to do that—I thought it would be the other
way around with *her* waking *me* up—but it made me realize and I
told her, "Baby, I would never get upset if you wake up in the
night and need to eat and you're keeping me awake, because this
is a reminder that I'd rather have that than you not *wanting* to
eat."

Notice that the explanation Maria gives for not being particularly cautious with Rosa is that, during the phase when her baby was still unable
to regulate her own temperature and there was a freezing storm and a
broken heater upstairs, there nevertheless was a solution at hand. In fact,
the fire, the space heater, and Maria sleeping with the baby all worked
together to solve the problem of Rosa's thermal regulation in a way that
was cozy and pleasant. Rosa's *temperature* was the problem, and Maria
did not generalize that to a more wide-ranging sense of fragility in her
child. Notice, too, that Maria did not choose to take her baby to the doc-
tor when the baby failed to eat and did not see it as necessary to confer
with an expert to decide how to hydrate her. Rather, she thought her sister's idea to give the milk in the easiest possible way for the baby to drink
made sense, and she went with her instinct. Again, Maria did not interpret the hydration problem as an indicator that Rosa was fragile or
unhealthy. She just needed more fluids.

For the first two months, Maria had a number of female family members living with her and assisting: her mother, her sister, and two of her

nieces. She did not do any housework, cooking, or shopping for the first six weeks and was simply taken care of. It was a festive environment and Maria relished this time with her baby.

AV: What are your various emotional responses to having a baby?

MC: Oh my gosh, I just can't get enough of her. Every time I see her, my heart just *melts* and I just want to grab her and pick her up. That's the other thing; when she's around, I just want to hold her, have her next to me, and I'm constantly, constantly kissing her.

AV: Has that changed over time since she was born?

MC: That's how it's been since the beginning. The only difference is now I'm a little rougher; I squeeze her. When she was a newborn, I was more gentle, kissing her softer.

One of the biggest adjustments for Maria as a mother has been to adjust her pace of life. Already during pregnancy, she said, "One of the most difficult things for me is to have to slow down and be able to rest, even just a half an hour, 'cuz I'm a high-energy person, always on the go, another little project. Now everything takes me twice as long as before."

This adjustment continues as a mother: "Twice since Rosa has been born, I've noticed I'm rushing her, like rushing through a feeding so we can get out the door to the store. Both times, I became aware of how it was no longer fun and it was out of rhythm with Rosa. So I decided consciously to slow down, and that I didn't *need* to get to the store ten minutes faster."

At this point, the shift to a slower pace is nearly complete. In certain ways, Maria's mothering is very accommodating and child-centered. "If Rosa wants to engage with me, then I'm more than happy to stop brushing my hair or whatever in order to hold her and be with her. It's just not a big deal to keep to my own schedule, particularly when we are alone together. I'd rather be with Rosa than do just about anything else." Yet both Maria and Steven want Rosa to be adaptable and, in this way, their parenting is more *adult*-centered. "I never tell people to be quiet during Rosa's naps—and with the house full of talkative Latin women, there is a lot of noise at all times! And we don't keep to any particular schedule. . . . I sometimes bring her home late from evenings at friends and we plan to start using our cabin in the Sierras soon, and we don't want to have to leave at three on Sundays in order to get Rosa back for bedtime." Instead, she wants to keep to her original timing of getting home around eleven, and just let Rosa learn to sleep anytime, anywhere, with any noise level, and in any condition whenever she is sleepy.

Maria is so relaxed about Rosa's sleep, in fact, that after talking with me for two hours, she is impatient for me to see Rosa, who had fallen asleep in the bouncy seat upstairs just moments before I arrived. So Maria brings me upstairs, picks Rosa up, and wakes her so we can all be together. We talk and play with Rosa for a half hour, despite Rosa still showing signs of sleepiness—yawning and rubbing her eyes. Maria believes that if Rosa still wants to sleep more, she can do so later.

Despite her minimal concern for disturbing her baby's sleep, Maria does seem attuned to her baby's preferences. She shows me how Rosa most likes to be held. "She likes to have her legs free—she has never enjoyed being swaddled or to have her leg movement confined in any way. Even in the womb during the labor, she seemed to be trying to go spread eagle. And she likes to face out into the action." At three months, Maria generally holds Rosa up against her own torso, supporting her under her bottom with one hand, with the other hand stabilizing from the neck and shoulders, facing out. She sways at times, pats, and jiggles from this basic position. She kisses her a lot on the cheek and head, and talks to her in baby talk. "I love to hold her," she says. "Unless I am busy doing something such as cooking or cleaning, I would prefer to hold Rosa, and even when I put her down, I have her close by and continue to talk with her nearly continuously. I'm a talkative person and I enjoy having someone to talk to. I tell Rosa about every day, if it is sunny or rainy, and what I'm doing, like in the shower I say, 'Now I'm putting the shampoo on my head; ooh, it's dripping in my eyes, I better rinse!' It's fun."

Maria believes it runs in her family to just know how to calm a baby, how the baby wants to be held, and what kinds of voices will make the baby happy. By contrast, she says, "Steven has very little of this natural instinct." Maria then demonstrates to me how Steven holds the baby (upright and away from his body), and Rosa immediately begins to fuss. Maria then comforts her, whereupon she shows me another Steven hold (sideways, facing up, again away from her body), which again causes the baby to fuss. She does not seem to mind using Rosa as a prop to show me what Rosa does not like. Maria appears confident that if her baby is not content for a few seconds, she will be fine as soon as Maria responds appropriately to her needs.

Despite her holding style being more comforting to Rosa than her demonstration of Steven's hold, Maria is not physically gingerly with Rosa and handles her "more roughly than Steven." She is also somewhat clumsy and "accidentally bonk[s] Rosa sometimes" when she is carrying her around. This does not overly concern her and she just apologizes to Rosa and calms her tears with words and hugs. By contrast, she describes Steven as an alarmist regarding Rosa's health and well-being. He "thinks a runny nose or a five-minute bout of crying calls for a trip to the ER. I try to tell him those things are normal and fine."

Maria's actions—waking a sleeping child or making noise during the child's nap, using her as a prop to demonstrate positions she does not like, maintaining an adult schedule and having Rosa adapt to that, not being overly concerned about accidentally bumping into things while holding the child—could all potentially be seen as evidence of maternal insensitivity. Yet at the same time, Maria's ability to calm her child is highly developed.

I suggest that it is *because* Maria is so confident about her ability to calm her baby that she is less anxious about her baby's minor upsets. She believes in her own ability to take care of her child. Furthermore, she does not adhere to the one-false-move-and-you've-scarred-your-child-for-life school of thought and, in keeping with other women with light motherloads, she believes her child is robust, adaptable, and generally okay. Even after a potentially very scary birth experience in which Rosa's monitor revealed heart-rate problems, and Rosa's blood problems and jaundice, which required intensive care, Maria saw her as strong and healthy because of the strength of her cry. Maria heeded that cry as Rosa's direct daughter-to-mother message of okayness, rather than taking the monitors and diagnoses as the correct indicators of Rosa's overall health.

Parenting is simply not an ordeal for Maria, who was born into a different cultural context and who has steered clear of what she sees as the expert-propagated US cultural model of frightening parenting. She says, "When I think of people having a baby thinking it's going to become so hectic—it really *doesn't*. You just have to drop the things that aren't so important in your life, and then it's the same."

Two years later, Maria's sister is living with the family and caring for Rosa while Maria is at work. When Rosa wakes in the night, she calls out, "Tía! Mamá!" as the mothering role is split down the middle between mother and aunt. Other women from Maria's extended family also frequently visit and actively participate in child care. As with Barb, the care work in Maria's family is truly shared.

At this point, Rosa is a toddler and is into *everything*. She swats at the large potted plant every time she goes by and demands to go outside when it starts raining. She is both independent (happily plays by herself, feeds herself, and dresses herself) and connecting (very talkative and prefers to play in whatever room her mother or Tía are in). "[S]he has a strong will. When she wants something, she's very tenacious. She will do whatever it takes. And if we automatically say no, then she'll start screaming angrily. . . . Sometimes I want to laugh, but I don't. So I tell her very patiently, 'That's not nice,' so I try to explain why she can't do that. She never frustrates me. I've never been frustrated with her. I guess I have enough help or a lot of patience, so I can distract her . . . and she's fine."

Rosa hit her developmental milestones early. She used a fork at ten months, spoke fifteen words by eleven months, and began walking at just nine months.

AV: [Where] does she tend to move towards?

MC: *EVERYWHERE!* The first day she started to walk, she started running, and you know that she's going to lose her balance and end up on the floor. And she would run to me with her arms up, and I think she knew that she was *free* and she would smile and raise her arms and go, "Yay!!!" She's very expressive.

Being with Maria, I am struck—as I am when I am with Barb Winters— by how different she is than most of the women I followed for this research. It is unusual to encounter a mother for whom mothering is not an emergency, for whom fear is not a prominent driving force in how to mother, and who exudes a belief that she and her baby are both fine.

As a secure, nonanxious mother with a light motherload, she may do things with which other mothers would take issue. She parodies her husband's caregiving. She is rougher with her child than many would feel comfortable with. Her adult-centered schedule may be inconsiderate of some of her child's needs for regularity. I do not mean to convey that she or Barb or J. T. (the connection-oriented woman with a light motherload whom we met in chapter 4) or the other women with light motherloads are somehow better mothers than the mothers whose love and protectiveness drives them to enhance the family's security through a more strategic mother-child relationship. Light-motherload mothering is simply not driven by fear or insecurity.

We might suspect that the increased perception of societal insecurity in our culture is the whole story of what is causing the heavy motherload. Yet Maria was raised by a single mother of six—in a family with little money that fled from a war-torn country when Maria's brother was a target for assassination. Maria has seen more than her share of physical danger, economic insecurity, and the results of divorce within her own family of origin, yet she carries a light motherload.

An alternative hypothesis to explain a light motherload is that some women's more moderate expectations of themselves may result from lower mothering standards. However, Maria's admiration for her own mother—who was the family's sole breadwinner yet still managed to hold her six children as they fell asleep and breast-feed them into their second years—indicates her regard for rather high standards.

How, then, can we explain Maria's light motherload, given her high mothering standards and an upbringing seemingly riddled with insecurity? One clear difference between Maria and most mothers in this study is her low exposure to advice literature. Maria had never heard of parenting advice books in Guatemala and was shocked to see how ubiquitous they are in the United States. She was also shocked to see the American depiction of frightening parenting, especially compared to her family's assumption of maternal competency—women using their own minds and hearts to figure out what to do with their children in most circumstances. In general, women in this study who have the lightest motherloads are also those who have the least to do with expert parenting literature and with medical experts.[10]

Additionally, Maria, like other women with light motherloads, has help. She has a whole flock of Latinas in her family who are willing and able to be there for her and the baby. Her sister moved in with her in order to coparent. Barb has both her own and David's parents living nearby and regularly caregiving, in addition to a deeply trusted paid caregiver. Both Barb and J. T. have very hands-on partners who are fully engaged in parenting. These women are not alone in their responsibility for their children.

Finally, Maria's relationship with her child does not appear to detract from the other elements of her life that give her security and meaning. She generally maintains and nurtures these other elements—such as partnership, other relationships, and meaningful work—alongside nurturing her baby.

Women with light motherloads, like all mothers, face challenges—their babies teethe, get sick, and wake up crying at night. Yet they show an acceptance of these occasional bumps, a sense of humor about their own mistakes, and a playfulness about the (shared) work of mothering. Whether they are connection oriented, independence oriented, or truly dual in their orientations—and even when they do extraordinary amounts of mothering work—women with light motherloads simply do not experience the same level of burden in their mothering as women with heavy motherloads.

8 Conclusion

Across the social spectrum, most parents feel that they are
parenting on their own desert island. . . .

—Margaret Nelson[1]

We hear a lot about today's over-the-top intensive mothers or, more sym-
pathetically, how the expectations of motherhood have become unrealistically high. Academics, bloggers, social commentators, and our own acquaintances all seem to recognize that a generation ago, mothering was not
as stressful or labor-intensive and the mothering enterprise did not inspire
the same fear and intimidation. But key questions remain unanswered.

1. *Why is mothering such an ordeal in the twenty-first century,* for the
   rich and poor alike, for single as well as married women, and for whites,
   African Americans, Chinese Americans, Latinas, and others? What has
   changed since the 1970s to explain this intensity? Mothers are working
   for pay and have plenty of other things to do with their time and energy,
   so why get so fixated on mothering now? We lack powerful data-driven
   understandings of why this is happening.

2. *What various forms does this intensity take?* Probably the most
   common image of intensive mothering is of a white, middle-class,
   heterosexual, US-born woman racing her children to too many activities,
   keeping them indoors so they won't be snatched by a kidnapper, or
   texting them about how to deal with a friend's potentially slighting
   comment. While there are indeed such mothers, there are many other

mothers whom we would also have to call intensive but who look and act quite differently. Their mothering strategies have been understudied. Annette Lareau and Margaret Nelson have begun this important research on differences in mothering by demonstrating that social class is one pivot on which a number of strategic differences turn.[2] However, my findings reveal great within-class variation that has been previously unaccounted for. Additionally, I find other pivots, such as job insecurity and partnership insecurity, that overlap with class only partially and that profoundly affect mothering expectations and strategies. Furthermore, these insecurities may reflect more than we can ascertain by looking at a person's current circumstances, such as their social class or marital status, since one's insecurities include fears of what *might* occur, not simply what *is* occurring. What varieties of intensive mothering do these different types of fear bring forth?

3. *What are the outcomes of these various forms of high-intensity mothering?* Prior discussions of consequences have been mostly speculative. Some observers suggest today's highly involved mothering is making life increasingly demanding, hectic, and stressful for mothers and their families. Some suggest intensive mothering (undifferentiated in any way) is to blame for our current generation of overindulged, easily bored, un-launchable children. However, to truly reveal the consequences and how they differ among women adopting different strategies, we need to follow mother-child relationships over time to see how the dynamics actually play out.

4. *Are there less stressful alternative ways of mothering?* Are there mothers—living in the same place and time and equally privileged or underprivileged—who do *not* have unrealistically high expectations of the mother-child relationship? If so, what gives these women their special capacity for moderation? And how is family life different when mothers are not the sole security guards?

This book addresses all of these unanswered questions regarding high-intensity, high-expectations mothering—why it is happening, the different ways it can manifest, its consequences, and its alternatives—through developing an understanding of the motherload.

1. *Why is mothering such an ordeal in the twenty-first century?*

I argue that the motherload—the expectation that the mother-child relationship can produce security—has gotten heavier. The intensification of mothering we have seen in the last four or five decades is the intensification of *protection*, which takes a variety of forms. The woman in public housing struggling to shield her child from violence, the stay-at-home mother uncomfortably married to a high-earning spouse and seeking a best friend in her child, and the career woman obsessed with germs, toxins, accidents, or child abduction may look very different on the surface and would seem to have very different motivations. In fact, they are each trying to do the same thing: create security. They all perceive the world as threatening or insecure, they all want to make it better for themselves and their families, and they all are attempting to do so through the perceived power of the mother-child relationship.

Several factors align in contemporary American society to propel these high expectations of mother-child security, a sort of perfect storm of social, psychological, and economic pressures adding weight to the mother-load. These pressures are: (1) an increased perception of economic, social, and physical security threats (some of which really have become more threatening and some of which may only seem so); (2) the decreased availability of personally or publically available safety nets to deal with these threats; (3) a culture that trumpets the importance of the impressionable years and sees children as breakable if they are improperly handled; and (4) advice literature that places responsibility for how children turn out squarely upon the shoulders of the parents, especially the mothers. In simplest terms, threat perception is up, alternative safe havens are down, children's lives are at stake, and the mother is responsible for making all this better.

The following recaps each of the pieces of this argument: First, there is the climate of insecurity. Changes in the economy in the past several decades, more bankruptcies and foreclosures, fiercer competition for college admissions and jobs, the spike in the divorce rate in the 1970s, nuclear proliferation, large-scale terrorist acts, and an increasing globalization of environmental risk are stacked on top of a cultural shift toward greater risk consciousness and the social amplification of certain dangers.[3] The result is an increasing preoccupation with crime and physical safety and increasing anxiety over the possibility of losing one's job, health, or relationships. Taken together, these objective and subjective risks make up the threat.

Attachment theory predicts that a sense of threat will send most people on quests for safe havens. However, many women find few places to turn.

A romantic partner is one possibility. Indeed, a solid partnership has remarkable protective powers and women who are able to find emotional solace with their partners prior to child rearing tend to carry light motherloads. Yet dubiousness about heterosexual marriage and divorce anxiety make partnership an iffy bet for many women.

Paid work and financial independence from men are other forms of security many women seek, and given the volatility of romantic relationships, this quest often takes on great emotional vehemence. However, in the flexible workplace of the new economy, jobs themselves are increasingly volatile or temporary, and layoffs are of greater concern than they were in the past. This destabilizes the rock of financial independence on which millions of women landed in the 1970s, a time when the divorce rate also reached its all-time high. So the solution to one form of insecurity has itself become insecure.

With dwindling faith in either partnership or work as lasting sources of security, there is a great need for *something* to hold onto. In this book, I argue that there is one saving relationship held apart from the rest: that of mother and child. Whereas children were ascribed great preciousness with the advent of industrial capitalism,[4] the new preciousness in the postindustrial risk society is not children themselves but rather the mother-child relationship. This relationship is not subject to divorce, layoff, or dissolution due to declining common interests. And, perhaps by attrition, this one remaining precious connection can seem like one's only guaranteed bond. It can therefore be loaded with expectations to remedy a world of ills and make everything better. This expectation is the motherload.

The reason why *women* are the ones left in charge of dealing with insecurity—that there is a motherload but no comparable fatherload—is partly due to what sociologist Kathleen Gerson calls the unfinished revolution: egalitarian family ideals but neotraditional realities in which women remain primarily responsible for parenting.[5] It is also partly the result of popular psychology's infusion into our culture through parenting advice books, expert Web sites, self-help talk shows, mothering magazines, medical doctors, and other sources of authoritative knowledge. Popular psychology's premises are loosely based on Freud, who traced patients' maladaptive behaviors back to maternal roots, and on Bowlby, who established the link between children's security and how they were mothered. Both of these central figures attributed incredible determinative powers to early motherhood.[6]

Interestingly, "the assumption that early caregiving experiences foreshadow adult development is quite controversial in contemporary psychology,"[7] so the science itself is changing—but not its popularized version. The seeds of maternal determinism have been sown beyond the halls of academia and have taken root in the taken-for-granted assumptions one finds throughout the cultural landscape in mothers' groups, grocery stores, hospitals, and homes.

The explanation of the increasing motherload in the last several decades is thus multistranded and includes a risk society that focuses on potential threats, a perceived shortage of reliable resources to deal with those threats, a sense of children's extreme vulnerability in the early years, and a belief in individual maternal control reinforced by an explosion of expert-driven models of correct mothering. This explanation is drawn from the testimony of the mothers I interviewed but also corroborated, strand by strand, by other research. Weaving these strands together, we see why contemporary mothering is so intensive: it is thought to bring security to both children and their mothers.

2. *What various forms does this intensity take?*

Most of the mothers in this study carry heavy motherloads. They take on the weighty challenge of privately remedying social uncertainties by drawing on the mother-child relationship to scaffold together a new edifice of security. How this looks varies widely. If you ask a hundred people to do something that is clearly possible, there may be convergence around the easiest or most obvious way to do it. If you ask them to do the impossible, their efforts will likely call forth more ingenuity and may diverge considerably. Solving the problems of society through a single just-right relationship is impossible. Looking in from the outside, it may seem absurd that a woman would take on *personal responsibility*—simply by mothering in the right way—for dealing with such external or uncontrollable threats as terrorism, economic insecurity, and her child's (or her own) future divorce. There is clearly no way to create certainty even for one person in an uncertain world. However, sheer impossibility is not a deal breaker and, in this book, we see that many women try and they try hard. They cannot stop the nuclear blast, but they can live far from an urban center. They cannot make their own lives secure in every way, but they can create little people who will remain their children through the thick and thin of divorce or layoff. They cannot ensure their daughters will never get divorced, but they can help them become career women so they will be financially okay if they ever do divorce. And if all else fails, they can redirect their anxieties toward a single, potentially conquerable enemy, such as germs or emotional abandonment, and fight all their wars on that front. They can focus on their babies' pacifiers falling on the ground or their babies' pain at being set down in their cribs—and at least right *that* wrong.

Every mother is unique, yet the methods by which mothers cope with a sense of threat fall into several basic patterns. In broad strokes, this book illustrates five security strategies women draw on, either singly or in combination, in their efforts to extract the most security possible from the mother-child relationship:

SHIELDING STRATEGY

In this form of classic protectiveness, mothers focus on their children's physical safety and use the mother-child relationship as an all-encompassing cocoon to separate their children from harmful influences, physical threats, and information about negativity in the world.

ANTIDOTE STRATEGY

These mothers focus almost exclusively on emotional security and attempt to create such an intensive connection with their children that the mother-child relationship will suffice in and of itself for what they see as their children's security needs. This relationship is intended to serve as an internalized antidote for presumably ubiquitous ills.

COMPENSATORY-CONNECTION STRATEGY

Mothers who use this strategy magnify the connection with their children to such a degree that this one seemingly secure connection can appear to fill their otherwise insecure attachment-scapes. This allows the women to feel more subjectively secure despite meeting nearly the entirety of their own attachment and security needs through a single bond.

INOCULATION STRATEGY

Mothers who inoculate attempt to protect children by intentionally exposing them to risk in gradually increasing doses, toughening them up, and teaching them how to confidently navigate a threatening world on their own.

FRIENDSHIP STRATEGY

These mothers find their own security through independence (even if financially dependent on men), first by avoiding direct caregiving as much as possible during their children's infancies, then by turning their children into friends, which reduces the women's emotional dependence on men.

On the surface, these security strategies are completely different from one another. Letting one's six-month-old go headfirst down the slide or eat dirt is different from either gating the stairs or becoming one's toddler's best friend. Underneath these differences, however, the dynamic remains the same: the mother feels the world is insecure and she takes on that load of insecurity with utter determination to counter it through the power of a properly executed mother-child relationship.

Since mothers cannot, in fact, make it all better and create ultimate security, they are often forced do the next-best thing—to try to create a *feeling* of security. At least in the realm of feelings, they stand a chance. To accomplish this feeling, mothers often turn a laser focus toward a security realm in which harm is statistically improbable (such as child abduction or SIDS) or toward one they feel confident in addressing (such as exposure to certain toxins, or an emotional sense of security rooted in the mother-child relationship). In both cases, this realm takes on dire importance and acts as a sort of stand-in for all the other forms of insecurity.

3. What are the outcomes of these various forms of high-intensity mothering?

Do these strategies work? For all the stress and responsibility they bring, do they at least provide the intended security? The short answer is no. The unintended consequence of viewing the mother-child relationship as the single safe harbor for both mothers and children is the *perpetuation* of insecurity in three realms: the personal, the familial, and the political.

On the personal level, by placing all of their security chips on the mother-child relationship, women are sometimes shortchanging other aspects of their lives. This is especially the case when a woman's sense of alarm is displaced from, say, the economic realm to a threat that feels less probable or more surmountable, such as germs, child abduction, or emotional abandonment. An overzealous focus on combating such threats, either on behalf of one's child or oneself, may make one's life feel better or more secure in the short term, but often actually makes it less secure. For example, a woman may drift from former friendships and involvements because she sees her own emotional security as so tightly bound to the mother-child relationship. Or an unemployed woman may cease her job search because the anxiety of that search can be avoided by an amplified focus on some other security issue, such as the child's physical safety. The motherload can thus interfere with a woman creating a stable ground on which she (and her family) can stand.

On the familial level, the motherload can destabilize family relationships. Just as fragile partnerships that do not provide much security often increase the security women expect in the mother-child relationship, a heavy motherload can, in turn, divert a woman from the work needed to build or maintain a strong adult partnership. If she feels that her security needs are already met through motherhood or if she is exclusively focused on her child's security, she may not seek or have room for an emotionally open relationship with her partner. Thus, a heavy motherload can compromise partnerships.

Furthermore, a heavy motherload can destabilize the mother-child relationship. In some cases, the woman tries so hard to give her children security at her own expense that she ends up feeling resentment and rage, which can lead to erratic and volatile behavior with her children. In some cases, she holds onto her children so tightly for her own security that she experiences their growth into autonomous personhood as a form of abandonment from which she may self-protectively withdraw. In still other cases, she may be so daunted by her expectations of the responsibilities of motherhood that she backs away from her children from the onset.

We know from history that when people disproportionally direct their security needs onto a single relationship, it destabilizes that relationship.[8] Recall that during the Victorian era, when kin ties weakened and middle-class women largely stopped working, women's broad base of security condensed into the male-female couple, which became romanticized in a wished-for intimacy intended to make up for all that women had lost. So how did marriage fare this projected centrality? Marriage could not take the pressure. Divorce rates immediately began to increase as the symbol failed to live up to the high expectations put upon it. This failure of expectations should give us pause as we again shift the center of security and importance, this time onto the mother-child relationship. If the mother-child relationship fails to live up to the life-redeeming expectations put upon it, what correlate of an increasing divorce rate will take the pressure off *this* relationship?

On the political level, the motherload deflects our attention from collective action. As we ascribe ever greater redemptive powers to the mother-child relationship, the pressure is off society to create a more secure social system for all children. Children are assumed to be saved by their individual parents. In addition, the emergency conditions under which some women attempt this saving leave them little time or will for political action or for attention to concerns beyond their own families. Instead of creating security, then, placing the burden of social problems on the backs of individual mothers is a symbolic gesture. It is a way to feel better about social problems without doing much about them.

As we see in each of these realms—the personal, the familial, and the political—the urge to *feel* secure can sometimes work against the urge to actually *be* secure. Just as an addictive substance may subjectively appear to make it all better, we may feel a decline in pressure and heave a great collective sigh by placing impossibly high security expectations on the mother-child relationship. It may help us feel that things are still okay and that, as a society, the mothers are watching our backs. Mothers themselves, faced with impossible expectations, may also breathe easier when their focus is primarily on felt security, which may create a sense of personal control otherwise lacking.

However, an emphasis on the feeling of security can sometimes lead to a deterioration of people's actual circumstances. In the end, addictive substances make things worse, and attempting to extract impossible amounts of security from the mother-child relationship not only fails to provide but also may undermine security in the long run.

The security backfire this research documents in mothering may be simply one instance of a broader phenomenon. Risk scholars discuss how humanity's elaborate and far-reaching efforts—arguably to gain a semblance of control over nature, to gain *security*—are sowing the seeds of our own destruction. Massive attempts to accumulate resources, to dominate other individuals or societies, or to develop nuclear weapons, for example, might well be regarded as large-scale security strategies, perhaps even attempts to stave off the ultimate insecurity: death. Yet these strategies—which in the short run make us *feel* more secure and in control—can likewise ultimately backfire, making the world even more dangerous. So it is, after fighting against natural forms of destruction for most of human history—hunger, disease, fire, flood, and so on—we find ourselves having turned a historical corner in which the greatest threats to human life are now of our own making.[9] And these new threats are almost without fail the unintended consequences of our quite understandable struggles for security.

Even when our efforts to guarantee security don't produce life-threatening consequences, they can still be problematic. For example, in the seemingly blameless realm of concern over health, sociologist Shulamit Reinharz notes that "prevention itself [sometimes] intrudes on the quality of life, foregrounds danger, and makes it harder to enjoy everyday experiences." Reinharz's sociological question is: "[C]an prevention become so overdone that it becomes deleterious in and of itself?"[10] Just as the medicine can sometimes be worse than the ailment, so, too, it may be with mothering. The presumed stakes have grown too high, the ills that the mother-child relationship is intended to deflect are too numerous, and the purported consequences of maternal missteps are too terrible. The solution to the security crisis has begun to look like a crisis itself.

4. *Are there less stressful alternatives to intensive mothering?*

I was only able to discern the costs of a heavy motherload because of the countermodel I found in mothers who are *not* overwhelmed by the scary world *or* by motherhood—two facts that are quite possibly related. For these women with light motherloads, the mother-child relationship is simply that—a relationship—one of several in their own and their children's lives and one they intend to enjoy. These women do not imbue the mother-child relationship with redemptive powers. Furthermore, by *not* taking the mother-child relationship to be the source of all security, they maintain a broader base of security in their lives, they enlist greater support in the mothering project, and they are less likely to be overwhelmed by the ups and downs of motherhood. This paradoxically *enhances their family's security*. While these women are in the minority, they offer an illuminating contrast to the more typical mothers in this research who carry heavy motherloads.

Given such a distinction, it is of utmost importance to understand what factors distinguish women carrying light motherloads from their overburdened counterparts. One of the interesting findings of this research is that the burden does not reside in specific mothering practices. While intensive mothering practices and psychic stress often do go together, this is not always the case. Some women who spend relatively little time with their children feel completely overwhelmed by motherhood. Conversely, some mothers who sleep with their babies, hold them nearly continuously, attend to their every whimper, and breast-feed around the clock do not experience motherhood as particularly burdensome. Likewise, there are both working and stay-at-home mothers with both heavy and light motherloads. The divide between arduous and less arduous mothering, then, is neither defined by connection- versus independence-oriented mothering philosophies nor by high- versus low-intensity mothering practices. Rather, it is defined by the magnitude of a mother's expectations of security those practices are intended to create. That is, it is defined by the motherload.

While sociologists have been studying what women *do* as mothers, the real story may be what they *expect* from motherhood—the security they intend to create by mothering the way they do. New insights may emerge as we focus greater attention on that piece of the story. This research begins that undertaking and brings to light four factors underlying high-expectation mothering (i.e., mothering with a heavy motherload).

First, women carrying heavy motherloads tend to be preoccupied with various forms of danger in the world at large. They worry more than women with light motherloads about such things as crime, germs, automobile accidents, and terrorism.

Second, women with heavy motherloads tend to have insecure attachment-scapes. Whereas women with light motherloads usually have at least one very secure aspect of their lives as they enter motherhood—such as a strong, mutually supportive partnership—women with heavy motherloads often doubt the stability (or worthiness) of their partnerships or are not partnered at all. They may also carry an image of themselves as wounded and draw repeatedly on their own childhoods—especially their feelings of being improperly mothered—to explain their current life troubles. They may be anxious about finding or maintaining jobs with steady paychecks. In sum, their lives feel insecure.

Pairing the first factor (impersonal risk-society fears) with the second (a lack of security resources in their own personal lives), the result is a need for some sort of security intervention.

Third, women carrying heavy motherloads often view children as breakable, so the stakes feel very high. Thus, the lives of their children appear to require more regulation than those of women with lighter motherloads, who see children as resilient and likely to grow up mentally and physically healthy.

Fourth, women with heavy motherloads often rigidly adhere to well-developed correct mothering models. They tend to read more how-to books and consult more Web sites than women with light motherloads, and once they land on their own mothering model—typically before their babies are even born—they are more apt to generalize it as correct mothering and to view other models judgmentally.

All of this results in women looking at the mother-child relationship as a highly potent security-source capable of making it all better—*if* mothers get it right. Yet when motherhood is imbued with such great power and becomes so heavily loaded, this can inadvertently *destabilize* families.

Looking beneath the admittedly mesmerizing phenomenon of intensive mothering, then, we have found that the real problem is the motherload. Yet it is imperative to pause here for clarification: in all my years of research, I found no evidence that heavy-motherload mothering is bad for children and that light-motherload mothering is good for them. Every one of the mothers in my research cared deeply for her child(ren) and did her best, as the vast majority of mothers do. And perhaps because of that, the children I met in the course of my interviews were—at least three years into their lives with their mothers—mostly happy, healthy, curious, and engaged. They rode tricycles, spilled juice, showed off their latest drawings, laughed, and cried—regardless of how they were mothered. In fact, while child outcomes were not a primary focus of my research, I was certainly paying attention, and I saw no discernible differences between children whose mothers carried heavy versus light motherloads.

What I did find is that much of the *struggle* of mothering is related to carrying a heavy motherload. This struggle is not inherent in raising a child, nor is it inherent in raising a child in a risk society. Rather, it occurs when women take on (or are handed) responsibility for resolving the insecurity and fearfulness of our society through a single just-right relationship. Heavy-motherload mothering is *difficult*. Raising children has always been hard, of course, and has brought some of life's greatest challenges along with some of its most exquisite joys. Yet today's unrealistic expectations of mothers makes it more difficult and less joyful. It does not appear to be a good deal.

However life enriching, meaningful, and heart-poundingly real the mother-child relationship is, when we view it as the one piece of solid ground left in a crazy, tumultuous world, we turn that solid ground into a tiny island occupied only by two—and that makes it harder to stand on.

APPENDIX A   Research Participants

	Mothering strategy/ Approach	Race/ ethnicity	Partnership status at baby's birth	Prepregnancy work and annual salary	Age at study onset	Study child's birth order
HEATHER DOVER*	Antidote	White	Long-term boyfriend	Apartment manager, $3,600 + rent	32	Second
PATRICIA TATE*	Antidote	White	Married	Unemployed	24	First
PENNY WALTON	Antidote	White	Married	Magazine intern, $18,000	29	Second
TRUDY COGAN	Antidote	African American	Long-term boyfriend	Secretary, $28,000	31	First
FRAN POLOKOW	Antidote	White	Married	Full-time mother to first child	31	Second
BECK FARROW*	Antidote	White	Long-term lesbian partnership	Pharmacy worker, $25,000	34	Second
AMY ROTHSCHILD*	Shielding	White	Long-term boyfriend	Nurse's assistant, $18,000	28	First
JORDAN COUSINS	Antidote	White	Married	Unemployed/ playwright	35	First
JESSICA TASKER*	Antidote/ friendship	White	Married	Dance instructor, $18,000	35	First
SAMANTHA PRITIKIN	Antidote/ compensatory connection	White	Single	Unemployed	36	Second
SHIRLEY MATHESON	Shielding	White	Married	Unemployed	27	First
PAT ROGERS	Shielding	White	Married	Preschool teacher, $20,000	30	First and second (twins)

	Shielding					
LOTTIE FINCH		White	Married	Third-grade teacher, $32,000	34	Second
MARY ANN CARRINGTON*	Compensatory connection/antidote	White	Married	Temporary clerical worker, $12,000	26	First
MOROWA FRANKLIN*	Compensatory connection	African American	Single	Unemployed	22	First
GINA HALEY*	Compensatory connection	White	Married	Child-care provider, $12,000	33	Fourth
IGNACIA CRUZ*	Compensatory connection→light-ML connection	African American–Filipina	Long-term boyfriend	Recently fired factory worker	18	First
SHEENA GOSWAMI*	Compensatory connection	Indian American	Married	Gardener, $18,000	28	First
KATIE GARBER*	Compensatory connection	White	Boyfriend (elsewhere in the state)	Bus driver, $28,000	29	First
JENNY GUTIERREZ	Compensatory connection	Chicana	Single	Nurse, $30,000	29	First
MISTY FEUTZ	Compensatory connection	White	Long-term boyfriend	Waitress, $18,000	22	First
ALMA PEREZ*	Light-ML connection	Chicana	Married	Community college teacher, $44,000	34	First
HANNAH SHETLAND*	Light-ML connection	White	Married	Social worker, $30,000	27	First
SAM PEARLMAN*	Light-ML connection	White	Married	Student, $15,000	35	First

(continued)

(continued)

	Mothering strategy/ Approach	Race/ ethnicity	Partnership status at baby's birth	Prepregnancy work and annual salary	Age at study onset	Study child's birth order
J. T. MILES*	Light-ML connection	White	Long-term boyfriend	Bookstore worker, $12,000	26	First
LENA WASSERMAN*	Light-ML connection	German immigrant	Married	Weekend German teacher, $7,200	29	First
JESSICA YOUNG	Light-ML connection	White	Long-term lesbian partnership	Personal trainer, $30,000	32	First
TAMMY WONG*	Inoculation	Chinese American	Married	Accountant, $80,000	32	Second
MADDY WINGFIELD*	Inoculation	White	Married	Office worker, $40,000	28	First
GEORGIA SHEEVES*	Inoculation	White	Married	Entrepreneur/ saleswoman, $24,000	41	First
VIVIAN YEE*	Inoculation/friendship	Chinese American	Married	Scientist, $55,000	28	First
GWEN SAVAGE	Inoculation	White	Married	Editor, $42,000	30	First
JULIA FREITAG	Inoculation	German immigrant	Married	Photographer, $36,000	33	Third
SARAH GORDON	Inoculation	White	Married	Reporter, $24,000	35	Second

DAPHNE FETROLIS*	Inoculation/compensatory connection	Greek immigrant	Married	Secretary for husband, unpaid	31	First
DEB FELDMAN*	Inoculation/compensatory connection	White	Married	Unemployed business manager	35	Second
AMIRA BLANKENSHIP*	Inoculation/compensatory connection	White	Married	Attorney, $150,000	31	First
AMELIA MCDANIELS*	Inoculation→ light-ML connection (minor)	White	Married	Vice president of marketing, $120,000	31	First
MYRA ROSSI*	Friendship	White	Long-term boyfriend	Unemployed	41	First
PADNUNI GUPTA*	Friendship	Indian American	Married	Office worker, $36,000	32	First
BECCA LANDSWORTH	Friendship	White	Married	Temporary clerical worker, $18,000	25	First
ELLIE RYDER*	Antidote→friendship	White	Married	Unemployed	36	First
MARIA CASTILLO*	Light-ML independence	Guatemalan immigrant	Married	Hospice manager, $40,000	34	First
BARB WINTERS*	Light-ML independence	White	Married	Fund-raiser, $60,000	36	Second
LILY SHERMAN*	Light-ML independence	White	Married	Facilities manager, $42,000	29	First
WANDA FERRINA*	Light-ML independence	White	Married	Real estate salesperson, $30,000	28	First

(continued)

(continued)

	Mothering strategy/ Approach	Race/ ethnicity	Partnership status at baby's birth	Prepregnancy work and annual salary	Age at study onset	Study child's birth order
LAURA ENGLAND*	Light-ML independence	White	Married	Full-time mother to first children	33	Third
RUDY FIRESTONE*	Light-ML independence	White	Married	Wine shop manager, $39,000	36	First
TERRY MCDONALD*	Light-ML independence	White	Long-term boyfriend	Graphics designer, $40,000	30	First
DIANE CHANG	Light-ML independence	Chinese American	Married	Travel agent, $28,000	30	First
MAYA WASKOW	Light-ML independence	White	Married	Database programmer, $50,000	32	Second

* = participant in longitudinal component of the study

APPENDIX B Research Methods

This research is based on a total of 168 in-depth interviews conducted between 2003 and 2009 with fifty-one primary caregivers of young children in the United States. I followed thirty-four of these mothers longitudinally for the first three years of their children's lives, starting in late pregnancy. These longitudinal research participants engaged in semi-structured, in-depth, face-to-face interviews that generally took place before the birth, again during early infancy, and approximately once per year thereafter until the child was three years old.[1] In this manner I was able to see not only what drove women's mothering and how they mothered but also the early outcomes both in family dynamics and in women's satisfactions with their parenting, partnerships, and work lives. Interviews typically took place in the informants' homes, or occasionally a public setting, and mother-child interactions were also observed on approximately the same schedule. The nonlongitudinal participants were interviewed toward the end of the study, either once or with a single follow-up, and their interviews were specifically targeted around the issues of security emergent from the longitudinal data.

Studying mothers of very young children is an ideal way to investigate the motherload for a number of reasons. First, these are the so-called critical years in which mothers are especially likely to consider themselves responsible for their children's security. Second, this is the phase in which mothers are most steeped in advice literature. And third, this is a time when many partnerships shift from egalitarian ideals to neotraditional realities[2] and women begin bearing the brunt of what Arlie Hochschild calls the second shift of domestic and child rearing labor.[3] This increase in women's responsibilities at home often necessitates changes in their work lives, including reduced work hours and less availability for travel or for night and weekend work. This, in turn, frequently results in fewer promotions, lower pay, and lessened financial independence—with great security implications for women.[4] For all these reasons, early motherhood is a life stage in which security may be particularly salient and security expectations of the mother-child relationship, for both the mother and child, may be particularly high. This may make the motherload particularly visible in mothers of young children.

Research participants were recruited primarily at five birth-preparation classes during late pregnancy where they were told this was a study of how caregivers balance independence and connection with their children—which was, in fact, how the project began. The focus on security was emergent from the interview process.

MY POSITION IN THE FIELD

I became pregnant early in the research process, just as I was recruiting pregnant study participants. Having a child at about the same time as many of the women I studied complicated my relationships with them. Some of the study participants looked to me as a fellow mother in the trenches and assumed a high degree of insider knowledge and empathy for the travails of motherhood. Some seemed to view me in my scholarly capacity as a mothering expert and wanted to know how they should be mothering (a question I regularly deflected). As I often brought the women meals when their children were born, ran into them at the park, or watched their babies as they dashed to the pharmacy before an interview, the line between research and friendship was not always a clear one. I believe that is often the case in qualitative work, though it might not always be acknowledged, and given the intimate subject matter and long-term nature of my research, the sense of personal connection with my informants was probably stronger than is typical. Furthermore, as one segment of the population I was studying was attachment mothers who would welcome me bringing my own baby to interviews (and who might see it as worrisome if I did not), my young son sometimes accompanied me to interviews and would lie across my lap or rest on the couch beside me as I asked my interview questions and took notes.

To be transparent about my own incoming assumptions, I entered motherhood with a natural affinity for attachment parenting. I wanted to have my baby close for the sake of both his well-being and my own. My ideologies and mothering models were constantly shifting, however, due to my mothering experiences as well as what I was learning in my research, which led me to wrestle with various questions. For example, when my research uncovered compensatory connection, I began to consider how I felt about my own needs for physical comfort and emotional intimacy being met through the mother-child relationship. (I ultimately resolved this as acceptable to me as I see both my child and myself as subjects in the mother-child relationship, and as I had other well-established sources of security in my life and therefore did not feel I was *overly* dependent on mothering to meet my needs.)

My husband and I had twin girls a year and a half after having our son, so were parenting three children under the age of two at the same moment that I was in the thick of very intense and deeply personal research about motherhood. This meant both my professional work and private life were intensely focused on the same thing, making it feel as if every cell in my body was pulsing with early motherhood. In my private life, the powerful experience of loving and caring for three human babies—what my twins group called extreme parenting—was utterly transforming me, humbling me, melting me, and forcing me to call upon deep internal resources I didn't realize I had. I often felt raw as I struggled with sleep deprivation, mastitis, one baby's colic, and another's repeated ear infections. I had also longed for children all my life, had lived and worked in two orphanages for a total of four years, had taken on a foster baby for a year in Mexico, and now felt blessed beyond comprehension and moved to new heights of joy and meaning as I lay on the couch covered by the warm, breathing bodies of my own litter of little ones. I grappled fiercely with the irony of having these dearly loved ones in child care by day—cared for by other women—while I was off researching motherhood.

The research experience was itself intense as mothers sobbed with me, laughed with me, asked about my babies, and confided with me things they had never shared with any other person such as their shame, rage, lack of bonded feelings, or what they saw as overidentification with their babies. I entered these completely other worlds of motherhood, spilling over with emotion, and then at four o'clock the workday was over and I went and picked up my own kids and was back in my own mothering experience. I was certainly living up close to the data, and there was a blur between the scholarly and the personal about which I frequently debriefed with fellow family scholars to minimize projecting my own experiences onto my informants.

Ultimately, I believe this inundation with early motherhood enriched my work and was fruitful to my scholarly understandings. Being a mother of young children prompted me to ask follow-up questions of research participants I might not have known to ask if I weren't in the throes of my own mothering experiences. And while my social position as a mother was very specific—as an older, educated, married Latina—I knew the sounds, smells, common embarrassments, physical challenges, and spiritual highs of this enterprise. I knew how much grocery stores charged for formula and where to get it for free. I sometimes arrived at interviews with vomit on my blouse or took research notes while twin fetuses did circus performances inside my body. I was deeply embodied within my area of study and very much an insider, but freshly so, which meant none of it was yet taken for granted or romanticized by the passage of time.

Focusing on motherhood in both my research and my personal life was also fruitful to my understandings as a mother as I was able to witness up close a vast and diverse array of mothering experiences, which helped liberate me from many of my own narrow beliefs about good mothering. This gave me deep compassion for mothers as a whole and freed me to feel my way through my own experiences with more openness to possibilities, as well as a greater peace with ruptures in what I had originally expected in my own mother-child relationships.

LONGITUDINAL SUBJECTS

Most of the data in this book comes from the longitudinal subjects, with whom I had repeated contact throughout their initial years with a new child. As I began this research deeply interested in the tension between independence and connection in motherhood, I hoped to research mothers with a range of differing approaches to parenting. Thus, the birth classes I recruited from consisted both of hospital-based classes geared toward physician-assisted births and also classes at a lactation and doula center geared toward natural births with a midwife. Because midwife-assisted births have not been mainstream in the United States since the early twentieth century, I was oversampling women committed to what Bobel calls natural mothering: giving birth without drugs, breastfeeding, co-sleeping, and carrying children in arms more frequently than is currently typical in the United States.[5] This oversampling of women who selected a midwife-attended birth means there are probably more connection-oriented mothers in my sample than in the population at large.

Drawing the longitudinal participants primarily from birth-preparation classes, even such differently oriented classes, limited the study in two ways: (1) The study omitted adoptive mothers, and (2) using an educationally focused recruitment setting introduced a middle-class bias. This bias was mostly evident in the women's education levels, as most participants attended at least some college—although one in ten did not, including one high school dropout. In other regards, such as in type of work and incomes, the participants had a broader range. At the onset of the study—prior to the birth of their children—the participants' median earnings were slightly below the median real earnings for full-time working women in the United States.[6] For about a third of the participants, there was some struggle to pay monthly bills, and about one in five women was not employed in the labor market at the onset of the study, including one woman who was homeless. For those doing paid work, their jobs included both those associated with the middle class (e.g., graphics designer, social worker, and teacher) and those associated with the working class (e.g., bus driver, factory worker, and retail worker).

The mothers also diverged in other respects, which was my hope as I did not seek a homogenous sample.[7] Twenty-six were married to (or in a long-term committed lesbian relationship with) the other parent of their children at the point of the first interview, and eight were unmarried. Twenty-four were American-born whites, two were white immigrants to the United States, two were Latinas (one US-born, one immigrant), two were African American (one was mixed race but identified as black), two were second-generation Chinese, and two were second-generation East Indian. While these numbers approach the diversity of US mothers, they are not meant to exactly match the proportions of single versus married, immigrant verses US-born, or varieties of racial identities in the US population at large. Rather, my intentions with the sample were simply to include a variety of perspectives in the research. For a full listing of the research participants, along with various characteristics, see appendix A.

RACE AND CLASS

Using a heterogeneous sample in a qualitative study has its own limitations. The advantage of a homogenous or otherwise controlled sample is greater power to draw social locational conclusions. For example, in a study where all of the informants are US-born and working class, or where the study is a two-way comparison between, say, whites and African Americans, one may be able to draw out highly nuanced racial or socioeconomic understandings.

However, the advantage of this study including a greater variety of mothers—diverse not only by race but also by age, ethnicity, immigration status, gender, sexual orientation, partnership status, work status, and income—is it is inclusive of the perspectives of mothers living in entirely different social worlds. I hoped this might allow me to ascertain which aspects of their lives mattered most to them regarding both security and mothering and whether these were similar to or different from the assessments of mothers whose lives were very different. My intentions were therefore to understand how a broader-than-typical range of issues informs mothering, to draw insights from a wide variety of sources that might be missed in a more controlled sample, and to see if there were any overarching patterns either because of or despite these social locational differences.

Pausing for a moment over race and ethnicity, we know that both how one identifies racially and how one is racially perceived by others have profound implications for security and for parenting. For example, black children—systematically disadvantaged by higher-than-typical infant mortality, professionals' attempts to curb their birthrate, suboptimal schooling, racial profiling, and unfair hiring practices when they grow up—must either be protected from or prepared to cope with such challenges.[8] Over the generations, therefore, African American parents have developed multiple racially specific parenting methodologies to protect their children from or tool them to survive such harsh realities.[9]

Nonetheless, given the broad mix of races and ethnicities among the women I studied and the small number of informants of particular racial identities, I hesitate to make racial arguments on the basis of my data lest the analysis imply racial determinism. To say, for example, that Chinese American women mother in a particular way (even with the caveat that I am discussing only women in this sample) would be egregiously misleading and would risk essentializing whole groups of people based on very limited information. This is particularly problematic when, as is often the case, within-group differences exceed between-group differences.

In general, one of the difficulties I wrestle with in creating concepts and building theory is that to do so one needs categories, which are often assumed to be more clearly bound than they really are, including such standard-use categories as race and class. If one places ten people into a particular category, such as Latina or working class, each of those ten people is a *unique individual* with a varying degree of fit within the parameters of the given category. A Latina may have fair skin and green eyes. A man with a working-class job may marry an attorney and parts of him suddenly live in two different classes. It sometimes feels a little presumptuous to have the categories at all.

But as sociologists, we are category-making creatures. If a sociologist's map of the world were to include exactly the same level of detail and individual differences as the world itself, it wouldn't be a map. Thus, the research analyst tries to extract and accentuate what she sees as most important from the data, what appears to be responsible for the different outcomes in the observed situations, and why the world works the way it does. She draws lines around particular attributes, settings, or experiences, and uses those now-parceled bits of social reality in her efforts to make sense of and make more visible the underlying dynamics.

In drawing such lines within this research, I do occasionally make limited racial arguments, as I recognize race has a profound effect. For example, in chapter 5 on the inoculation security strategy, I discuss the literature on race socialization and the parenting strategy of risk exposure. I show how this strategy of risk exposure, once viewed as prevalent among poor and working-class African Americans, may be extending into professional white and Chinese American families, and I conjecture as to why. However, for the most part, just as Lareau's data were more conclusive regarding the effects of class than race on her particular parenting typology,[10] my own data are more conclusive regarding the effects of women's personally controlled material resources than their racial identification on which security strategies they use. My analysis therefore focuses on those issues about which I have the most conclusive evidence. This also includes how women's work and partnership securities affect their approaches to mothering. While these forms of security may to some degree map onto social class—and, to a lesser extent, race—they do so imperfectly. Thus, this study is not about class differences in parenting per se but may be considered a refinement of such studies, investigating the underlying insecurities that may partially contribute to certain previously observed class differences, but which may also occur, albeit differently, among women in any class.

DATA ANALYSIS

Analytically, this work falls into the interpretive sociological tradition of such researchers as Arlie Hochschild and Annette Lareau who use in-depth analysis of case studies to uncover meanings, dynamics, and conceptual understandings.[11] The strength of such a methodology is creating new understandings of dynamics at play: theory building. However, the small sample size does not lend itself to testing its own theoretical contributions, which would be a welcome next step with a larger sample.

When I initially embarked on this research, I did not know I would find different security strategies. I certainly did not anticipate that moth-

Table 1   Mothering security strategies

Security strategy intended to enhance:	Independence Oriented	Connection Oriented
CHILD'S security	Strategy A	Strategy B
MOTHER'S security	Strategy C	Strategy D

ers' overzealous attempts to create security could backfire. My approach was grounded theoretical, meaning I entered mothers' lives with a degree of openness not only regarding what answers I would find but also regarding what questions were most worthy of asking. As I began interviews and observations, however, the finding that became almost immediately apparent was that for most mothers of young children, security is an issue of great importance. Due to the longitudinal nature of the study, I was able to engage in deeper pursuit of this finding and document the unfolding dynamics as women struggled to live up to varying expectations of the security the mother-child relationship would provide to their children and themselves.

One unfortunate fact is that while security leaped out from the data unmistakably, I did not initially recognize the motherload. Prior to recognizing and naming it, like many of my informants, I had a somewhat taken-for-granted assumption that women create security for their families, and my question was *how* they do it, not *whether* they take on that role. Recall table 1, which depicted the two-by-two chart I created in my early analysis to analyze the security strategies, reproduced above.

Each of the cells of this chart corresponds to a strategy (sometimes more than one) and contains some number of women who use that strategy. I assigned one book chapter to each cell and thought I had fairly well mapped out my argument. There were, however, a sizable number of women who did not appear in this chart. They were the outliers: the women who did not talk much about security. It was unclear how to deal with them, and eventually rather than simply presenting them as exceptions, I began to analyze them in their own right. It was only by delving into the analysis of these particular women that the main concept of the book, the motherload, came into focus and I began to recognize the assumption of security in the mother-child relationship was actually a variable. The exceptional cases were critical to this understanding.

The danger of grounded theory—going into the field with openness about what is most important to study—is that one could spend literally years not recognizing the story within one's piles of data—and there is always some nonzero probability that one will *never* recognize the "something of great significance." If there is a lesson for other qualitative researchers from my own tale of delayed discovery, it is not to sweep the exceptional cases under the carpet or set them aside to deal with later. These cases may, in fact, hold the keys to the kingdom.

On the other hand, the greatest hope of this sort of work is that one may strike upon something of great significance. As one is not limited by the scope of the research question, the answer does not have to fit into a particular box, shaped by social convention or prior knowledge. This allows for the possibility that one can find something one wouldn't have even known to look for. In the case of this research, this unexpected finding was the motherload.

Notes

1. To maintain the anonymity of the research participants, I have changed their names as well as much of their identifying information. I also insert pseudonyms, adjusted job titles, changed place names, and so on into direct quotes.

2. I put "make it all better" in quotes because this research has uncovered how problematic it is to expect mothers to, in fact, make it all better. These high expectations often lead mothers to take on more responsibility than is realistic, bringing about a host of negative consequences which do not ultimately make it all better. Henceforth, however, I will omit the quotes.

3. McGee, "The 'Ideograph,'" 6. McGee uses the term *ideograph* to describe a particular family of politically relevant concepts, such as *freedom* and *equality*, that are ill-defined yet ideologically powerful. Because the elasticity of such concepts makes them useful in persuading others in the political arena, they become a form of rhetorical social control. Since the time of his writing in the early 1980s, *security* could surely be added to this list. In my own observation, security is a concept people use to understand various aspects of their own lives—such as their parenting, romantic relationships, or job choices. But security is also a politically charged concept of the type McGee describes used persuasively in the public sphere for political gain (or, one could certainly add, to sell products).

4. Bianchi et al., *Changing Rhythms*.

5. Bianchi et al., *Changing Rhythms*; Hsin, "Mother's Time with Children."

6. Pew Research Center, "Motherhood Today."

7. Coontz, "The Family Revolution," 12.

8. Hays, *Cultural Contradictions of Motherhood*; Nelson, *Parenting Out of Control*; Rosenfeld and Wise, *Over-Scheduled Child*; Wolf, *Is Breast Best?*; Warner, *Perfect Madness*. Note that "Mommy Madness" is the title of a February 21, 2005, *Newsweek* piece excerpted from Judith Warner's (2005) book, *Perfect Madness: Motherhood in the Age of Anxiety*, and while the book itself is sympathetic to mothers and critical of the expectations put upon them, the term *madness* has cultural resonance in an era where intensive mothering is mostly pathologized. Warner's arguments themselves, however, overlap with my own. She writes: "Women today mother in the [*Newsweek* excerpt adds here the words "excessive, control-freakish" that are not in the book] way that they do . . . because, to a large extent, *they have to*, because they are unsupported, because their children are not taken care of, in any meaningful way, by society at large, because there is right now no widespread feeling of social responsibility—for children, for families, for *anyone*, really—and so they must take everything onto themselves. And because they *can't*, humanly, take everything onto themselves, they simply go nuts" (277).

9. Cooper, *Cut Adrift*; Ehrenreich, *Fear of Falling*.

10. Annette Lareau, *Unequal Childhoods*.

11. Nelson, *Parenting Out of Control*.

12. Edin and Kefalas, *Promises I Can Keep*.

13. Boudia and Jas, "Risk and Risk Society," 317; Beck, *Risk Society*; Giddens, "Risk and Responsibility"; Hacker, *Great Risk Shift*.

14. Hays, *Cultural Contradictions of Motherhood*, 8. The seeds of the recent intensive mothering phenomenon were actually sown earlier than the 1970s. Hays traces their early emergence to the Victorian era, when family based productivity was replaced by centralized workplaces and middle-class women therefore sought their new *raison d'être* in child rearing. However, it is only in the recent decades of which I am speaking, and which Hays studied, that parenting has intensified during a period of middle-class female economic productivity and has intensified to such a degree, becoming what so many scholars and public figures have recognized as "out of control" (Nelson 2010).

15. See Blum (1999) and Wolf (2011) for further discussions of the high stakes of motherhood and how various authorities oversell the benefits of breast-feeding, which they present as a form of risk management, with the implication that non-breast-feeding mothers are endangering their children.

16. For an in-depth discussion of both children's assumed vulnerability and parents' assumed power over child outcomes, see sociologist Frank Furedi's theoretically rich 2002 book, *Paranoid Parenting*.

17. Pew Research Center, "Motherhood Today."

18. Several sociologists from the feminist psychoanalytic tradition, including Nancy Chodorow, Ilene Philipson, and Daphne de Marneffe, although not studying intensive mothering per se, do bring mothers' own needs and desires into their analyses. My own research furthers their pioneering work by focusing on security as a central motivator in mothering and showing that many women specifically seek an *intensive* mother-child relationship as the best type of relationship to meet their own security needs.

19. Nelson (2010) has already initiated this much-needed conversation. Although she finds that the professional middle-class parents whom she classifies as "parenting out of control" do so in part to help prevent their children from slipping down the class ladder, she recognizes these parents' own satisfactions from parenting are often relationship-centered, stemming from their open communication and emotionally close relationships with their children (103). This contrasts with the less intensive nonprofessional middle-class and working-class parents for whom she finds "satisfactions less often hinge on their relationship with their children" (101) and instead stem more purely from the successes of the children themselves.

20. Hays, *Cultural Contradictions of Motherhood*.

21. I use quotes around these commonly used concepts to indicate that I do not ascribe to them. In the remainder of the book, I will omit quotes around "good mothering" and "correct mothering" to make the writing less cumbersome, however I remain critical of these concepts throughout.

22. Nelson, *Parenting Out of Control*, 6.

23. Hacker, *Great Risk Shift*.

24. Harvey, *Brief History of Neoliberalism*.

25. Cooper, *Cut Adrift*, 23.

26. Much as with "good mothering," I take a highly critical stance toward the common use of the concept of "bad mothering." However, I will henceforth omit quotes.

27. "Proper" and "improper" mothering are likewise concepts to which I do not ascribe yet will henceforth not mark with quotes.

28. Caplan, "Mother Blaming," 135.

29. Wylie, *Generation of Vipers*, 196.

30. As Douglas and Michaels (2004) point out, idealizing mothers—such as by seeing them as the solution to society's woes—is no great favor to them either, and ultimately undermines women every bit as much as viewing them as the problem.

31. Ainsworth, *Infancy in Uganda*.

32. Bowlby, *Attachment and Loss*.

33. Harlow, "Nature of Love."

34. See, for example, Klaus and Kennel (1976).

35. Sociologist Arlie Hochschild (1983) describes this absorption into public consciousness as the adoption of new "feeling rules," or culturally specific scripts we use to assess and manage our feelings. In another example of authority-driven feeling rules in parenting, sociologist Amy Schalet (2011) argues that the alleged inevitability of conflict between teenagers and parents and the idea that "raging hormones" cause teenagers to make immature sexual choices are not biological facts but rather US-specific cultural understandings. When US teenagers themselves adopt this understanding, it creates the conditions under which they do indeed rebel. Thus, teen rebellion is an example of a feeling rule that is propagated by those in positions of authority and that affects how people interpret and then live their lives. I argue that the assumption of the all-encompassing importance of the mother-child bond is another such authority-driven feeling rule that likewise changes lives on the ground for families.

36. Sociologist Frank Furedi (2002) notes: "Getting parents used to the idea that what they do is decisive is the hidden agenda behind a lot of the advice [literature]. . . . Its main purpose is to inculcate its readers with the thesis of parental determinism" (71).

37. Sharone, *Flawed System/Flawed Self.*

38. Anthony Giddens (1991) refers to this phenomenon, wherein scientific knowledge affects the object of study, as a "double hermeneutic"; quantum physicists, similarly discussing the effect observation itself has on quantum wave-particles, describe this as the "observer effect."

39. Beck, *Risk Society*; Giddens, "Risk and Responsibility"; Hacker, *Great Risk Shift*; Wallulis, *New Insecurity.*

40. Hacker, *Great Risk Shift*, 18; Kalleberg, "Precarious Work, Insecure Workers."

41. In the Panel Study of Income Dynamics conducted in 1996, 46 percent of workers indicated that they felt this concern frequently (cited in Hacker 2006, 18).

42. When I began my data collection in 2003, the ratio of unemployed persons to job openings in the United States was approximately two. By the end of my data collection in 2009, it was six. At the same time, competition for colleges also became fiercer, as the mass influx of children of the baby boomers meant many more young people were suddenly vying for each admissions spot to the most desirable colleges (Bureau of Labor Statistics 2012).

43. Durkheim, *Division of Labor.*

44. Giddens, "Post-Traditional Society," 75.

45. Farber, "Company Man an Anachronism?"

46. American Management Association Workforce Survey, "Workforce Growth Slows."

47. Hacker, *Great Risk Shift*, 25.

48. The average drop in income was 25 percent in the early 1970s and 40 percent in the late 1990s. Income swings for the college-educated today are compa-

rable to those for the less-educated in the 1970s (findings from the Panel Study of Income Dynamics, cited in Hacker 2006, 31).

49. Hacker, *Great Risk Shift*, 13.

50. Between 2007 and 2011, for example, bankruptcy nearly doubled again (Flynn and Kearns 2011).

51. Hacker, *Great Risk Shift*, 32.

52. The actual divorce rate is a contested statistic depending greatly on how one measures it. However, Furstenberg (1990, 382) calculates that "at least half of all those marrying will divorce" and Martin and Bumpass (1989) calculate that of those who married in the 1980s, almost two-thirds will separate or divorce.

53. Skolnick, "Marriage."

54. Putnam, *Bowling Alone*, 107.

55. Ibid., 105, 107.

56. Bellah et al., *Habits of the Heart*.

57. Furedi, *Culture of Fear*.

58. Glassner, *Culture of Fear*, xi.

59. Reinharz, "Enough Already!" 36, 38.

60. Furedi, *Culture of Fear*.

61. Wilkinson, *Anxiety in Risk Society*, 5.

62. Glassner, *Culture of Fear*, xxvi–xxvii.

63. Starr, "Technological Risk."

64. Slovic, "Perceptions of Risk."

65. Search conducted at Galegroup Expanded Academic ASAP on October 10, 2007.

66. Villalobos, "Mothering in Fear."

67. Hackstaff, *Culture of Divorce*, 137, emphasis deleted.

68. Ibid., 135.

69. Bourdieu, "Job Insecurity," 84.

70. Mead, *Culture and Commitment*; Bellah et al., *Habits of the Heart*; Wallulis, *New Insecurity*.

71. Coontz, *Way We Never Were*.

72. See chapter 6 for a discussion of how the paths to women's valuing independence were very different among African American and working-class women than they were for white middle-class feminists. Yet this great variety of women did all arrive at independence ideals—particularly financial independence from men—by the late twentieth century.

73. Roper Starch Worldwide, "American Women's Opinion Poll."

74. Lynd and Lynd, *Middletown*; Caplow et al., *Middletown Families*.

75. Alwin, "Obedience to Autonomy"; Johnson et al., "Cross-Cultural Parenting"; Roper Starch Worldwide, "Kids and Moms Speak."

76. See Bowlby ([1969] 1982) for attachment theory's foundational text.

77. Certainly some women straddle the middle, use one type of strategy for their own security and another for their children's, or switch from one strategy to another as they mother in response to the children's growth or other changing circumstances. Yet typically, the heavier a woman's motherload, the more vehemently she holds to either independence or connection as the "correct" way to mother for security and the more polarized her parenting becomes into that particular camp.

78. I do not see this expectation as mothers' faults, but instead it is frequently foisted upon them when partners, communities, and others are unwilling or unable to play a more active role in creating security for families.

CHAPTER 2. SHIELDING AND ANTIDOTE STRATEGIES

1. In 1999, according to the US Department of Justice (2002), there were 115 "stereotypical kidnappings" of US children by strangers or slight acquaintances, in contrast with the finding by the National Center for Injury Prevention and Control (2009) that 6,019 US children died of motor vehicle accidents in the same year.

2. Rosa, "Social Amplification of Risk," 55.

3. Slovic, "Perceptions of Risk."

4. This is not to suggest that mothers today do not fear automobile accidents. Many speak with great concern about accidents involving their child as a *pedestrian*. However, they rarely express worries about accidents involving the child as a motor vehicle *occupant*. This is despite the fact that 89 percent of motor vehicle fatalities are of vehicle occupants and only 11 percent are of pedestrians (Legalcatch 2008). Thus, again we see social factors either amplifying or diminishing certain risks, in this case probably because a stranger's car striking a pedestrian child elicits more dread than having an accident in the family car with an occupant child.

5. Huddy, Feldman, and Weber, "Felt Insecurity," 136.

6. Ibid., 138.

7. Beck, *Risk Society*, 138.

8. Giddens, "Risk and Responsibility," 3.

9. Beck, *Risk Society*, 21.

10. Ruddick, "Maternal Thinking," 99.

11. Huddy, Feldman, and Weber, "Felt Insecurity," 132.

12. Furedi, *Paranoid Parenting*; Nelson, *Parenting Out of Control*; Rosenfeld and Wise, *Over-Scheduled Child*; Skenazy, *Free-Range Kids*.

13. Note that there are exceptions to almost any generalization I (or any researcher) can make. So, for example, there are women who work long hours on

the labor market and are also ideologically committed to very hands-on, time-intensive mothering, and there are unemployed women committed to independence for their children. Despite the existence of exceptions, recognizing trends can often still be useful (appendix B includes a brief discussion of why this is so).

14. It is interesting to note that Nelson (2010) finds upper-middle-class professional parents to be *more* oriented toward mother-child connection, and middle- and working-class parents to be more concerned with imparting skills of self-sufficiency. This finding—seemingly opposite to my own—could be due to the fact that she examines social class of the family as a whole whereas here I am looking at a mother's individual connection to work. Thus, for example, a mother who does not have a secure job but is married to a high-earning spouse would likely fall into the connection-oriented category in my study, and the same woman would likely hyperconnect to her child in what Nelson calls "parenting out of control," thus resolving the apparent differences for those cases. Also Nelson's finding that privileged parents seek friendship with their children is something I find as well and explore in chapter 6.

15. Lareau, *Unequal Childhoods*; Nelson, *Parenting Out of Control*.

16. For example, Balbus (1990), Bundesen (1998), Furedi (2002), Levy (1970), and Paul (2008) all discuss overprotective parenting as a variant of what I call the shielding strategy.

17. Recall that the security strategies I outline in this research are only general approaches to the mother-child relationship and are not rigid types that define a person. They are therefore fluid and overlapping; a person may embody aspects of a number of strategies, or shift from primarily one to another over time. When I refer to frequencies of occurrence in this book, I include only the longitudinal research participants with whom I was able to see more complex and changing dynamics than with the nonlongitudinal participants. (See appendix A for a complete listing of informant characteristics and strategies used.)

18. Attachment parenting is a movement popularized in the United States by Dr. William Sears in his numerous parenting books, most notably *The Baby Book* (1992), coauthored with his wife, Martha Sears. He and other attachment parenting advocates espouse the benefits of (a) wearing your baby—that is, holding it continuously, often in a sling, (b) co-sleeping, and (c) breast-feeding on demand for longer than is typical in the United States.

19. Sociologist Rosanna Hertz's (2006) study of primarily middle-class women who find themselves unpartnered as their ovaries age shows that while these women would ideally like a career, partner, and children, if they can't have it all, they'll settle for a career and children. These single mothers by choice remain a rarity in US family formation, yet Hertz's bottom line that "we can no longer deny that the core of family life is the mother and her children" (xviii) holds true more broadly.

20. DaCosta, "Marriage and Motherhood," 8.

21. Ibid., 10.

22. Ibid., 6.

23. Ibid., 16.

24. Douglas and Michaels, *Mommy Myth*; Ehrenreich and English, *For Her Own Good*; Furedi, *Paranoid Parenting*; Thurer, *Myths of Motherhood*; Warner, *Perfect Madness.*

25. Sears and Sears, *Baby Book*, 8.

26. Ibid., 9.

27. One very famous example of such research is Klaus and Kennel's 1976 book, *Maternal Infant Bonding.*

28. Liedloff, *Continuum Concept*, 59.

29. Ibid., 59, 60.

30. Ibid., 63.

31. Ibid., 60.

32. Ibid., 63.

33. Note that Heather's part-time job as an apartment manager makes *her* a "working parent" as well. However, she does not identify herself as such possibly because it could emphasize her separation from her children, which does not fit with her correct mothering model of total availability.

34. Keller and Goldberg, "Co-Sleeping." While Keller and Goldberg find co-sleeping babies require nighttime assistance for longer than solitary sleepers, during the day co-sleeping young children become self-reliant *earlier* than solitary sleepers, such as by dressing themselves and making friends without assistance.

35. Bobel, *Paradox of Natural Mothering*, 142.

36. Ibid., 142.

37. Ibid., 144.

38. Fraley and Brumbaugh, "Change in Attachment Security."

39. Balbus, "Engendering Change"; Bundesen, "Overprotective Mother"; Furedi, *Paranoid Parenting*; Levy, "Maternal Overprotection"; Paul, *Parenting, Inc.*

40. Otte, "Perils of Parental Projection."

41. Glassner, *Culture of Fear.*

42. The dependence on the expert for one's certainty usually begins in pregnancy when a woman may consult written sources merely to understand how to have a safe pregnancy. Furedi (2002) points out that an "insidious effect of the preconception and antenatal advice is that many women take to heart its message— that they are responsible for the healthy outcome of a pregnancy" (73). From this, she graduates to parenting advice and, since many pregnancy books include at least one chapter at the end on early parenting, this transition is often seamless. This expert parenting advice promulgates, with authority, correct mothering models of how to raise a safe, healthy, smart, nonfussy, socially competent, psychologically well-adjusted child.

CHAPTER 3. COMPENSATORY CONNECTION
STRATEGY

1. Beck and Beck-Gernsheim, *Normal Chaos of Love*, 37.

2. Bowlby, *Affectional Bonds* and *Attachment and Loss*; Huddy, Feldman, and Weber, "Felt Insecurity"; Main, "Field of Attachment."

3. Huddy, Feldman, and Weber, "Felt Insecurity," 132.

4. Hays, *Cultural Contradictions of Motherhood*, 99.

5. Ibid., 175.

6. Lareau, *Unequal Childhoods*; Nelson, *Parenting Out of Control*.

7. Bianchi et al., *Changing Rhythms*; Furedi, *Paranoid Parenting*; Nelson, *Parenting Out of Control*.

8. Pew Research Center, "Motherhood Today."

9. De Marneffe, *Maternal Desire*.

10. Shumway, *Modern Love*, 23.

11. Coontz, *Way We Never Were*; D'Emilio and Freedman, *Intimate Matters*.

12. Gillis, *World Own Making*, 7.

13. See, for example, Dizard and Gadlin (1990) and Rosen (1982).

14. Philipson, "Narcissism and Mothering," 38.

15. Ibid., 36.

16. Coontz, "The Family Revolution"; Douglas and Michaels, *Mommy Myth*; Hays, *Cultural Contradictions of Motherhood*; Thurer, *Myths of Motherhood*; Warner, *Perfect Madness*.

17. Intensive mothering among full-time employed mothers is evident in the scholarship of Blair-Loy (2003), Garey (1995, 1999), and Hays (1996), among others.

18. Sennett, *Corrosion of Character*.

19. DaCosta, "Marriage and Motherhood," 1.

20. Ibid., 11.

21. Edin and Kefalas, *Promises I Can Keep*, 201–2.

22. Ibid., 11.

23. Marianne Cooper's (2014) *Cut Adrift* likewise uncovers rampant insecurity among the privileged.

24. Sroufe and Waters, "Attachment as Organizational Construct," 3.

25. Joan Acker's 2006 book *Class Questions: Feminist Answers* also points out this disconnect between many stay-at-home mothers' privileged class positions and their experiences of insecurity. She writes: "They had few economic worries, but they felt insecure. . . . The women's own efficacy in assuring their economic security was weak" (49).

26. Some of the framing, data, and analysis in this book, and especially in this chapter, was formerly published in my 2014 *Journal of Family Issues* article, "Compensatory Connection: Mothers' Own Stakes in an Intensive Mother-Child

Relationship." In that article, I compare a highly independence-oriented respondent (not case studied in this book) with Gina Haley, highlighted in this chapter.

27. One exception in the expert literature, a critique of overholding infants, is Ezzo and Bucknam's (1998) book *On Becoming Baby Wise*. This popular parenting book advocates setting clear limits with babies and children and fostering independence by not overindulging them, not responding overly quickly to protest cries, and not holding them excessively. *Baby Wise* expresses ardent opposition to attachment parenting, both for children's and parents' sakes.

28. See Crittenden (2001) for a detailed discussion of the financial costs of motherhood both for stay-at-home and employed mothers.

29. Nelson, *Parenting Out of Control*, 11, emphasis deleted.

30. Allen and Hawkins, "Maternal Gatekeeping," 200.

31. Hawkins et al., "Dual-Earner Couples Share"; Lamb, "Fathers and Child Development."

32. Angier, "Social Glue," 1, discussing Hrdy *Mothers and Others*.

33. Hrdy, *Mothers and Others*.

34. Bobel, *Paradox of Natural Mothering*, 139.

35. de Marneffe, *Maternal Desire*, xi.

36. Ibid., 14, emphasis in original.

37. Ibid., 14.

38. Fraley et al., "Assessing Attachment," 617.

39. Ibid.

40. Hazan, Gur-Yaish, and Campa, "To Be Attached," 73.

41. Bowlby, *Attachment and Loss*.

42. Allen and Hawkins, "Maternal Gatekeeping," 202.

43. Damaske, *For the Family?*

44. In Ofer Sharone's 2013 book, *Flawed System/Flawed Self*, he describes how one's very sense of self can feel on the line in the job search, so rejections feel personal, and even people without parenting as an alternative pursuit sometimes stop job searching entirely when the pain and fear of rejection becomes too intense.

45. Nelson, *Parenting Out of Control*, 69.

46. Ibid., 67, emphasis deleted.

47. In highlighting sociological understandings, I disaggregate (1) the degree to which one draws on psychotherapeutic framings of one's life (a socially and culturally influenced construct) and (2) the degree of harm caused by childhood events themselves (more purely psychological). In doing so, I do not mean to disavow the latter or the actual influence of traumatic life histories. I am merely drawing attention to the former—that is, I am sociologically contextualizing people's use of psychological frames—and showing how that influences the motherload.

48. The case study in this chapter, Gina Haley, exhibits issues beyond those attributable to her heavy motherload, which are surely psychological in nature. This is a disadvantage of highlighting an extreme case. The advantage of the extreme case is that the dynamics are amplified and very clear, so it works well for illustrative purposes.

49. Bobel, *Paradox of Natural Mothering*, 138, emphasis added.

50. Philipson, "Narcissism and Mothering," 38.

51. Bellah et al, *Habits of the Heart*; Mead, *Culture and Commitment*.

52. Wilkinson, *Anxiety in Risk Society*, 30.

53. Edin and Kefalas, *Promises I Can Keep*.

54. Hays, *Cultural Contradictions of Motherhood*; Lareau, *Unequal Childhoods*; Nelson, *Parenting Out of Control*; Thurer, *Myths of Motherhood*; Warner, *Perfect Madness*; Wolf, *Is Breast Best?*

CHAPTER 4. LIGHT-MOTHERLOAD CONNECTION

1. Sonkin, "Attachment Theory."

2. Pearson et al., "Earned- and Continuous-Security."

3. Denying painful childhood events occurs among what attachment researchers call dismissive individuals (an insecure attachment status), and dwelling on past events that regularly intrude into present discussions occurs among similarly insecurely attached preoccupied individuals (Sonkin 2005, 1).

4. Rutter et al., "Adult Outcome."

5. Cowan and Cowan, *When Partners Become Parents*, 147.

6. One could argue this is due to J. T.'s working-class background and her assuming what Lareau (2003) describes as a natural growth model of parenting (in which working-class parents assume children can grow without the need for the parents' constant supervision, intervention, and scheduling). However, we must not wrongly infer from this that those with fewer economic resources *lack* a model of good mothering. For example, working-class parents often express that well-behaved children reflect good parenting, as they have been taught to obey rules and respect authority (Lareau 2003). It is simply a different model of what good parenting looks like.

7. Rukeyser, *The Life of Poetry*.

CHAPTER 5. INOCULATION STRATEGY

1 Furedi, *Paranoid Parenting*; Nelson, *Parenting Out of Control*; Wolf, *Is Breast Best?*

2. Rosenfeld and Wise, *Over-Scheduled Child*; Warner, *Perfect Madness*.

3. Brown and Lesane-Brown, "Race Socialization Messages," 201; Feagin and Sikes, *Living with Racism*, 17.

4. Carothers, "Catching Sense," 321.

5. Pugh, *Longing and Belonging.*

6. Feagin and Sikes, *Living with Racism*, 97.

7. Wright, *I'm Chocolate, You're Vanilla.*

8. Moraga, "La Guera."

9. Lareau, *Unequal Childhoods.*

10. Nelson, *Parenting Out of Control*, 120.

11. Some of the data and analysis from this chapter previously appeared in my (2010) piece "Mothering in Fear: How Living in an Insecure-Feeling World Affects Parenting," though Daphne, who will be the primary case study in this chapter, did not appear in that piece.

12. Due to idiosyncratic personal details that might compromise anonymity, Julia is the only case study I present in *Motherload* that is actually a composite of two respondents (though almost all of her quotes are attributable to the primary respondent).

13. Skenazy, "Subway Alone," 1.

14. See www.freerangekids.com, Stephanie Pringhipakis comment posted April 10, 2008, 1:34 a.m., emphasis added; Rabbmari comment posted April 10, 2008, 3:56 a.m.

15. Van Epps, "Racist World," 1.

16. Carothers, "Catching Sense," 321–22.

17. Beck, *Risk Society.*

18. Douglas, *Risk and Blame.*

19. As we saw in the introductory chapter, this common belief in an increasing crime rate is actually incorrect.

20. Wilkinson, *Anxiety in Risk Society*, 68.

21. Nelson, *Parenting Out of Control*, 103, 93.

22. Winnicott, "Parent-Infant Relationship."

23. Urdang, *Human Behavior*, 94.

24. In fact, among light-motherload mothers (highlighted in chapters 4 and 7) who view the world as generally safe and children as generally resilient, independence and connection become almost indistinguishable, interwoven moment to moment. These women's parenting becomes very difficult to classify as either primarily independence oriented or primarily connection oriented.

CHAPTER 6. FRIENDSHIP STRATEGY

1. Furman, *Kiss and Run.*

2. Blair-Loy, *Competing Devotions*; Crittenden, *Price of Motherhood*; Stone, *Opting Out?*; Williams, *Unbending Gender.*

3. Pew Research Center, "Motherhood Today."

4. Crittenden, *Price of Motherhood*; Edin and Kefalas, *Promises I Can Keep*; Williams *Unbending Gender.*

5. Hirshman (2007) and Rich (1980) each argue why this financial independence from men is so crucial for women.

6. Such theories include those of Bellah et al. (1985), Wallulis (1998), and Wilkinson (2001).

7. In chapter 5, I described the security bind that occurs when a woman wants one type of relationship for her child and another type for herself. For example, Daphne, the case study I highlighted in that chapter, believes independence is best for her child but wishes for connection for herself. Ellie has the opposite security bind: she believes connection is best for her child but wishes for independence for herself. In both cases, the woman's desires are pitted against what she sees as the child's needs, creating tension in the relationship.

8. Almost sixteen million families had at least one adult child living at home in 2003, up 14 percent since 1985, and between 2003 and 2011 these numbers further increased (Census Bureau 2004, 2011a, 2011b). Silvia Rose Honig (2008) finds that a high level of parental investment in the future career success of one's adolescent children (such as strictly overseeing their homework, hiring tutors, or writing their college entrance essays for them) is associated with prolonged financial support into adulthood and may actually impede future career success and the financial independence the parents are hoping to impart.

9. Quoted in Douglas and Michaels, *Mommy Myth*, 319.

10. Census Bureau, "Who's Minding the Kids?"

11. Blair-Loy, *Competing Devotions.*

12. See Arlie Russell Hochschild's (2012) *The Outsourced Self: Intimate Life in Market Times* and Allison Pugh's (2005) article "Selling Compromise: Toys, Motherhood, and the Cultural Deal," both of which address using consumption to buy one's way out of certain aspects of intimate life.

13. Coontz, *Marriage*; de Beauvoir, *Second Sex*; Friedan, *Feminine Mystique*; Hirshman, *Get to Work*; Rich, "Compulsory Heterosexuality."

14. hooks, *Feminist Theory.*

15. Collins, "Shifting the Center."

16. Blum and Deussen, "Negotiating Independent Motherhood"; Damaske, *For the Family?*; hooks, *Feminist Theory.*

17. Roper Starch Worldwide, "American Women's Opinion Poll."

18. Ibid.

19. Damaske, *For the Family?*

20. Nelson, *Parenting Out of Control*, 9.

21. Ibid. Nelson finds that parents today, across social class, view a baby monitor as an essential and taken-for-granted aspect of child safety when the baby is not physically at hand.

CHAPTER 7. LIGHT-MOTHERLOAD INDEPENDENCE

1 Stack, *All Our Kin.*

2. Newman, *No Shame.*

3. Ibid., cited in Sarkisian and Gerstel, *Nuclear Family Values*, 29.

4. Sociologist Karen Hansen (2005) likewise finds that middle-class families today, including white families, often rely on kin in ways formerly associated with working-class or poor families or families of color.

5. De Luccie, "Mothers as Gatekeepers."

6. Allen and Hawkins, "Maternal Gatekeeping," 203.

7. Gerson, *Unfinished Revolution.*

8. Furedi, *Paranoid Parenting*, 46.

9. Ibid., 46.

10. It is unclear whether low engagement with parenting advice literature is a cause or an effect of a light motherload.

CHAPTER 8. CONCLUSION

1. Nelson, *Parenting Out of Control*, 68.

2. Lareau, *Unequal Childhoods*; Nelson, *Parenting Out of Control.*

3. Furedi, *Paranoid Parenting*; Giddens, "Risk and Responsibility"; Hacker, *Great Risk Shift*; Slovic, "Perceptions of Risk."

4. Zelizer, *Pricing the Priceless Child.*

5. Gerson, *Unfinished Revolution.* Gerson's analysis is sympathetic to men insofar as she finds their lesser involvement in caregiving is often the result of their deep-seated sense of responsibility for breadwinning and fears that more intensive caregiving on their part will jeopardize their work and ability to financially provide. In a prior and related analysis, Arlie Hochschild (1989) introduced the *stalled* revolution: the lack of revolutionary change in either workplace structures or men's parenting or domestic behavior to accommodate the second-wave feminist revolution in which throngs of middle-class women joined the workforce. Decades later, women remain disproportionately responsible for children, and while responsibility does not always translate to a heavy motherload, it certainly contributes.

6. Because early childhood is seen as the most crucial time for mothers to get it right—and because public schools only take the baton after this purportedly critical period has passed—the motherload may be particularly visible in early mothering. Had my research focused instead on mothers of ten-year-olds or of teenagers, the findings may have been quite different and the motherload may have been less clearly visible (or perhaps not). Research on the motherload in mothers of older children would be a welcome next step.

7. Fraley and Brumbaugh, "Dynamical Systems Approach," 119–20.

8. Coontz, *Marriage*; D'Emilio and Freedman, *Intimate Matters*.

9. Giddens, "Risk and Responsibility," 3.

10. Reinharz, "Enough Already!" 36.

APPENDIX B. RESEARCH METHODS

1. I interviewed and observed some informants more frequently than this, and some less frequently depending on availability. The project began with thirty-six longitudinal informants, two of whom moved away early in the study and could not be located. Two additional informants were likewise difficult to locate, but I was able to connect sporadically and thus include their data.

2. Gerson, *Unfinished Revolution*.

3. Hochschild, *Second Shift*.

4. Crittenden, *Price of Motherhood*; Williams, *Unbending Gender*.

5. Bobel, *Paradox of Natural Mothering*.

6. The national average is drawn from the real median incomes for full-time working women, taken from 2005 census data (http://www.census.gov/prod/2006pubs/p60-231.pdf, p. 11).

7. In fact, while I refer to the research participants collectively as mothers, I studied parents with the primary responsibility for caregiving, and in two of the longitudinal families, this included a stay-at-home father. I welcomed this form of diversity in my informants, yet because in the vast majority of families I studied it was the woman who had primary caregiving responsibility, I decided that using a gender-neutral term such as *primary caregiver* throughout the book would mask the gendering of parental responsibilities that persists today and the fact that ours is still a primarily female-reared society. (Note: With so few men in the sample, I was unable to distinguish gender differences in the use of the security strategies.)

8. Noguera, "Trouble with Black Boys"; Roberts, "Killing the Black Body."

9. Brown and Lesane-Brown, "Race Socialization Messages"; Carothers, "Catching Sense"; Collins, "Shifting the Center."

10. Lareau, *Unequal Childhoods*.

11. See Hochschild (1997) and Lareau (2003) for examples of this method.

References

Acker, Joan. 2006. *Class Questions: Feminist Answers*. Lanham, MD: Rowman & Littlefield Publishers, Inc.

Ainsworth, Mary. 1967. *Infancy in Uganda: Infant Care and the Growth of Love*. Baltimore: Johns Hopkins University Press.

Allen, Sarah M., and Alan J. Hawkins. 1999. "Maternal Gatekeeping: Mothers' Beliefs and Behaviors that Inhibit Greater Father Involvement in Family Work." *Journal of Marriage and Family* 61(1): 199–212.

Alwin, Duane F. 1988. "From Obedience to Autonomy: Changes in Traits Desired in Children, 1924–1978." *Public Opinion Quarterly* 52 (Spring): 33–52.

American Management Association's Workforce Survey. 1999. "Workforce Growth Slows, AMA's 13th Annual Workforce Survey Shows More Hiring, More Firing, More Companies Doing Both at Once; Corporate Restructuring and Reengineering Result in Both Job Cuts, Additions." October 26. http://www.amanet.org/press/archives/growthsurv.htm.

Angier, Natalie. 2009. "In a Helpless Baby, the Roots of Our Social Glue." *New York Times Online*, March 2. http://www.nytimes.com/2009/03/03/science/03angi.html.

Balbus, Isaac D. 1990. "Engendering Change: A Psychoanalytic Preface to a Feminist Theory of the History of Parenting." Paper presented at the annual meeting of the American Sociological Association, August.

Beck, Ulrich. (1986) 1992. *Risk Society: Towards a New Modernity*. Translated by Mark Ritter. London: Sage Publications.

———. 2002. "The Silence of Words and Political Dynamics in the World Risk Society." *Logos* 1(4): 1–18.

Beck, Ulrich, and Elisabeth Beck-Gernsheim. 1995. *The Normal Chaos of Love.* Cambridge: Polity Press.

Bellah, Robert, Richard Madsen, William M. Sullivan, Ann Swidler, Steven M. Tipton. 1985. *Habits of the Heart.* Berkeley: University of California Press.

Bianchi, Suzanne M., John P. Robinson, and Melissa A. Milkie. 2006. *Changing Rhythms of American Family Life.* London: Russell Sage.

Blair-Loy, M. 2003. *Competing Devotions: Career and Family among Women Executives.* Cambridge, MA: Harvard University Press.

Blum, Linda M. 1999. *At the Breast: Ideologies of Breastfeeding and Motherhood in the Contemporary United States.* Boston: Beacon Press.

Blum, Linda M., and Theresa Deussen. 1996. "Negotiating Independent Motherhood: Working-Class African American Women Talk about Marriage and Motherhood." *Gender & Society* 10(2): 199–211.

Bobel, Chris. 2001. "Bounded Liberation: A Focused Study of La Leche League International." *Gender & Society* 15(1): 130–51.

———. 2002. *The Paradox of Natural Mothering.* Philadelphia: Temple University Press.

Boudia, Soraya, and Nathalie Jas. 2007. "Risk and Risk Society in Historical Perspective." *History and Technology* 23(4): 317–31.

Bourdieu, Pierre. 1999. "Job Insecurity Is Everywhere Now." In *Acts of Resistance: Against the Tyranny of the Market*, translated by Richard Nice. New York: New Press.

Bowlby, John. 1979. *The Making and Breaking of Affectional Bonds.* London: Tavistock Publications.

———. (1969) 1982. *Attachment and Loss: Vol. 1, Attachment.* New York: Basic Books.

Brown, Tony N., and Chase L. Lesane-Brown. 2006. "Race Socialization Messages across Historical Time." *Social Psychology Quarterly* 69(2): 201–13.

Bundesen, Herman. 1998. "The Overprotective Mother." In *"Bad" Mothers: The Politics of Blame in Twentieth-Century America*, edited by Molly Ladd-Taylor and Lauri Umansky, 268–70. New York: New York University Press.

Bureau of Labor Statistics. 2012. "Job Openings and Labor Turnover Survey Highlights." http://www.bls.gov/web/jolts/jlt_labstatgraphs.pdf.

Caplan, Paula. 1998. "Mother Blaming." In *"Bad" Mothers: The Politics of Blame in Twentieth-Century America*, edited by Molly Ladd-Taylor and Lauri Umansky. New York: New York University Press.

Caplow, Theodore, Howard M. Bahr, Bruce A. Chadwick, Reuben Hill, and Margaret Holmes Williamson. 1985. *Middletown Families: Fifty Years of Change and Continuity.* Minneapolis: University of Minnesota Press.

Carothers, Suzanne C. 1998. "Catching Sense: Learning from our Mothers to be Black and Female." In *Families in the U.S.: Kinship and Domestic Politics*, edited by Karen Hansen and Anita Garey. Philadelphia: Temple University Press.

Census Bureau. 2004. "American Housing Survey for the United States: 2003." Released September 2004. http://www.census.gov/prod/2004pubs/H150-03 .pdf.

———. 2005. "Who's Minding the Kids? Child Care Arrangements: Winter 2002." Released October 2005. http://www.census.gov/prod/2005pubs/p70 -101.pdf.

———. 2011a. "More Young Adults Are Living in Their Parents' Home." Released November 3. http://www.census.gov/newsroom/releases/archives/families _households/cb11-183.html.

———. 2011b. "Percent of Adults 25–34 Who Are the Child of the Householder: 1983–2011." Released November 4. http://www.census.gov/newsroom /releases/pdf/cb11-183_figs1-4.pdf.

Collins, Patricia Hill. 1994. "Shifting the Center: Race, Class, and Feminist Theorizing about Motherhood." In *Mothering: Ideology, Experience, and Agency*, edited by Evelyn Nakano Glenn, Grace Chang, and Linda Rennie Forcey. New York: Routledge.

Coontz, Stephanie. 2000. *The Way We Never Were*. New York: Basic Books.

———. 2005. *Marriage, a History: How Love Conquered Marriage*. New York: Penguin.

———. 2007. "The Family Revolution." *Greater Good* (Fall).

Cooper, Marianne. 2014. *Cut Adrift: Families in Insecure Times*. Berkeley: University of California Press.

Cowan, Carolyn Pape, and Philip A. Cowan. 1992. *When Partners Become Parents: The Big Life Change for Couples*. New York: Basic Books.

Crittenden, Ann. 2001. *The Price of Motherhood: Why the Most Important Job in the World Is Still the Least Valued*. New York: Metropolitan Books.

DaCosta, Kimberly. 1995. "Marriage and Motherhood: A New Perspective on Commitment, Sacrifice and Self-Development." MA thesis, University of California–Berkeley.

Damaske, Sarah. 2011. *For the Family? How Class and Gender Shape Women's Work*. New York: Oxford University Press.

de Beauvoir, Simone. (1949) 1989. *The Second Sex*. New York: W. W. Norton & Co.

De Luccie, Mary F. 1995. "Mothers as Gatekeepers: A Model of Maternal Mediators of Father Involvement." *The Journal of Genetic Psychology* 156(1): 115–31.

de Marneffe, Daphne. 2004. *Maternal Desire: On Children, Love, and the Inner Life*. New York: Little, Brown and Company.

D'Emilio, John, and Estelle B. Freedman. 1988. *Intimate Matters: A History of Sexuality in America*. Chicago: University of Chicago.

Dizard, Dan, and Howard Gadlin. 1990. *The Minimal Family*. Amherst: University of Massachusetts Press.

Douglas, Mary. 1992. *Risk and Blame*. New York: Routledge.

Douglas, Susan J., and Meredith W. Michaels. 2004. *The Mommy Myth: The Idealization of Motherhood and How It Has Undermined Women*. New York: Free Press.

Durkheim, Emile. (1893) 1964. *The Division of Labor in Society*. New York: Free Press.

Edin, Kathryn, and Maria Kefalas. 2005. *Promises I Can Keep: Why Poor Women Put Motherhood before Marriage*. Berkeley: University of California Press.

Ehrenreich, Barbara. 1985. *Fear of Falling*. New York: HarperPerennial.

Ehrenreich, Barbara, and Diedre English. 1978. *For Her Own Good: 150 Years of the Experts' Advice to Women*. Garden City, NY: Anchor Books.

Ezzo, Gary, and Robert Bucknam. 1998. *On Becoming Baby Wise: Learn How Over 500,000 Babies Were Trained to Sleep through the Night the Natural Way*. 2nd ed. Sisters, OR: Multnomah Publishers.

Farber, Henry S. 2007. "Is the Company Man an Anachronism? Trends in Long-Term Employment in the U.S. 1973–2006." In *The Price of Independence: The Economics of Early Adulthood*, edited by Sheldon Danziger and Cecilia Rouse. New York: Russell Sage.

Feagin, Joe, and Melvin P. Sikes. 1994. *Living with Racism: The Black Middle-Class Experience*. Boston: Beacon Press.

Flynn, Ed, and Thomas C. Kearns. 2011. "Assessing the Data: Filing Trends in Bankruptcy, 2007–2011." *ABI Journal* 30(9).

Fraley, R. Chris, and Claudia C. Brumbaugh. 2004. "A Dynamical Systems Approach to Understanding Stability and Change in Attachment Security." In *Adult Attachment: Theory, Research, and Clinical Implications*, edited by W. S. Rholes and J. A. Simpson, 86–132. New York: Guilford Press.

Fraley, R. Chris, Marie E. Heffernan, Amanda M. Vicary, and Claudia C. Brumbaugh. 2011. "The Experiences in Close Relationships—Relationship Structures Questionnaire: A Method for Assessing Attachment Orientations across Relationships." *Psychological Assessment* 23(3): 615–25.

Friedan, Betty. (1963) 2001. *The Feminine Mystique*. New York: W. W. Norton & Co.

Furedi, Frank. 1997. *Culture of Fear: Risk-Taking and the Morality of Low Expectation*. London: Continuum Press.

———. 2002. *Paranoid Parenting*. Chicago: Chicago Review Press.

Furman, Elina. 2007. *Kiss and Run: The Single, Picky, and Indecisive Girl's Guide to Overcoming her Fear of Commitment*. New York: Simon and Schuster.

Furstenberg, Frank F. 1990. "Divorce and the American Family," *Annual Review of Sociology* 16: 379–403.

Garey, Anita. 1995. "Constructing Motherhood on the Night Shift: 'Working Mothers' as Stay-at-Home Moms." *Qualitative Sociology* 18: 414–37.

———. 1999. *Weaving Work and Motherhood*. Philadelphia: Temple University Press.

Gerson, Kathleen. 2011. *The Unfinished Revolution: Coming of Age in a New Era of Gender, Work, and Family*. New York: Oxford University Press.

Giddens, Anthony. 1991. *Modernity and Self-Identity: Self and Society in the Late Modern Age*. Stanford, CA: Stanford University Press.

———. 1994. "Living in a Post-Traditional Society." In *Reflexive Modernization: Politics, Traditions, and Aesthetics in the Modern Social Order*, edited by Ulrich Beck, Anthony Giddens, and Scott Lash, 56–109. Cambridge: Polity Press.

———. 1999. "Risk and Responsibility." *Modern Law Review* 62(1): 1–10.

Gillis, John. 1997. *A World of Their Own Making: Myth, Ritual, and the Quest for Family Values*. Cambridge, MA: Harvard University Press.

Glassner, Barry. 2000. *The Culture of Fear: Why Americans Are Afraid of the Wrong Things*. New York: Basic Books.

Hacker, Jakob S. 2006. *The Great Risk Shift: The Assault on American Jobs, Families, Health Care, and Retirement and How You Can Fight Back*. New York: Oxford University Press.

Hackstaff, Karla B. 2000. *Marriage in a Culture of Divorce*. Philadelphia: Temple University Press.

Hansen, Karen. 2005. *Not-So-Nuclear Families: Class, Gender, and Networks of Care*. New Brunswick, NJ: Rutgers University Press.

Harlow, Harry. 1958. "The Nature of Love." *American Psychologist* 13: 673–85.

Harvey, David. 2007. *A Brief History of Neoliberalism*. New York: Oxford University Press.

Hawkins, Alan J., Tomi-Ann Roberts, Shawn L. Christiansen, and Christina M. Marshall. 1994. "An Evaluation of a Program to Help Dual-Earner Couples Share the Second Shift." *Family Relations* 43: 213–20.

Hays, Sharon. 1996. *The Cultural Contradictions of Motherhood*. New Haven, CT: Yale University Press.

Hazan, Cindy, Nurit Gur-Yaish, and Mary Campa. 2004. "What Does It Mean to Be Attached?" In *Adult Attachment: Theory, Research, and Clinical Implications*, edited by J. Simpson and S. Rholes, 55–85. New York: Guilford Press.

Hertz, Rosanna. 2006. *Single by Chance, Mothers by Choice: How Women are Choosing Parenthood without Marriage and Creating the New American Family*. New York: Oxford University Press.

Hirshman, Linda. 2007. *Get to Work: . . . And Get a Life, Before It's Too Late*. New York: Penguin.

Hochschild, Arlie Russell. 1983. *The Managed Heart: The Commercialization of Human Feeling.* Berkeley: University of California Press.

——. 1989. *The Second Shift: Working Parents and the Revolution at Home.* New York: Viking Penguin.

——. 1997. *The Time Bind.* New York: Metropolitan Books.

——. 2012. *The Outsourced Self: Intimate Life in Market Times.* New York: Metropolitan Books.

Honig, Sylvia Rose. 2008. "Socialization, Parental Dependence, and Hindered Development in Career," paper presented at the annual meeting of the American Sociological Association, August.

hooks, bell. 1984. *Feminist Theory: From Margin to Center.* Cambridge, MA: South End Press.

Hrdy, Sarah Blaffer. 2009. *Mothers and Others: The Evolutionary Origins of Mutual Understanding.* Cambridge, MA: Harvard University Press.

Hsin, Amy. 2006. "Mother's Time with Children: Does Time Matter?" Working paper for California Center for Population Research. Released December 1. http://www.escholarship.org/uc/item/2vn214z3.

Huddy, Leonie, Stanley Feldman, and Christopher Weber. 2007. "The Political Consequences of Perceived Threat and Felt Insecurity." *The Annals of the American Academy, AAPSS* 614: 131–53.

Johnson, Laura, Jenny Radesky, and Barry Zuckerman. 2013. "Cross-Cultural Parenting: Reflections on Autonomy and Interdependence." *Pediatrics* 131(4): 631–33.

Kalleberg, Arne L. 2009. "Precarious Work, Insecure Workers: Employment Relations in Transition," *American Sociological Review* 74(1): 1–22.

Keller, Meret A., and Wendy A. Goldberg. 2004. "Co-Sleeping: Help or Hindrance for Young Children's Independence?" *Infant and Child Development* 13(5): 369–88.

Klaus, Marshall H., and John H. Kennel. 1976. *Maternal Infant Bonding.* St. Louis, MO: CV Mosby.

Lamb, Michael E. 1997. "Fathers and Child Development: An Introductory Overview," In *The Role of the Father in Child Development*, 3rd edition, edited by M. E. Lamb, 1–18. New York: Wiley.

Lareau, Annette. 2003. *Unequal Childhoods: Class, Race, and Family Life.* Berkeley: University of California Press.

Legalcatch, 2008. "Pedestrian Accident Statistics." Posted March 18. http://legalcatch.wordpress.com/2008/03/18/pedestrian-accident-statistics/.

Levy, David M. 1970. "The Concept of Maternal Overprotection." In *Parenthood: Its Psychology and Psychopathology*, edited by E. James Anthony and Therese Benedek, 387–409. Boston: Little, Brown and Company.

Liedloff, Jean. 1977. *The Continuum Concept.* Reading, MS: Addison-Wesley.

Lynd, R. S., and H. M. Lynd. 1929. *Middletown: A Study in American Culture.* New York: Harcourt, Brace and Company.

Main, Mary. 1996. "Introduction to the Special Section on Attachment and Psychopathology: Overview of the Field of Attachment." *Journal of Consulting and Clinical Psychology* 64(2): 237–43.

Martin, Teresa Castro and Larry L. Bumpass. 1989. "Recent Trends in Marital Disruption." *Demography* 26(1): 37–51.

McGee, Michael Calvin. 1980. "The 'Ideograph': A Link between Rhetoric and Ideology." *Quarterly Journal of Speech* 6(1): 1–16.

Mead, Margaret. 1970. *Culture and Commitment.* New York: Natural History Press.

Moraga, Cherrie. 1979. "La Guera." In *This Bridge Called My Back: Writings by Radical Women of Color,* edited by Cherrie Moraga and Gloria Anzaldua, 27–34. Watertown, MA: Persephone Press.

National Center for Injury Prevention and Control. 2009. "WISQARS (Web-based Injury Statistics Query and Reporting System) Leading Causes of Death Reports, 1999–2005." Query conducted February 12, 2009. http://webappa.cdc.gov/sasweb/ncipc/leadcaus10.html.

Nelson, Margaret K. 2010. *Parenting Out of Control: Anxious Parents in Uncertain Times.* New York: New York University Press.

Newman, Katherine S. 1999. *No Shame in My Game: The Working Poor in the Inner City.* New York: Alfred A. Knopf, Inc. and Russell Sage Foundation.

Noguera, Pedor A. 2003. "The Trouble with Black Boys: The Role and Influence of Environmental and Cultural Factors on the Academic Performance of African American Males." *Urban Education* 38(4): 431–59.

Otte, Mary Jane. 1999. "The Child Psychoanalyst as Clinician: The Perils of Parental Projection." *Annual of Psychoanalysis* 26: 201–17.

Paul, Pamela. 2008. *Parenting, Inc.* New York: Times Books.

Pearson, Jane L., Deborah A. Cohn, Philip A. Cowan, and Carolyn P. Cowan. 1994. "Earned- and Continuous-Security in Adult Attachment: Relation to Depressive Symptomatology and Parenting Style." *Development and Psychopathology* 6(2): 359–73.

Pew Research Center. 2007. "Motherhood Today: Tougher Challenges, Less Success." Pew Research Center for the People and the Press. Released May 2. http://www.people-press.org/2007/05/02/motherhood-today-tougher-challenges-less-success/.

———. 2010. "Childlessness Up Among All Women; Down Among Women with Advanced Degrees." Pew Research Social and Demographic Trends. Released June 25. http://www.pewsocialtrends.org/2010/06/25/childlessness-up-among-all-women-down-among-women-with-advanced-degrees/.

Philipson, Ilene. 1982. "Narcissism and Mothering: The 1950s Reconsidered." *Women's Studies International Forum* 5(1): 29–40.

Pugh, Allison. 2005. "Selling Compromise: Toys, Motherhood, and the Cultural Deal." *Gender & Society* 19(6): 729–49.

———. 2009. *Longing and Belonging: Parents, Children, and Consumer Culture.* Berkeley: University of California Press.

Putnam, Robert D. 2000. *Bowling Alone: The Collapse and Revival of American Community.* New York: Simon and Schuster.

Reinharz, Shulamit. 1999. "Enough Already!: The Pervasiveness of Warnings in Everyday Life." In *Qualitative Sociology as Everyday Life*, edited by Barry Glassner and Rosanna Hertz, 31–40. Thousand Oaks, CA: Sage Publications.

Rich, Adrienne Rich. 1980. "Compulsory Heterosexuality and Lesbian Existence." *Signs* 5(4): 631–60.

Roberts, Dorothy. 2007. "Killing the Black Body: Race, Reproduction and the Meaning of Liberty." In *Maternal Theory: Essential Readings*, edited by Andea O'Reilly, 482–99. Toronto: Demeter Press.

Roper Starch Worldwide. 1997. "Kids and Moms Speak Survey." iPOLL Databank, Roper Center for Public Opinion Research. October. University of Connecticut.

———. 1999. "The 2000 Virginia Slims American Women's Opinion Poll." iPOLL Databank, Roper Center for Public Opinion Research. May. University of Connecticut.

Rosa, Eugene A. 2003. "The Logical Structure of the Social Amplification of Risk Framework (SARF): Metatheoretical Foundations and Policy Implications." In *The Social Amplification of Risk*, edited by Nick Pidgeon, Roger E. Kasperson and Paul Slovic, 47–79. Cambridge: Cambridge University Press.

Rosen, B. C. 1982. *The Industrial Connection.* New York: Aldine Publishing Company.

Rosenfeld, Alvin, and Nicole Wise. 2000. *The Over-Scheduled Child: Avoiding the Hyper-Parenting Trap.* New York: St. Martin's Press.

Ruddick, Sara. 2007. "Maternal Thinking." In *Maternal Theory: Essential Readings*, edited by Andrea O'Reilly, 96–113. Toronto: Demeter Press.

Rukeyser, Muriel. 1996. *The Life of Poetry.* Ashfield, MA: Paris Press.

Rutter, Michael, David Quinton, and Jonathan Hill. 1990. "Adult Outcome of Institution-Reared Children: Males and Females Compared." In *Straight and Devious Pathways from Childhood to Adulthood*, edited by Lee N. Robins and Michael Rutter, 135–57. New York: Cambridge University Press.

Sarkisian, Natalia, and Naomi Gerstel. 2012. *Nuclear Family Values, Extended Family Lives: The Power of Race, Class, and Gender.* New York: Routledge.

Schalet, Amy. 2011. *Not under My Roof: Parents, Teens, and the Culture of Sex.* Chicago: University of Chicago Press.

Sears, William, and Martha Sears, with Robert Sears and James Sears. 1992. *The Baby Book: Everything You Need to Know about Your Baby from Birth to Age Two*. Boston: Little, Brown and Company.

Sennett, Richard. 1998. *Corrosion of Character: The Personal Consequences of Work in the New Capitalism*. New York: W. W. Norton & Co.

Sharone, Ofer. 2013. *Flawed System/Flawed Self: Job Searching and Unemployment Experiences*. Chicago: University of Chicago Press.

Shumway, David R. 2003. *Modern Love: Romance, Intimacy, and the Marriage Crisis*. New York: New York University Press.

Skenazy, Lenore. 2008. "Why I Let my 9-Year-Old Ride the Subway Alone," *New York Sun*, April 7.

———. 2009. *Free-Range Kids, How to Raise Safe, Self-Reliant Children (without Going Nuts with Worry)*. San Francisco: Jossey-Bass.

Skolnick, Arlene. 2008. "Marriage." Microsoft Encarta Online Encyclopedia. http://encarta.msn.com.

Slovic, Paul. 1987. "Perceptions of Risk." *Science* 236: 280–85.

Sonkin, Daniel J. 2005. "Attachment Theory and Psychotherapy." *Therapist: A Publication of the California Association of Marriage and Family Therapists*, January/February. http://www.daniel-sonkin.com/attachment_psy chotherapy.htm.

Sroufe, L. Alan, and Everett Waters. 1977. "Attachment as an Organizational Construct." *Child Development* 48: 1184–99.

Stack, Carol. 1974. *All Our Kin: Strategies for Survival in a Black Community*. New York: Harper.

Starr, Chauncey. 1969. "Social Benefit Versus Technological Risk," *Science* 165: 1232–38.

Stone, Pamela. 2007. *Opting Out? Why Women Really Quit Careers and Head Home*. Berkeley: University of California Press.

Thurer, Shari. 1995. *Myths of Motherhood: How Culture Reinvents the Good Mother*. New York: Penguin.

Urdang, Esther. 2002. *Human Behavior and the Social Environment: Interweaving the Inner and Outer Worlds*. Philadelphia: Haworth Press.

US Department of Justice. 2002. "National Incidence Studies of Missing, Abducted, Runaway, and Thrownaway Children," October. http://www.ncjrs .gov/pdffiles1/ojjdp/196467.pdf.

Van Epps, Sharon. 2012. "Teaching My Son to Protect Himself in a Racist World." http://www.adoptivefamilies.com/articles/2348/.

Villalobos, Ana. 2010. "Mothering in Fear: How Living in an Insecure-Feeling World Affects Parenting." In *21st Century Motherhood: Experience, Identity, Policy, Agency*, edited by Andrea O'Reilly. New York: Columbia University Press.

———. 2014. "Compensatory Connection: Mothers' Own Stakes in an Intensive Mother-Child Relationship." *Journal of Family Issues*. Prepublished January 21, 2014, as doi: 10.1177/0192513X13520157.

Wallulis, Jerald. 1998. *The New Insecurity: The End of the Standard Job and Family*. Albany, NY: State University of New York Press.

Warner, Judith. 2005. *Perfect Madness: Motherhood in the Age of Anxiety*. New York: Penguin Group.

Wilkinson, Iain. 2001. *Anxiety in a Risk Society*. London: Routledge.

Williams, Joan. 2000. *Unbending Gender: Why Family and Work Conflict and What to Do about It*. New York: Oxford University Press.

Winnicott, Donald. 1960. "The Theory of the Parent-Infant Relationship," *International Journal of Psycho-Analysis* 41: 585–95.

Wolf, Joan B. 2011. *Is Breast Best? Taking on the Breastfeeding Experts and the New High Stakes of Motherhood*. New York: New York University Press.

Wright, Marguerite A. 1998. *I'm Chocolate, You're Vanilla: Raising Healthy Black and Biracial Children in a Race-Conscious World*. New York: Jossey-Bass.

Wylie, Philip. (1942) 1955. *Generation of Vipers*. New York: Pocket Books.

Zelizer, Viviana. 1981. *Pricing the Priceless Child: The Changing Social Value of Children*. Princeton, NJ: Princeton University Press.

Index

abandonment issues: intense compensatory connection prompted by, 79–80; mother's, and antidote strategy, 48–49

abduction, efforts to inoculate child against, 149

Acker, Joan, 259n25

adoptee, themes continuing in motherhood, 48

adult attachment studies, 87

advice literature: eschewing, 212–13, 220; insidious effect of, 258n42; and maternal determinism, 15; susceptibility to, 66. *See also* social amplification of risk; parenting books

African Americans: implications of, in research, 247; inoculation strategy by, 143–46; use of "community-based independence" by, 188–89

Ainsworth, Mary, 14

antidote security strategy, 42–44, 46–62, 64–65; case study, 46–62; compared to light motherload, 136–37; defined, 227; difficulties caused by, 52, 57–62

attachment: criteria of, 87–88; responsive, 113–19

attachment parenting, 50–57, 257n18; and aching desire to be with child, 86–87;

being flexible about, 113–119; and constant infant holding, 77–79; with full-time work, 55–56; as imperative, 15; judgmental attitude toward working mom, 55–57; "mom counts" attitudes within, 62; shift to, after divorce, 78; toll on mother, 57–61

attachment relationships, child vs. partner, 87

attachment theory, 14–16; and connectedness, 24; and quest for safe haven, 224–25

attachment-scape, 108–9, 166; elements of, 96; secure, 126–30, 146, 166–67; weak, 81–83, 99, 107, 153–55, 157, 233

baby: ambivalent feelings toward, 179; appearance of, mother's criticism of, 178–79. *See also* children

Baby Book, The, and attachment parenting, 53, 257n18

babysitter: difficulty leaving child with, 51; high-quality, 208; outsourcing care to, 182–87, 196; reluctance to use, 93

Beck, Ulrich, 34, 35, 156

birth, healing, 47–48

Bobel, Chris: and maternal sacrifice, 60; study of "natural mothers," 86

bonding research, 15

mother's groups, social connections through, 173

natural growth model of parenting, 261n6
neglect, inoculation viewed as, 153
Nelson, Margaret, 7–8, 96, 223, 257n14
newborn, relaxed approach to, 205–8
9/11 attacks: effects of, and inoculation strategy, 141; and risk perception, 34, 36

On Becoming Baby Wise, 260n27
overprotective parenting. *See* shielding security strategy

pain tolerance, efforts to achieve through inoculation, 147–48
parenting advice, susceptibility to, 66
parenting books: eschewing, 132; *Generation of Vipers*, 13; *The Baby Book*, 53, 66; *The Continuum Concept*, 53. *See also* advice literature
parenting model, working-class, 261n6
parenting style: family's disagreement with, 78; fluid approach to, 130; judging others', 119–20
partner: ambivalence toward, 73–74, 78, 82–83, 154, 177, 192; and jealousy toward baby, 187; solutions to dependence on, 191–93
partnership: costs to, with attachment parenting, 58–59; motherload as destabilizer, 229; parenting as, 201–3; prioritizing, 198, 203–5, 211–12; stable, 127; view of, by women using compensatory connection, 91–94; wariness of, 105–6
Perez, Alma, and responsive attachment, 115–17
Petrolis, Daphne: case study of inoculation strategy, 146–48; motherhood compensating for unemployment, 89
Philipson, Ilene, and rise of narcissistic children, 72
physical intimacy, with baby vs. husband, 83
physical security: concerns about, 9; preoccupation with, 233. *See also* inoculation security strategy
physical security, focusing on, 2–3; child's, 32–38; displacing job insecurity, 40–41, 64
political action, replaced by maternal responsibility, 66, 230
Polokow, Fran, as widowed mother, 45
popular psychology: and maternal determinism, 15–16; role of, in heavy

motherload, 225–26. *See also* advice literature
pregnancy: enjoyment of, 212; insecurity with, 177–78
Pritikin, Samantha, and antidote strategy, 43–44
protection. *See* security
psychology: within sociological context, 260n47. *See also* popular psychology

race: financial dependence on men, 188–89; implications for research, 247–48; and inoculation strategy, 143–46; white women and compensatory connection, 71–72
realism theory, 156
Reinharz, Shulamit, 19, 231
rejection, experiencing child's independence as, 160–61
religion, children as substitute for, 71–72
research findings, preview of, 24–27
research methods, 241–50; author's position and background, 242–50; frequency of interviews and observation, 265n1
research participants: listing, 235–40; race and class of, 246–48; variety in, 4
responsive attachment, 113–19
risk: ability to alter, 156–57; defined, 34; inoculating against, by tough mother vs. tough world, 163; intentionally exposing to, as inoculation, 142–43; measured response to, 200–201; protecting from vs. exposing to, 149–52; social construction of, 156
risk perception, 34–38
risk scholarship, 231
risk society, 9; defined, 35; and shielding strategy, 33–38, 63; shift of responsibility for, 16
Rossi, Myra, 35; and financial dependence, 188–91; and friendship strategy, 170–72, 175–78, 181; use of babysitters by, 183–87
Ruddick, Sara, 36
Ryder, Ellie: and attachment parenting, 59; and friendship strategy, 172–73, 178, 181; use of babysitters by, 183, 187

sacrifice. *See* maternal deprivation
safety, efforts to achieve through inoculation, 148–49
Savage, Gwen, 33
Sears, Martha, 53
Sears, William, 53, 257n18

www.ingramcontent.com/pod-product-compliance
Lightning Source LLC
Chambersburg PA
CBHW020841270326
41928CB00006B/501